Thomas Merton and
Thich Nhat Hanh

Thomas Merton and Thich Nhat Hanh

Engaged Spirituality in an Age of Globalization

Robert H. King

Continuum

New York • London

The Continuum International Publishing Group Inc
370 Lexington Avenue, New York, NY 10017

The Continuum International Publishing Group Ltd
The Tower Building, 11 York Road, London SE1 7NX

Printed in the United States of America

Library of Congress Cataloging in Publication Data

King, Robert Harlen, 1935–
   Thomas Merton and Thich Nhat Hanh : engaged spirituality in an age of globalization / Robert H. King.
     p. cm.
   Includes bibliographical references.
   ISBN 0-8264-1340-4
   1. Religion and social problems. 2. Spirituality. 3. Merton, Thomas, 1915–1968. 4. Nhât Hònh, Thâch. I. Title.

   BL65.S62 K56 2001
   291.1'7—dc21   2001032565

Contents

Acknowledgments

THIS BOOK BEGAN with an invitation from my friend Hideo Mineshima, a member of the faculty of Waseda University in Tokyo, Japan, to present a paper at an international conference on comparative thought. Because I had recently taught a graduate seminar on the topic of contemplation and action, I decided to make that the theme of my paper. I chose Thomas Merton and Thich Nhat Hanh as examples of Christian and Buddhist approaches to this subject, not realizing just how exemplary they were. Without the opportunity to present that paper and the enthusiastic response it elicited, this book probably would not have been written.

I also want to express my appreciation to Patrick Henry and the Institute for Ecumenical and Cultural Research at St. John's University in Collegeville, Minnesota, for providing a wonderful setting in which to begin my research. Going from Mississippi to Minnesota in the middle of winter was a bit of an adjustment, but the hospitality was as warm as the climate was cold. My semester as a resident scholar at the institute was crucial to my work. My colleagues there were very supportive, but I especially want to acknowledge the assistance I received from David Hackett, who read early drafts of three of the chapters and offered helpful criticism as well as encouragement.

There are many fine biographies of Thomas Merton, but the one that ranks highest in my estimation is William Shannon's *Silent Lamp: The Thomas Merton Story*. It was invaluable to me in my work, as was his collection of Merton's social writings, *Passion for Peace*. As if that were not enough, he was kind enough to read my main chapter on Merton and offer insightful comments. There is no biography of Thich Nhat Hanh in English, but the nearest thing to it is Chan Khong's memoirs entitled *Learning True Love*. Because she has been closely associated with Nhat Hanh since the late 1950s, one learns a great deal about him and his work by reading about her experiences. I was especially grateful for the opportunity to meet Chan Khong and talk with her during my visit to Plum Village.

Two people who read the Nhat Hanh chapter for accuracy provided useful corrections. They were Arnold Kotler, founder of Parallax Press and editor of several of Nhat Hanh's works, and Sister Annabel Laity, a close associate of Nhat Hanh for nearly twenty years and currently abbess of Forest Monastery in Vermont. Sister Annabel also shared with me her unpublished translation of Nhat Hanh's history of Vietnamese Buddhism.

Jim Forest is one of the few people who knew both Merton and Nhat Hanh personally. He has also written about them—in *Living with Wisdom*, a moving account of Merton's life, and *Only the Rice Loves You*, his recollections of a month spent with Nhat Hanh at the height of the Vietnam War. Jim responded generously to my inquiries regarding several matters he had firsthand knowledge of. He also helped me locate the photograph that appears on the cover.

Finally, I want to express my special gratitude to two people who assisted me throughout the project: Richard Freis, my former colleague at Millsaps College and a longtime friend; and Elizabeth, my wife and beloved companion on the spiritual journey. Both offered valuable suggestions and gave much-needed encouragement at key points along the way. I cannot imagine this book's having come to completion without them.

Permissions

The Asian Journals of Thomas Merton by Thomas Merton. Copyright 1975 by the Trustees of the Merton Legacy. Reprinted by permission of New Directions Publishing Corp.

Call Me by My True Names: The Collected Poems of Thich Nhat Hanh (1993) by Thich Nhat Hanh. Reprinted by permission of Parallax Press, Berkeley, California.

Fragrant Palm Leaves: Journals 1962-1966 (1968) by Thich Nhat Hanh. Reprinted by permission of Parallax Press, Berkeley, California.

In the Footsteps of Gandhi: Conversations with Spiritual Social Activists (1990) by Catherine Ingram. Reprinted by permission of Parallax Press, Berkeley, California.

Love in Action: Writings on Nonviolent Social Change (1993) by Thich Nhat Hanh. Reprinted by permission of Parallax Press, Berkeley, California.

New Seeds of Contemplation by Thomas Merton. Copyright 1961 by The Abbey of Gethsemani, Inc. Reprinted by permission of New Directions Publishing Corp.

Passion for Peace: The Social Essays of Thomas Merton, edited by William H. Shannon. Copyright 1995 by the Trustees of the Merton Legacy Trust. Reprinted by permission of The Crossroad Publishing Company.

The Raft Is Not the Shore by Daniel Berrigan and Thich Nhat Hanh. Copyright 1975 by Daniel Berrigan, S.J., and Thich Nhat Hanh. Reprinted by permission of Beacon Press, Boston.

Prologue

A Personal Perspective

O N A COLD WINTER morning in the Upper Hamlet of Plum Village in southern France, Thich Nhat Hanh had just finished a talk on anger when I approached him with a request. I told him I was writing a book about Thomas Merton and Thich Nhat Hanh and would like an opportunity to talk with him. He looked at me very intently for a moment and then asked, "Why do you want to write a book about Merton and me? You should write about your own practice." When I explained that this book was an outgrowth of my spiritual practice, he said I should write about how he and Thomas Merton have affected my practice. I never did get the meeting I asked for, but I have tried to take his advice to heart.

In this book I have not taken the standard academic approach, which would have been to make an objective comparison of the ideas of these two exceptional individuals, one Christian and the other Buddhist, and then conclude with some generalizations about their religions. I have chosen instead to take a more personal approach and to draw on my own experience to interpret the life and work of these men whom I have come to see not only as important religious thinkers, but also as singular human beings who developed in significant ways—intellectually and spiritually—over their lifetimes. Writing about Thomas Merton and Thich Nhat Hanh really has been an outgrowth and an expression of my own spiritual practice. They have come to represent for me a new kind of spirituality that I believe may be the best hope for religious renewal in our day. This new spirituality is not the prerogative of any particular religious tradition, but can be found in all of the world's great living religions. It is an "engaged spirituality" that combines traditional meditative practice with social

1

action directed at the eradication of the most deeply rooted, intractable problems of contemporary life. It is, moreover, a spirituality particularly well-suited to this age of globalization, a period in history when genuine dialogue among the world's leading religions may be crucial for human survival.

One could write about this new spirituality without reference to Merton or Nhat Hanh, for they are certainly not its only exemplars. Yet they have been at the forefront of this development from the beginning and are remarkably adept at articulating it for others. Their books have been translated into many languages and are read by persons of many different religious traditions; communities of practice in all parts of the world have formed around their teachings; and they are themselves regarded as embodying this new spirituality. In the thirty-plus years since his death, Merton's popularity has not diminished. His journals and letters have been edited and published posthumously, and books about him abound. Nhat Hanh lectures and gives workshops in all parts of the world and receives over a thousand visitors a year at his community in the south of France. Both men are seminal thinkers, whose influence can be expected to extend well into the twenty-first century. Individually they are important, but together they may be considered even more significant. For although their lives developed independently of one another and took quite different shapes, they shed light on each other in wonderful and unexpected ways. By approaching the new spirituality that they represent from these two distinct perspectives, we should be better able to understand it.

My own perspective is different from either of theirs. Although like Thomas Merton I am a Christian, I am neither a Catholic nor a monastic. I was raised as a Protestant and educated in the liberal reformed tradition of Christianity. My teachers included Paul Tillich and H. Richard Niebuhr, both well known for their creative reinterpretations of the historic Christian faith. I have also been influenced by the writings of other nineteenth- and twentieth-century theologians who grappled with the question of how to make the Christian faith relevant to the modern world. My theological education, however, did not include the writings of Merton or the contemplative tradition he represents. Indeed, the very idea of contemplative practice was alien to the tradition in which I was educated. There is a strong emphasis in traditional Protestantism on ethics and social responsibility, but very little attention is devoted to spiritual practices of any kind. When

I discovered a contemplative longing in myself, it was like coming home—yet to a home I had never known.

I entered the teaching profession in the early 1960s at the time of the civil rights movement, lived through the period of the Vietnam War, and shared with my students the anguish of that tragic conflict. I was teaching a course on Buddhism at the time and was aware of Buddhist opposition to the war, but I did not learn about Thich Nhat Hanh until many years later. Then an article in the *New York Times* about his work with American veterans of the war who were suffering from posttraumatic syndrome piqued my interest. I was intrigued by the idea of a Buddhist monk who had been a leader in the peace movement ministering to men who had fought in the very war that he opposed, men who once believed passionately in the rightness of their cause but now suffered from the moral and psychological effects of being agents of death for many of his fellow Vietnamese. It struck me as the kind of ministry of reconciliation that we like to associate with Christianity, but do not always find exemplified in Christians. I wondered what it was about his form of Buddhism that made this reconciliation possible. I thought it might have to do with the practice of meditation, but I did not know enough about the subject to make a judgment.

Only later did I decide to take up the practice of meditation, and then it was a Jesuit priest who introduced me to Zen meditation. He had lived for a time in Japan and had trained with a Zen Buddhist priest. He saw no contradiction between the Zen practice of meditation and certain contemplative practices in his own tradition, so he had no problem teaching it to others. For me it was a painful, frustrating experience just to sit on the floor in a manner approximating the traditional posture of Buddhist practitioners. But eventually I found a way to sit for extended periods of time and began to practice regularly on my own. By now I had begun to reevaluate my own religious training and to inquire into the contemplative tradition that had been largely absent from my theological education. I began reading people like Merton and the Christian mystics who preceded him and actually taught a seminar on Buddhist and Christian approaches to contemplation. Still, I was not satisfied that I really understood this tradition in either its Buddhist or Christian manifestations.

In the fall of 1994, I took a two-month leave from my position as academic dean at Millsaps, a liberal arts college in Jackson, Mississippi, to travel to Japan and experience firsthand a religion I had

known until then only through books and lectures. In the course of
several weeks I visited a number of Buddhist temples, attended a
variety of Buddhist services, and spoke with priests, teachers, and
students about current Buddhist religious practices. My most memorable experience, however, was living for two weeks as a monk at
Sogenji, a Zen Buddhist monastery on the outskirts of Okayama. In
certain respects Sogenji is not a typical Japanese monastery. It is an
international community with representatives from at least ten different countries, including lay men and women. Shodo Harada Roshi,
the teacher and abbot of the monastery, spends several weeks each
year in the United States and Europe, carrying the message of Zen
to the West. When he is in residence, the community follows a
traditional schedule of meditative practice, devoting as much as nine
hours a day to sitting meditation. The emphasis of the training is on
breathing, or as the Roshi once said to me "returning to one's original
breath." At the conclusion of my first week, I told the Roshi's assistant
that I felt as if I had just completed a course in remedial breathing.
It was as difficult as anything I had ever done in my life, but it was
worth it. In many ways the experience changed my life.

I have continued to practice meditation and following my retirement
spent three months at this same monastery deepening my practice.
Immediately after that I spent five months as a resident scholar at
the Institute for Ecumenical and Cultural Research in Collegeville,
Minnesota. The institute is affiliated with St. John's University and
with a Benedictine abbey, where I was invited to join the monks in
their morning and evening prayers, so my contemplative experience
has been varied. I do not consider myself an accomplished practitioner
by any means, but I do believe that meditation has deepened my
understanding of both Christianity and Buddhism. Now when I read
Thomas Merton or one of the classical Christian mystics, I do so with
much greater appreciation and understanding. I approach them from
an experiential perspective that was lacking previously. As for Thich
Nhat Hanh, I can see how his meditative practice supports and informs
his social action. I can also appreciate his ability to communicate
with individuals outside his own religious tradition because I have
had a similar experience myself.

This study of Merton and Nhat Hanh should not be considered a
comprehensive treatment or definitive assessment of either man's
work or contribution. It is a personal exploration of a particular
theme within their work: the theme of contemplation and action. I

am interested in how they came to understand the relationship between contemplative practice and social action in the context of their own religious traditions. I am especially interested in discovering any commonality in their approaches to engaged spirituality, a form of practice that could serve as a unifying paradigm for the world's religions in this age of globalization. If the world's religions are inevitably to confront one another in unprecedented ways in the years ahead, it would be good to know that constructive engagement is possible, that persons deeply committed to their own religious faith can learn from those of other faiths and grow through the experience. That seems to be the message of Merton and Nhat Hanh, but it needs to be fleshed out, and that can only come from a close examination of their work.

To carry out this assignment, we have primarily to consider their published work. Both men have written extensively and in ways that are often quite self-revealing. Some of Merton's best writing is taken directly from his journals, for instance, *The Sign of Jonas*, covering a period of intense vocational crisis in the early 1950s, and *Conjectures of a Guilty Bystander*, dealing with the tumultuous decade of the sixties. Both books appeared during his lifetime and were purposefully edited for the reading public. The journals from which these selections were taken and his extensive personal correspondence have been published since his death. This body of work may be more revealing in some respects than his previously published works, but it does not have, in my judgment, the public standing of work published in his lifetime, so I have not given it as much prominence. My purpose in studying Merton and Nhat Hanh is to learn what they have to say to us about engaged spirituality. For this purpose their published writings are our best source. Both are deeply committed teachers: they teach us through their lives and especially through what they have to say about their lives.

In the case of Nhat Hanh, there is much less to consider in the way of personal writing. Until recently his journals were not available in English. Then in 1998, *Fragrant Palm Leaves* appeared. Based on journal entries from 1962 to 1964 and first published in Vietnamese more than thirty years ago, this book expresses the personal anguish he felt at that time and reveals something of the personal transformation he went through during the early years of the Vietnam War, when he was living in the United States and teaching at Columbia University. Apart from this work, which specifically focuses on his personal

development at a critical stage in his life, there are passages interspersed throughout his writings that provide a window into his personal
life, places where he draws upon personal experience to illuminate
a particular point he wants to make. So it is possible to get some
sense of his inner, personal life as well as his outer, public life from
his published writings.

We need to acknowledge at the outset, however, that the material
at our disposal for considering the personal development of these two
men is quite different, and this fact will affect significantly the way
they are presented. The focus of Merton's writings is, for the most
part, his inner life. References to events in the larger world appear
only occasionally in his early writings. Later, as he assumes a more
public role and takes a more active interest in social issues, the focus
shifts somewhat. Through his letters, essays, and books, he becomes
an active participant in world affairs; yet even then he remains highly
introspective. Nhat Hanh, by contrast, engages the world around
him from the outset. We see him throughout his career attending
conferences, giving talks, writing books, organizing communities, and
developing programs of social action. When his efforts to effect institutional change are rebuffed, as they frequently were in the early years,
he will sometimes withdraw and turn inward. He has indicated that
these periods were necessary for healing and personal growth, yet we
hear very little about them, just as we hear very little about his inner
life. Compared with Merton, he is much more reserved.

It would be a mistake, however, to make too much of a distinction
between the "inner" and "outer" lives of men like Merton and Nhat
Hanh, whose vocation it has been to live for others. Their spirituality
is as real in what they *do* as in what they think or feel, and their
outer lives invariably draw on the resources of their inner lives. Thus
Merton, although he had doubts at first, came eventually to see that
his writing was not a distraction from his vocation: it *was* his vocation.
Nhat Hanh, committed as he was to ending the war in Vietnam,
discovered that opposition to the war only exacerbated the conflict if
it did not originate from a place of inner peace. Contemplation, if it
is genuine, must express itself in action on behalf of others, while
social action unaccompanied by contemplation invariably grows sterile
and unproductive. Contemplation *and* action are required for a fully
integrated spirituality. This is the central message of both men and
the over-arching theme of this book.

But there is another theme as well, another reason for writing this book, and that is interreligious dialogue. These men exemplify openness and a willingness to engage in serious dialogue with religions other than their own. This was not so earlier in their lives. Then, both regarded other religions with suspicion and misunderstanding. Outside of the teaching authority of the Catholic Church, Merton once wrote, he could see "only the void of nirvana, or the feeble intellectual light of Platonic idealism, or the sensual dreams of the Sufis"—hardly a basis for genuine dialogue. Nhat Hanh initially saw Christianity through the bitter experience of colonialism. "In such an atmosphere of discrimination and injustice against non-Christians," he later wrote, "it was difficult for me to discover the beauty of Jesus' teachings."

In time their views changed, until it could be said not only that they were able to respect one another's religion, but also that they learned from it. Merton probed deeply the teachings of Zen, corresponding for a time with one of its leading proponents and writing a number of insightful essays on the subject. Without ceasing to be a Christian or a Catholic, he discovered a deep inner resonance with this ancient religion, observing at one point in his correspondence with D. T. Suzuki that if he could not "breathe Zen" he would probably "die of spiritual asphyxiation." Nhat Hanh came to his current assessment of Christianity initially through contact with Christians who shared his social values and joined with him in the struggle for peace and social justice. He has come so far in his appreciation for the teachings of Jesus that he now has an image of Jesus on his personal altar alongside images of Buddha.

In a time when there is still a prevailing attitude of suspicion and a general lack of understanding toward other religions, we have much to learn from these two spiritual pioneers. They did not compromise their faith by being open to persons of other faiths. On the contrary, engagement with other faiths seems to have deepened and enhanced their own. For both of them, dialogue has led to personal transformation. There seems to be a widespread fear that genuine dialogue will lead to syncretism, the amalgamation of religions, and to a general loss of religious identity. But that fear is not borne out in their example. Over the objections of many within their own religious communities, they reached out to members of other religious communities while remaining rooted in their own traditions. Merton's inquiry into Buddhist spirituality took him eventually to Asia, where he engaged the Dalai Lama in dialogue, yet he did not cease to be a Christian monk concerned for the well-being of his religious order. Nhat Hanh welcomes persons of diverse faiths to his retreats and workshops, though not with the intention of converting them to Buddhism. If they find something of value in his teachings, he tells them to return to their own tradition and rediscover those same values there, values that they may not have been able to touch before.

The themes of this book are not unrelated. Contemplative practice can open the way to interreligious dialogue. Dialogue, in turn, can lead to greater mutual understanding and a greater willingness to cooperate with persons of other faiths in addressing the pressing social issues of our day. These will almost certainly be global issues that will require cooperative action across national, ethnic, and religious lines. We humans have shown on occasion that in spite of our religious differences we can come together in a common effort to address major crises such as war, famine, plague, and other natural catastrophes. But to sustain such an effort in the face of the profound ethical problems that will surely confront us in the twenty-first century—the allocation of scarce resources, preservation of the environment, and care of an aging population—we will need to find common ground at the level of spiritual awareness. Merton and Nhat Hanh found a way of doing that through the practice of engaged spirituality. We would do well to learn from their example.

1

A Historic Meeting

THOMAS MERTON and Thich Nhat Hanh met only once, and then briefly, yet in this one meeting they established a deep spiritual bond. The meeting took place at the Abbey of Our Lady of Gethsemani, a monastic community in the remote hill country of Kentucky, on the evening of May 26, 1966. It had been arranged by the Fellowship of Reconciliation, an international pacifist organization to which both men belonged.

Nhat Hanh, a Vietnamese Buddhist monk, had recently arrived in the United States from Vietnam to begin a speaking tour in which he would present a view that most Americans had not heard of the war currently raging in his country—one that adhered neither to the official American nor to the Communist position, but that reflected the strong desire of vast numbers of Vietnamese for an immediate end to the conflict. Merton had not, at this time, spoken out publicly against this war but was opposed to war in general. He was best known for his spiritual autobiography, *The Seven Storey Mountain*, an account of his life to the age of 27, when he left a teaching position at a Catholic university to join this community of Trappist monks. His subsequent writings on the practice of contemplation had served to establish his reputation as an important religious thinker. He was 51 years old at the time of the meeting and somewhat controversial because of his writings on the subject of nuclear war.

The meeting almost did not come off, because Nhat Hanh was tired from his travels and on the verge of losing his voice. The following day he would cancel a planned talk to the whole community, but for a few hours that evening he was able to carry on a discussion with

the monastery's most famous resident. He remembers Merton as someone with a great deal of human warmth—*chaleur humaine.* Conversation with him was easy. "When we talked," the Buddhist monk later
recalled, "I told him a few things, and he understood the things I
didn't tell him." He could see that Merton had a good grasp of
Buddhism. "One of the most difficult things concerning the understanding between East and West," he observed, "is that the West
tends to think in a dualistic way." But this was not the case with
Merton. While he could not remember everything they talked about
in that historic meeting, Nhat Hanh was clearly impressed with his
host's "capacity for dialogue."[1]

Merton was likewise impressed with his guest from Vietnam. He
recorded his initial observations in his journal a few days later. Nhat
Hanh, he wrote, "is first of all a true monk; very quiet, gentle, modest,
humble, and you can see his Zen has worked."[2] He elaborated on
these comments in a talk he gave to a group of novices the following
day and in a public appeal he wrote on the monk's behalf a short
time later, an appeal in which he addressed Thich Nhat Hanh as
"my brother."

John Heidbrink, the representative of the Fellowship of Reconciliation who accompanied Nhat Hanh on his tour, remembers a "charis-
matic moment" in the meeting. The two men were very interested in
each other's religious practices, so Merton had recited one of the
daily offices used by the monks at Gethsemani and Nhat Hanh responded with a Buddhist chant in Vietnamese. Merton was so moved
that he began spontaneously to sing along with him. Recalling the
incident many years later, Heidbrink said: "The beauty of the moment
was the clear evidence that both were deeply and profoundly informed
of the other's culture."[3]

In the few hours they were together, a spiritual bond had formed
between these men: the well-known Christian contemplative with a
penchant for social criticism and the little-known Buddhist peace
activist committed to ending an unpopular war in his country. Neither
man, as it turned out, was at the height of his reputation. Although
Merton lived only two and a half more years, his influence has continued to grow, due in large part to the many posthumously published
writings. Nhat Hanh, who is now in his seventies, is still active and
widely known for his teachings on the Buddhist practice of meditation
and the way of peace. Both men, moreover, have contributed to one

of the most important religious developments of our time: the start of real *dialogue* among the world's great religions.

A Pioneer for the Contemplative Way

Merton's story is the better known of the two, a fascinating story that has been told many times—beginning with his own account in *The Seven Storey Mountain*. He was only 32 years old and living in the monastery at Gethsemani when he wrote this extraordinary narrative of his spiritual journey from a life of reckless abandon as a young intellectual with aspirations of being a writer to a life of discipline and self-sacrifice as a monk in one of the strictest religious orders of the Catholic Church. As he tells it, his is a classic tale of religious conversion, except that rather than ending with his conversion to the Christian faith, it concludes with his decision to enter a Trappist monastery. The central issue for Merton at this time in his life was not whether he would become a Christian but whether he had a vocation as a contemplative. He was convinced that if he did, the monastery was the only place for him. This way of framing the issue would have seemed odd to most Americans, who assumed at that time that the contemplative life had no place in the modern world. That so many people were drawn to his story is an indication that it touched something deep within them, an aspect of themselves not generally acknowledged.

Born in France in 1915, the son of artists who were only nominally affiliated with the church, Merton did not have a traditional religious upbringing. His mother, who died when he was six, was a Quaker, though as far as we know she was not actively involved with them at the time she was caring for him. It is no doubt significant that he knew of this affiliation and on at least one occasion, while in college, attended a Quaker meeting for worship; yet he did not choose to follow this path. His father, with whom he lived on and off until he was sixteen, showed some interest in Christianity, but was not drawn to the church as such. Merton claims that his father had a contemplative disposition, which was reflected in his art; and for a time the two of them lived together in a medieval village in France, where the influence of the Catholic Church could be felt in the surroundings, but they did not attend church services. It was not until many years later, while traveling by himself in Rome, that Merton encountered

Byzantine art for the first time and was moved to pray. Yet even then he did not show a particular inclination for the religious life. As a student at Oakham, the English preparatory school he attended, he took part in sports and debate, edited the school newspaper, and pursued an active social life. He was intellectually gifted, yet as a first-year student at Cambridge University he was so caught up in parties and other pastimes that he failed to make the grades necessary to keep his scholarship. He also got a young woman pregnant and was ordered back to America by his British godfather, hardly a propitious beginning for a future monk.

His true passion from an early age was writing. In his autobiography he says that he began writing novels while still a schoolboy living with his father in France. Later, as a student at Columbia University, where he matriculated after the disastrous year at Cambridge, he found his primary friends among those who wrote for student publications. He even spent a summer with several of them in a cottage in upstate New York writing novels, and for a time thought he might become a journalist and create fiction on the side. In spite of his carefree life, he also had a social conscience. He recalls getting into an argument with the captain of the football team at Oakham over the merits of Gandhi's practice of civil disobedience and taking the side of the Hindu radical. As a college student, he briefly considered joining the Communist Party, but became disillusioned rather quickly. His first choice of a religious order was the Franciscans, who were best known for their social work. In fact, shortly before leaving for the Trappist monastery, he was preparing to go to work for a Catholic relief agency in Harlem. Through it all, however, there was a growing sense that he should become a priest—more specifically, a monk.

Merton was drawn to a life of solitude and silence, which he thought could only be found in a monastery. He considered for a time which religious order he should enter, but the real question was whether he would be acceptable to any order in light of his previous behavior. His initial inquiry into the priesthood was rebuffed, and he became convinced that he was morally unfit for the priesthood. For a while he tried to live as a contemplative within the world. He purchased a Breviary and began reciting the daily offices, much as he would if he were living in a monastery. To support himself, he took a teaching position at St. Bonaventure, a Catholic university not far from where he and his friends had spent the summer writing novels. He enjoyed teaching and was happy to be in an environment that supported his religious practice, yet he continued to feel a pull toward the priesthood. During the Easter recess, at the suggestion of one of his professors from Columbia, he traveled to Gethsemani Abbey, an obscure Trappist monastery in rural Kentucky, for a weeklong retreat. This visit had a profound effect on him. He says he was especially moved by the silence and the holiness of the place. Returning to the world outside the monastery, he found everything insipid and slightly insane. "There is only one place," he concluded, "where there is true order."[4] On December 10, 1941, as America was preparing for war, Thomas Merton resigned his teaching position and returned to this place of silence and holiness—this time to stay.

He was prepared to give up his literary aspirations in order to become a monk, but that was not to be the case. With the encouragement of his abbot, he began writing soon after he entered the monastery. At first it was poetry, and he found that he wrote his best verse in "the interval after the night office, in the great silence, between four and five-thirty in the mornings of feast days."[5] Then, in November 1944, three years after joining the Trappists, Merton published his first book of verse, entitled *Thirty Poems*. Other publications soon followed, including a manual for initiates and a biography of a contemporary saint, but the book that changed his life was *The Seven Storey Mountain*. It made him, in spite of himself, a celebrated author and added to the tension he already felt between the demands of the active life and the attractions of the contemplative life.

The Trappists, he found, had their own way of resolving this tension; they called it active contemplation. Their monasteries, he concluded, produced very few "pure contemplatives." They were much too *active* for that. "Doing things, suffering things, thinking things, making tangible and concrete sacrifices for the love of God—that is what contemplation seems to mean here," he wrote.[6] This was not Merton's idea of contemplation; it was not what had brought him to the monastery in the first place. What he sought above all was union with God, and that union, he was convinced, could best be found in silence and solitude. Speaking to his brother, John Paul, at the time of their last meeting shortly before the younger man left for the war in Europe, he described what he called the gift of faith. "By the gift of faith," he said, "you touch God, you enter into contact with His very substance and reality, in darkness: because nothing accessible, nothing comprehensible to our senses and reason can grasp His essence as it is in itself."[7] He might as well have been speaking of the gift of contemplation, for this is how he understood it. Yet he had no real model for this austere form of spiritual practice; he would have to find his own way.

At the time of his solemn vows, a year before the completion of *The Seven Storey Mountain*, Merton acknowledged that he was "no longer sure what a contemplative was, or what the contemplative vocation was, or what [his own] vocation was."[8] Throughout his writings, really until the end of his life, we see him grappling with these issues. In 1948, the year his autobiography appeared, he wrote a booklet entitled *What Is Contemplation?* The following year he published *Seeds of Contemplation*, a more ambitious work consisting primarily of personal reflections on topics relating to the contemplative life. But that was not the end of it. By 1958 he had begun to rethink this work and in 1962 came out with a greatly revised and expanded version titled *New Seeds of Contemplation*. At the time of his death, six years later, he was considering publishing another work in the same genre.

Contemplative practice, as Merton conceived it, is dynamic and transformative. It raises questions that are never fully answered once and for all. For that reason, there is a quality of openness and self-questioning in nearly all of his writings, and this no doubt contributed to their appeal. It brought out his essential humanity and helped the reader to identify with him. This quality is especially evident in a book he published in 1953, *The Sign of Jonas*. Using journal entries from the five-year period beginning with his solemn vows and culminating in his ordination to the priesthood, Merton takes the reader through what he considers a "period of fervor" in his life and the life of the monastery.[9] He questions his vocation, his choice of a religious order, even his own sincerity. *Conjectures of a Guilty Bystander*, published twelve years later, is also a compilation of personal reflections drawn from his journals but is presented in a topical rather than chronological order. He insists that this book, unlike the previous one, is not a spiritual journal. It is his "personal version of the world of the 1960s." Yet he acknowledges that "in elaborating such a version one unavoidably tells something of himself, for what a man truly is can be discovered only through his self-awareness in a living and actual world."[10] Merton, the contemplative, could not get away from self-exploration—and with self-exploration came self-transformation.

The contemplative life, he concluded, "is first of all *life*, and life implies openness, growth, development."[11]

Readers who were drawn to this aspect of his writing were not prepared for all the changes he would undergo. In 1962, Merton surprised everyone by mounting a series of articles critical of America's role in the nuclear arms race. The Christian contemplative had suddenly become a social activist. Other pieces followed on topics relating to the Cold War, racism, and the treatment of Native Americans. This kind of writing did not fit the popular image of the monk as contemplative. Merton, the quintessential monk, was not expected to have opinions on such worldly matters. Besides, most of his views were contrary to official church teaching, especially those regarding war. He was ordered by his religious superiors to cease writing on this subject.

Merton had always been against war. As a student at Columbia, he took part in a peace strike and signed a pledge refusing to fight in any war. When it looked as if he might be drafted during the Second World War, he applied for noncombatant status. Yet as a monk he was not supposed to take a public stand on anything so controversial. It was a reflection of the wide separation that had occurred between the contemplative life and the active life that a monk could not express his conscience on so profound an ethical issue as nuclear war. Merton would not be silenced, however, and found ways to continue to write about this and other social issues until the climate in the Catholic Church eventually changed.

At the time of his meeting with Nhat Hanh, the situation with the church was still in flux. The Second Vatican Council, which began meeting in 1962, had concluded its work a year earlier. *Pacem In Terris*, the papal encyclical that signaled a major shift in church teaching on war, had appeared three years earlier, but *Gaudium et Spes*, an important document promulgated by the council that also addressed the subject of war, had only been out for a few months. Active resistance to the Vietnam War was still in its earliest stages, and priests such as Daniel Berrigan and his brother Philip were just beginning to voice their opposition. Because Merton's stance toward war was generally known and he commanded a wide following among intellectuals, it was natural that the Fellowship of Reconciliation would want to arrange a meeting for him with Thich Nhat Hanh, a leading spokesman for Buddhist opposition to this war. Although his views were controversial, Merton was highly respected both in and outside the church. He could be helpful to Nhat Hanh and the cause he represented.

Profile of a Peace Activist

Thich Nhat Hanh was virtually unknown in the United States at this time. Merton remembers having read an article by him in French, but on the previous Sunday when he announced to the monks at Gethsemani that they would have a visitor next week from Vietnam, he was not sure how to pronounce the name. Because Nhat Hanh was fatigued and unable to speak to the community as planned, Merton spoke for him. Fortunately, this talk has been preserved on tape, which gives us a record of Merton's initial impressions of his Buddhist visitor. Listening to it, one senses the excitement of the meeting and the strong affinity Merton felt for this "peace activist."[12]

"Who is this fellow?" he asks rhetorically. "He is one of us, a monk." Nhat Hanh, it seems, had entered a monastery in 1942, the same year that Merton did, although Merton was eleven years older at the time. He was subjected to the full rigors of Zen training, which Merton assures his fellow monks was much tougher than their own training. When asked about the practice of meditation, Nhat Hanh said that in his tradition they would not let you meditate until you had been at the monastery for several years. "First, you must learn to close doors without slamming them." Merton liked that response. What is the point, after all, of trying to meditate if you have been going around in a violent and uncontrolled manner all day? A person must be formed by the life of the community before he can benefit from meditation. Nhat Hanh, in Merton's judgment, was a "completely formed monk."

He was also an intellectual and a writer, which appealed to Merton. "He is one of the leading intellectuals and writers in Vietnam," according to this monk who felt he had a special mission to intellectuals. Nhat Hanh had taught at Columbia, studied at Princeton, and lectured in France. He had written books on Buddhist philosophy as well as poetry. Merton was especially taken with his poetry and read two of Nhat Hanh's poems to the gathering of monks at the close of the presentation. But most of the talk was about the war in Vietnam and Nhat Hanh's role as a leader of Buddhist opposition to the war. Merton reminded his audience that a few weeks earlier one of them had asked him what these Buddhist monks were up to. What was their attitude toward the war? Now they had a chance to find out. The war, Merton felt, was nothing short of a spiritual crisis, and it was their professional responsibility as monks to be realistically informed about it. What better way for them to learn about the war than from a "fellow monk" living under the conditions of war?

Nhat Hanh, as it turned out, was no longer living in a monastery; he was actively engaged in the struggle to end the war and prepare his country for peace. His brother had been killed in that war, as had people all around him. "Everything," he told Merton, "is destroyed." Yet he was not bitter; he was working with the young people of the country to restore peace. He was even working with Catholics, contrary to the picture presented by the media that Buddhists and Catholics were totally at odds. This Buddhist monk, according to Merton, had eleven Catholic priests working with him in a kind of Peace Corps project to prepare the peasants and poor people for eventual reconstruction. "He has this institution going where they have courses, elementary stuff that you need for living—hygiene, farming, practical stuff." In a crisis situation, where everything is being destroyed, "this is what you do." You try to save what can be saved and prepare to put the place back together again. But above all, Merton said, "you need to stop the killing."

He could see that his guest was deeply committed to ending the war by peaceful means. "The whole thing, the basic thing, that you find with him is an orientation toward peace, real peace, a peaceful reconstruction of the country." There were divisions within Buddhism, Nhat Hanh reported, and some of the more highly publicized leaders were very political, trying to get the Buddhists into a position to control things. But that was not his way. Nhat Hanh, according to Merton, was not a "political operator." He just wanted to stop the killing while there was still someone left alive. "Because he does not take sides," Merton said, "he has the Viet Cong against him, but also the government." Terrible things could happen to him if he went back, as he felt he must. He could be put in jail or killed by the Viet Cong. He could even be killed by his own government in a way that would make it look like the work of the Viet Cong. "We need to pray for him," Merton told the monks. Meanwhile, he assured them that there were persons with influence in the American government who would try to get some protection for him.

Soon after he gave this talk to the community at Gethsemani, Merton wrote an impassioned letter on Nhat Hanh's behalf. This letter first appeared two weeks later in the printed program of a public meeting that was convened to support his work and was subsequently published in the magazine *Jubilee*. It is an extraordinary tribute to a man he had known for only a few hours. The meeting for which Merton originally composed the letter was itself quite remarkable. Sponsored by the Fellowship of Reconciliation, it was held in the New York City Town Hall on June 9, 1966. The event was designed to introduce Nhat Hanh to the American public and promote his efforts to end the war. A distinguished group of writers and poets opened the meeting with personal tributes to Nhat Hanh. The panel included Daniel Berrigan, Abraham Heschel, Robert Lowell, and Arthur Miller. Their presentations were followed with an address by Nhat Hanh and a reading from his poetry. The event concluded with a Buddhist prayer for peace chanted in Vietnamese.

Merton titled his letter "Nhat Hanh Is My Brother." He begins with a disclaimer: "This is not a political statement. It has no ulterior motive, it seeks to provoke no immediate reaction 'for' or 'against' this or that side in the Vietnam war. It is on the contrary a human and personal statement and an anguished plea for Thich Nhat Hanh who is my brother." He goes on to say that they both deplore the hostilities that are ravaging his country, and for exactly the same reasons: "human reasons, reasons of sanity, justice and love." They lament "the needless destruction, the fantastic and callous ravaging of human life, the rape of the culture and spirit of an exhausted people." He acknowledges that his statement is a "plea for peace," but insists that it is primarily a plea for his brother Nhat Hanh, who is in mortal danger because of his role as a peacemaker. The Buddhist monk is not a communist and yet refuses to be identified with the government, so he is distrusted by both sides. "We who have met and heard Nhat Hanh, or who have read about him," Merton insists, "must raise our voices to demand that his life and freedom be respected when he returns to his country."[13]

The Trappist monk, author of *The Seven Storey Mountain* and other contemplative writings, then considers what it might mean that Nhat Hanh is a Zen Buddhist. His words are generous and appreciative, very different from what he might have said at an earlier time in his life. Nhat Hanh, in his opinion, is a truly free man, free to act on behalf of others and "moved by the spiritual dynamic of a tradition of religious compassion." He bears witness to the spirit of Zen, as others have before him, but in a way that is manifestly different. "More than any other," Merton writes, "he has shown us that Zen is not an esoteric and world denying cult of inner illumination, but that it has its rare and unique sense of responsibility in the modern world."[14] In his talk to the monks at Gethsemani, Merton had compared the Buddhist spirit to that of the Franciscans. Both traditions, he said, manifest a genuine respect for life—a constructive, creative reverence for life.

At the conclusion of this passionate appeal on behalf of his Zen Buddhist "brother," Merton speaks eloquently of the spiritual bond that had developed between them.

> I have said Nhat Hanh is my brother, and it is true. We are both monks, and we have lived the monastic life about the same number of years. We are both poets, both existentialists. I have far more in common with Nhat Hanh than I have with many Americans, and I do not hesitate to say it. It is vitally important that such bonds be admitted. They are the bonds of a new solidarity and a new brotherhood which is beginning to be evident on all the five continents and which cuts across all political, religious and cultural lines to unite young men and women in every country in something that is more concrete than an ideal and more alive than a program. This unity of the young is the only hope of the world. In its name I appeal for Nhat Hanh. Do what you can for him. If I mean something to you, then let me put it this way: do for Nhat Hanh whatever you would do for me if I were in his position. In many ways, I wish I were.[15]

Following Merton's untimely death two and a half years later, Nhat Hanh reciprocated with a tribute to his Catholic friend. Concluding his reflections on their historic meeting, he defends Merton's decision to remain in the monastery rather than join the active opposition to the war.

> Thomas Merton was there in the monastery but he cannot be confined to that place. When you are a man of peace, even if you hide yourself in a mountain, you are working for peace. If you are not peaceful, then how can you work for peace? Those who are in demonstrations, marches, like that, they may be less for peace than someone who is just in his quarters on a mountain. . . . Thomas Merton—his life, his feelings, his teachings, and his work—are enough to prove his courage, his determination, his wisdom. He did more for peace than many who were out in the world.[16]

Clearly a bond had formed between these two men. In spite of religious, historical, and cultural differences, they had found a way to communicate with one another on a deep spiritual level.

An Opening for Dialogue

Thomas Merton and Thich Nhat Hanh did not meet again following that memorable encounter in the spring of 1966. There was some correspondence, and a year later Merton wrote an introduction for a book by Nhat Hanh tracing the history of the Vietnam War and making the case for a peaceful resolution of the conflict. He also included a discussion of an earlier book by Nhat Hanh in the concluding chapter of his work *Mystics and Zen Masters*. But their interests were taking them in different directions. Merton was once again reassessing his vocation, considering moving to another location, and preparing to travel to Asia. This trip would be his longest period away from Gethsemani since entering as a postulant and an opportunity for him to pursue his growing interest in Asian religions. It would also be his last trip. The conference in Bangkok, Thailand, which was his primary reason for going, had scarcely begun when on December 10, 1968, exactly twenty-seven years from the date of his arrival at Gethsemani Abbey, he was accidentally electrocuted by a fan in the room where he was staying. At the age of 53, his life came to a sudden end.

Meanwhile, Nhat Hanh was becoming more and more immersed in the peace effort. He had expected to return to Vietnam following his speaking tour in the United States, but instead was persuaded by his friends back home to remain abroad as an emissary for the Buddhist peace movement. He took up residence in Paris and in 1969 was named head of the unofficial Buddhist Peace Delegation to the Paris Peace Accords. From his small office there, he mounted a large-scale effort to end the war and bring relief to its victims. He met with world leaders and spoke to legislative assemblies, but he also wrote personal letters to the sponsors of Vietnamese children rendered homeless by the war. Working through a network of monks and nuns in Vietnam, he established resettlement centers, orphanages, and educational programs for children and adults in his home country. He also provided information about conditions in Vietnam to the outside world. Yet as the war progressed Nhat Hanh became increasingly alienated from the antiwar movement in the United States. Young people within the movement were resorting to violence and openly calling for victory by the North Vietnamese. He could not support such a polarized position because it was contrary to his fundamental commitment to peace and reconciliation. He continued his opposition to the war, but in a way consistent with the practice of nonviolence.

When the war finally ended, Nhat Hanh turned his attention to efforts to rebuild his homeland. Yet once again he was prevented from returning, this time by the victorious North Vietnamese, who considered him a threat. For a brief time, he attempted to organize a relief effort on behalf of the boat people, refugees from South Vietnam who were refused entry into neighboring countries such as Thailand, Malaysia, Singapore, Indonesia, and Hong Kong. But these efforts were also thwarted. So in 1977, he entered a period of withdrawal from world affairs. By then he was living in a renovated farmhouse several hours' drive from Paris. His friends would sometimes gather there on weekends, but for the most part he was left to himself. These were the hermitage years, when his primary activities were meditating, writing, and gardening.

The contemplative life fully lived invariably leads one back into the world to serve others. And so it was with Nhat Hanh. In 1982, he accepted an invitation to attend a Reverence for Life Conference in New York. The following year he returned to the United States to lecture and hold retreats on subjects relating to Buddhism and peace work. The response was overwhelmingly positive, and in the years since then he has continued to travel, carrying his message to all parts of the world and to persons of diverse religious backgrounds. About the time he reentered public life, Nhat Hanh moved his residence to a new location in the south of France, another converted farm, which he named Plum Village. There he formed a community that now offers year-round religious training to monks and nuns, as well as spiritual retreats open to Buddhists and non-Buddhists alike.

No longer associated exclusively with the war in Vietnam, Thich Nhat Hanh is now best known for his spiritual retreats and his writings on meditation. He is a prolific writer whose works appear in many different languages. In the course of his ministry, he has developed a unique form of spiritual practice combining meditation and action. He is especially effective in relating the practice of meditation to daily life. Nhat Hanh has retained a concern for social issues but places a greater emphasis on personal relationships than he once did. He speaks eloquently of the need to care for the earth, seek alternatives to war, build community, and heal the wounds caused by anger, hatred, and greed; yet he insists that real change must begin with the individual. Only by "being peace," he says, can we hope to "make peace" in the world.[17]

Although they started from different places and speak out of different traditions, there is an unmistakable convergence of the life and thought of Thomas Merton with that of Thich Nhat Hanh. Early on, Merton pursued a form of contemplative practice that had practically disappeared from Christianity and only later became involved in one of the most divisive social issues of his day. Nhat Hanh first came to prominence as the leader of a movement of social protest and later developed a reputation as a teacher of meditation. At the time of their meeting Merton had begun to speak out against war, so he could appreciate Nhat Hanh's social activism, while the Buddhist monk, engaged as he was in the struggle to end the war in his own country, never lost touch with his meditative practice, so he could understand the Catholic's commitment to the contemplative life. Both have been pioneers in the integration of contemplation and action within the conditions of the modern world.

But they have also been leaders in the movement for greater interreligious dialogue. Merton's interest in Eastern religions goes back to his college days, when he read Aldous Huxley and made friends with a Hindu monk who was studying in the United States. In the late 1950s, he initiated a correspondence with D. T. Suzuki, the foremost interpreter of Zen Buddhism to the West. Merton's interest in Zen continued until his death and resulted in a collection of essays that was published the same year he died, a small but important work called *Zen and the Birds of Appetite*. One of the most striking features of these essays is what they reveal about the development of his understanding of Zen over a ten-year period. Primarily through reading, since he was not permitted to leave the monastery, Merton carried on an internal dialogue with this highly mystical religion and eventually achieved a deep personal understanding of it. When he was finally able to travel to Asia in 1968, he went with a prepared mind. He used the opportunity to extend his dialogue with Buddhism to living representatives, committed practitioners of the religion.

Foremost among the Buddhists Merton met on this trip was the Dalai Lama, leader of the Tibetan community in exile. The two men engaged in a lively conversation extending over three days, at the conclusion of which Merton noted that a "real spiritual bond" had formed between them—not unlike what had occurred earlier with Nhat Hanh. While prevented by his untimely death from pursuing his dialogue with Buddhism further, Merton's influence on the subsequent development of interreligious dialogue is indisputable. In 1978, a commission for Monastic Interreligious Dialogue was formed and exchanges between Buddhist and Christian monks begun. In the summer of 1996, thirty years after the meeting between Thomas Merton and Thich Nhat Hanh, another historic encounter of Buddhists and Christians took place at Gethsemani. Convened at the suggestion of the Dalai Lama, it brought together monks and nuns from the three main Buddhist traditions—Tibetan, Theravadin, and Zen—along with representatives of various Benedictine orders. At the conclusion of the conference, there was a memorial service honoring Thomas Merton at which the Dalai Lama called on everyone present, Buddhist and Christian alike, to follow Merton's example. "If all of us followed this model," he said, "it would become very widespread and would be of very great benefit to the world."[18]

Thich Nhat Hanh did not attend this conference, yet he has contributed in his own way to the cause of interreligious dialogue in the years since his meeting with Merton. His community at Plum Village is open to persons of all faiths, as are the many workshops and retreats he holds throughout the world. He does not look upon these encounters as occasions to proselytize, but rather as opportunities to learn from one another. When persons of other faiths express an interest in following the Buddhist path, he invariably refers them back to their own tradition, confident that if they look deeply enough they will find the same thing in a different form.

In recent years Nhat Hanh has written two books specifically devoted to Buddhist-Christian dialogue: *Living Buddha, Living Christ* and *Going Home: Buddha and Jesus as Brothers.* They show an unusual degree of understanding and appreciation for another religion, especially considering that the religion in question was for a long time that of his oppressors. Though he does not deny that there are important differences between Christianity and Buddhism, he is convinced that at the deepest level these two faiths can communicate. It is as though he were extrapolating from his experience with Merton. For although there have been other instances of interreligious communication of this sort, they are relatively rare. In the course of history, the world's great religions have not shown much understanding of or appreciation for one another. There must be something special about the meeting

of Thomas Merton and Thich Nhat Hanh, something that accounts
for the depth of their communication. Could it be that their integration
of contemplative practice and social action is what created this remarkable *opening for dialogue*? If so, it constitutes a major development
in the history of the two religions.

Contemplation and Action in Historical Perspective

Christianity and Buddhism originated in different parts of the world
at a time when there was very little global communication. Both were
expansive religions, but they expanded in different directions, so
there was not much opportunity for dialogue until the modern era.
Christianity began in the Middle East and gradually spread north and
west to become the dominant religion of Europe and later the Americas,
while Buddhism started in India and migrated eastward as far as
China and Japan. Buddhism has been at one time or another the
established religion of most of the countries of Southeast Asia; and
even when it was not the official religion, it has exerted a profound
influence on the culture. The same could be said for Christianity
with respect to the cultures of Europe, Russia, and North and South
America. Both religions have been a major force in the creation of
entire civilizations, yet until the nineteenth century they could afford
to ignore one another. For the most part they occupied separate spheres
of influence and did not have to engage in serious dialogue. But that
situation may be changing.

In the period since World War II, a genuine interest in dialogue
has begun to emerge among the world's religions. The Second Vatican
Council, convened by Pope John XXIII in 1962, helped prepare the
way for greater rapprochement between the Catholic Church and other
religions by reassessing the church's traditional exclusionary position.
At about the same time, the World Council of Churches, speaking
for the mainline Protestant denominations, began promoting greater
openness toward persons of other faiths and ideologies. Soon Christians
of various persuasions were meeting with Jews, Muslims, Hindus, and
Buddhists in a variety of settings for the purpose of achieving greater
understanding of one another. Not all of these meetings, moreover,
have been initiated by Christians. The Dalai Lama in particular has
been responsible for promoting a number of meetings with representatives of other religions.

Some of the most important developments along this line have come from monks and nuns, which might seem surprising because monastics are generally supposed to keep to themselves and not have much contact with the larger world. They are seen as deeply committed to their own religious practices and not particularly open to the practices of others. But this is not what has transpired. Through a program of monastic exchange begun in the late 1970s, Buddhist and Christian monks and nuns have found they have a great deal in common—more so than with some members of their own faith. In this respect, the meeting of Merton and Nhat Hanh was a harbinger of things to come.

I once heard my Zen teacher, Harada Roshi, speak to a group of Franciscan nuns about his experience as a participant in one of these monastic exchanges. Along with several other Japanese monks, he spent a month in 1979 at a Benedictine monastery in Holland. He found the way of life of these Catholic monks not greatly different from that of Zen Buddhist monks, even though the two traditions had developed independently of one another. The Benedictines emphasized prayer, work, and the study of scripture, whereas Zen monks stressed work, meditation, and the study of sutras. What the Benedictines called contemplative prayer, he considered similar to the Zen practice of meditation. He was especially touched by a 96-year-old monk who showed the effects of many years of practice. His purity of heart, the Roshi observed, was what one would expect from years of Zen practice.

In spite of these similarities, the history of monasticism in the two religions is quite different. The monastic community has been an integral part of Buddhism from the beginning. Buddha himself is credited with laying the foundation by forming communities of monks and setting down rules of community life that survive to this day. Meditation was at the heart of the religion he founded, and the monastic community has been a principal means of sustaining and transmitting this practice. In classic Buddhist thought, the *sangha,* or religious community, is of equal importance with the *dharma,* or teaching of Buddha. It is, in fact, considered equivalent to Buddha himself. Membership in the sangha is not in principle limited to monks, though in practice it has been so circumscribed for most of the history of the religion. Buddhist monks and nuns are considered the primary bearers of the tradition, the true embodiment of the spiritual ideal. It was primarily through their efforts that the religion spread beyond India, and until recently Buddhism without monasticism would have been practically inconceivable.

By contrast, monasticism has played a relatively minor role in Christianity. At first, the religion spread largely through the efforts of itinerant preachers such as the apostle Paul, who traveled from place to place forming congregations of the faithful. It was not until the fourth century that something like a monastic tradition began to form in the desert. These desert monks, epitomized by St. Antony of Egypt, were for the most part hermits living an austere life outside of society. Merton was fascinated by them and compiled a book of their stories and sayings. Monasteries, in the sense of intentional communities formed for the express purpose of promoting spiritual practice, did not begin to appear until the sixth century, in the waning days of the Roman Empire, and the true flowering of the monastic tradition in Christianity did not take place until the twelfth century. Christian monasticism flourished throughout the Middle Ages and produced some of the most profound mystical writings of all times, but then it began to decline.

The Reformation, beginning in the sixteenth century, mounted a major assault on the monastic tradition, which was criticized as corrupt, self-indulgent, and out of touch with the true source of faith, the Bible. Although some monastic communities survived in predominantly Catholic countries such as France and Spain, they largely disappeared in countries where Protestantism prevailed. Among Catholics, the institution of monasticism declined, until by the end of the eighteenth century it was nearly extinct. The rise of science and the growth of secularization in the modern period further contributed to its demise in the West. There was simply no place for this form of religious life in the modern world—or so it seemed.

The decline of Christian monasticism was accompanied by a general loss of interest in contemplative practices. The spiritual impetus once directed toward these practices began to take other forms. Its influence can be seen in the devotional poetry of the seventeenth century and the social idealism of the eighteenth century, but contemplative practice as such was largely abandoned at this time in favor of a more active life. For Protestants especially, social reform replaced it as the primary means of spiritual transformation. There were some attempts to revive the monastic movement in the nineteenth century, but by the time Merton came along those efforts were largely spent. Monasticism, and the contemplative life it represented, had become thoroughly marginalized within Christianity.

Monastic communities on the other hand continued to play an integral role in Buddhism well into the twentieth century. This was especially true of Theravada Buddhism, the more conservative branch of the religion, but even Mahayana Buddhism, with its more liberal attitude toward change, has continued to grant monastic life a prominent place. In most Southeast Asian countries, monasteries are the primary educational institutions for the religion, and monks are looked upon throughout the region as leaders and exemplars of the faith. Monks do not generally take an active role in the governance of the country, though there have been times when they did. In the period preceding the Vietnam War, for instance, Buddhist monks took an active part in the effort to achieve national independence, but this was the exception. The prevailing view has been that monks should devote themselves to spiritual practices and the laity should support them with gifts and institutional protection.

In both Christianity and Buddhism, the monastery has been the primary vehicle for the cultivation and transmission of advanced forms of spiritual practice—what Buddhists call meditation, and Christians contemplation. These practices have been largely confined to the monastery, though not exclusively so. Buddhist laity are encouraged to practice some form of meditation on a regular basis and are permitted to spend a period of time in the monastery in order to receive training in meditation. Because meditation is such an integral part of their religion, the practice has not been allowed to die out, even for the laity, but it is pursued more intently and with greater seriousness in the monasteries. There have been some efforts to extend Christian contemplative practice beyond the monastery, but these efforts have met with limited success until recently. In their exchanges, Buddhist and Christian monastics found the area of greatest commonality to be their spiritual practices. It remains to be seen whether the same common ground can be found outside the monastery, and if so whether it will provide a true opening for dialogue.

In the meantime, another area of mutual interest may be developing among the world's religions, one that is unique to our time: engagement in social action. In both Buddhism and Christianity, there are signs of greater social awareness and a willingness to work together for the common good. During my first visit to Japan in 1994, I was the guest of the School Sisters of Notre Dame, a Catholic religious order with a convent in Kyoto. When I told them of my interest in Buddhism, they offered to introduce me to some Buddhists of their acquaintance.

One of them, Sister Delores, took me to meet a Japanese priest belonging to the Jodo sect. She knew him because they had worked together on a suicide prevention hotline. While I was there, I also met the priest's son, a recent college graduate who was preparing to take over the family temple. Over tea we talked about what motivated him to go into the priesthood, and he said it was the opportunity to help people. Neither he nor his father had any objection to working with Christians to relieve human suffering. As for the Catholics, Sister Delores said that her community was happy to cooperate with the Buddhists on projects of this sort. She felt that besides being worthwhile in their own right, these joint undertakings helped them to understand and appreciate one another more. In the area of social ethics especially, they found that they had a great deal in common.

Christianity and Buddhism appeal to the highest ethical aspirations of human beings. There are important differences, to be sure, yet there is a considerable body of ethical teaching that the two religions have in common. The traditional Eight Precepts of Buddhism, accepted by monks and laity alike, are similar in many ways to the Ten Commandments of Judaism and Christianity. Followers of Buddha and of Christ are admonished to refrain from killing, stealing, lying, or misusing their sexuality. In the Sermon on the Mount, Jesus goes even further by calling on his followers to put aside anger and forgive their enemies. But Buddhists are also told not to indulge in anger and not to discuss the faults of others. It is generally agreed that the heart of Christian ethics is love, whereas in Buddhism compassion is central. Yet this is a minor difference, probably only a matter of emphasis. In any case, individuals of both faiths are expected to transcend self-interest and act for the greater good of others.

A more important difference, and one that until recently constituted a major divide between the two religions, is the absence in Buddhism of anything corresponding to the prophetic tradition in Christianity. The writings of the Hebrew prophets date from the eighth century before Christ and are particularly revered by Christians because they are thought to point to Christ. Seen in the context of their time, however, they are most notable for their social message. The prophetic sayings taken as a whole constitute a severe indictment of the ruling class for failing to live up to the social requirements of their religion. Amos, Hosea, Isaiah, and Jeremiah, along with other prophets, invoke the judgment of God against those in power because they do not rule justly and do not show mercy toward the poor and needy of the society.

The very authority of the rulers is called into question because they do not act ethically. This spirit of social criticism has not always found expression in Christianity but has been a major force for social reform when it has. It was particularly evident in the antislavery movement of the nineteenth century. More recently its influence can be seen in the liberation theologies of Latin America and in certain expressions of feminist theology.

There are Buddhist teachings having to do with society. They advance a social ideal similar in certain respects to that of liberal Christianity, though they do not challenge the established political order in the way prophetic Christianity does. The chief exemplar of the Buddhist social ideal is King Ashoka, a convert to Buddhism who ruled India in the fourth century before Christ. Prior to his conversion, Ashoka mounted a successful military campaign in which he unified his country as it had not been previously. Following his conversion, he renounced war and began instituting social reforms, such as the establishment of hospitals, schools, and other social services. Under his aegis Buddhism flourished, and for a time it was the dominant religion of India. But around the time of Christ, there was a resurgence of Hinduism, and later still the invasion and conquest of much of India by the Muslims, so that by the end of the twelfth century Buddhism was virtually extinct in the country of its origin. By then, however, it was well established in most of the neighboring countries to the east, many of which in fact had Buddhist monarchs. Ashoka represented the ideal of kingship for these societies, even though Buddhist social values were not always adhered to. It was hoped that these values would permeate the society, but Buddhists themselves were not expected to question or in any sense defy the social order based on these values. On the contrary, they were expected to be submissive to authority, whether it be that of the king or the abbot.

But this attitude may be changing. There is now a movement within Buddhism that is prepared to challenge the status quo. Known as engaged Buddhism, it is a movement of social reform grounded in traditional Buddhist values but directed toward the transformation of society. Thich Nhat Hanh is regarded as one of its founders, though he is not presently involved in direct social action. He is credited with coining the term "engaged Buddhism," and his early work in Vietnam is frequently cited as a model of Buddhist-inspired social action. One might expect to find such a movement in the West, where Buddhism is relatively new and there is a history of social reform, but it has actually made its greatest headway in Southeast Asia, where Buddhism has been around for a long time and where there has not been a history of social activism.

Sarvodaya Sharamadana, a spiritually inspired rural-development movement in Sri Lanka, is a prime example of this new social activism. Under the leadership of a Buddhist layman by the name of A. T. Ariyaratne, the Sarvodaya movement has had a transforming effect on village culture in this small, underdeveloped country. At the same time, it has posed a challenge to the national government, which at first opposed it but later agreed to work with Sarvodaya. In the current conflict between the Tamils and the Sinhalese, it is one of the few voluntary organizations in which members of the two sides have been able to work together.

So there is reason to think that Christians and Buddhists could conceivably join forces to address some of the most intractable social problems of our time, such as war, poverty, disease, and the environment. But it will not be easy. It will require a spirit of openness and a willingness to engage in serious dialogue. It may also require the joining of contemplative practice and social action. Until recently these two aspects of religion—the contemplative and the active—have largely been kept separate and have even been in some quarters regarded as incompatible. It was assumed, at least in the West until recently, that those who followed the contemplative path would have to renounce the world and withdraw into a life of inner solitude. The contemplative might choose to live in a monastery or convent but was not expected to concern himself or herself with the affairs of the larger society. That was the province of those who remained in the world and pursued the active life, who were responsible for doing the world's work and maintaining the social order. Though the divide between contemplation and action may have been greater in Christianity than in Buddhism, the idea of a contemplative engaged in social action has been fairly much of an anomaly in both traditions until lately.

It is important to recognize this historic separation in order to grasp the full significance of what Merton and Nhat Hanh have accomplished for our time. Their personal integration of the contemplative and active dimensions of their two religions, especially their engagement with social issues, goes against the grain of both traditions. Each of them drew upon elements from his own tradition to create this integration and did so in a way that was truly original. They did so, moreover, in response to the events of their own day. Their spiritual vision did not emerge full-blown, but developed over time in the context of world events of epic proportions. Both men were reflective about what they were doing. Merton, for instance, appended an essay on the subject of contemplation and action to the conclusion of his spiritual autobiography, while Nhat Hanh, at the height of the war, addressed one of his most important writings on meditation to young activists. Yet, articulate as they have been, these two religious visionaries did not just talk about the integration of contemplative practice and social action; they lived it. They have come to exemplify *engaged spirituality* in a time of extraordinary change.

The Challenge of Globalization

Thomas Merton and Thich Nhat Hanh came of age in times of international upheaval. For Merton it was the period between the two World Wars. Hitler's rise to power roughly coincided with his own attempt to find himself. He was traveling in Germany in the spring of 1932 when the Nazi party first began to attract international attention; he was a student at Columbia University when Hitler's troops occupied the Rhineland and a recent convert to Catholicism when the German army invaded Czechoslovakia; and he was preparing to become a monk as the United States prepared to enter the war. It is surely no accident that the one manuscript he took with him to the monastery— and the only novel he eventually succeeded in publishing—was originally entitled "The Journal of My Escape from the Nazis." By becoming a monk, Merton was not just seeking a more contemplative life for himself; he was fleeing a world at war.

Nhat Hanh entered the monastic order about the same time Merton did, when most of the world was embroiled in war. But for him the war did not end with the surrender of Japan in 1945. A year later it raged in his own country, as the French struggled to hold on to their colonial empire. He was twenty years old at the time and training at a monastery in central Vietnam. Because large numbers of Buddhist monks and nuns supported the resistance movement, the monastery was not a particularly safe place to be. French soldiers came with guns, and many of his brothers and sisters in the order were killed. The Geneva Peace Accords of 1954 marked an official end to the war and to French occupation of Vietnam, but before the decade was over fighting had broken out again, this time between the North and

the South. American forces replaced the French, and what had begun
as a war of national liberation became a major focal point of the
Cold War. Nhat Hanh, who wanted to support the aspirations of the
Vietnamese people as well as the modernization of Buddhism, found
himself caught in an international power struggle.

In the end, neither man was able to disengage from international
issues. Without leaving the monastery, Merton took up the cause of
nuclear disarmament and eventually added his voice to the growing
opposition to the war in Vietnam. Nhat Hanh, discouraged from returning to Vietnam following his speaking tour in the United States,
became a leader in the international peace effort and later acquired
an international reputation as a teacher of meditation. The engaged
spirituality of Merton and Nhat Hanh was formed within a global
context, which was largely shaped by war, so their global engagement
was initially directed toward issues of war and peace. But they could
see that the world was becoming increasingly interconnected and
looked for ways to utilize this connection to advance the cause of peace.

Prior to leaving for Vietnam, Nhat Hanh addressed an open letter
to Martin Luther King, appealing to the well-known civil rights leader
to support the peace effort. Later he met personally with the Pope
and with other world leaders, seeking their help and influence to
bring an end to the war. Merton initiated a correspondence with
Russian poet and novelist Boris Pasternak even before he began
writing on the subject of war and eventually developed an international
correspondence with some of the leading intellectuals, writers, and
artists of the day. Both men found ways to communicate across national
and cultural boundaries: both were global citizens before there was
any talk of globalization.

With the end of the Cold War, we are coming to realize how globally
interconnected we are. The extraordinary advances in technology of
the past half-century, combined with fewer trade restrictions and
greater democratization of commerce, has created a global marketplace
unprecedented in human history. Global communication is perhaps
the most outstanding feature of our time as national boundaries are
no longer the barriers they once were, and cultural enclaves are no
longer impervious to outside influences. Goods and services flow from
one place to another more freely and rapidly than ever before and so
do ideas. People are exposed to other cultures, other systems of
thought, other values and ideals, from all over the world as never
before. If there was a time when religions could afford to ignore one

another, they can no longer. There are not only Muslim mosques and Hindu temples in most of our major cities, but a Methodist living in the mountains of Colorado can communicate via the Internet as easily with a Buddhist in Japan as with his Catholic neighbor next door. In this electronically linked world, the encounter of religions is inevitable. The only question is, What form will it take?

It could take the form of open warfare. In a controversial paper written at the time of the war in Bosnia, Samuel P. Huntington, a Harvard professor of government, has argued that religion rather than politics or economics could be the primary source of conflict in coming years.[19] He sees religion as the glue that holds whole civilizations together. By "civilization," he means a coherent culture with a unifying set of values. He regards India and China as distinct civilizations, along with those countries whose cultures were shaped by them. He sees Western civilization as defined largely by Christianity, though he distinguishes Eastern Orthodoxy (and countries like Russia where it once predominated) from Catholicism and Protestantism, which he groups together and associates with Europe and North America. Islam serves to define a civilization encompassing most of the Arab world, while Japan, he thinks, has its own unique civilization incorporating elements of Buddhism and Shintoism. The Bosnian war epitomized for him the "clash of civilizations," involving as it did conflict between Bosnian Muslims, Croatians (who are predominantly Roman Catholic), and Serbs (who along with Russians belong to the civilization rooted in Eastern Orthodoxy). Huntington sees what happened in Bosnia as a portent of what could happen on a global scale.

Even setting aside this highly pessimistic view, it is clear that religious conflict is by no means a thing of the past. The persistent and seemingly intractable warfare between Protestants and Catholics in Northern Ireland, Arabs and Jews in the Middle East, and Hindus and Muslims in Kashmir is a constant reminder that religion can be a very divisive factor. Buddhists, with their tradition of pacifism, have not altogether succeeded either in avoiding violent conflict with their neighbors, as witness the current struggle in Sri Lanka between Tamil Hindus and Sinhalese Buddhists. It would appear sometimes that conflict is endemic to religion, with its universal claim to truth yet close identification with the culture and values of a particular people. Sooner or later, it seems, one religious community convinced of its own rightness is going to come up against the contradictory claims of another community equally convinced of its rightness. In an age of global interdependence, encounters of this kind will be difficult to avoid; and unless we can find an alternative to conflict, they will almost certainly be destructive.

Thomas L. Friedman, foreign affairs columnist for the *New York Times,* has written extensively about the phenomenon of globalization, although he prefers to think of it as a system rather than a phenomenon. In his recent book, *The Lexus and the Olive Tree,* he identifies two related developments associated with globalization: a trend toward greater cultural homogenization and resistance to this trend by those who see their cultural identity threatened by it. Homogenization comes about, he thinks, because globalization, with its "inexorable integration of markets, nation-states, and technologies," has its own dominant culture, which tends to absorb or obliterate local, indigenous cultures on a worldwide scale.[20] Resistance to this homogenization comes from the human need for roots. Local culture "roots us, anchors us, identifies us and locates us in this world," Friedman writes. Few things, he believes, enrage people more than to have their cultural identity stripped away. "They will die for it, kill for it, sing for it, write poetry for it and novelize about it." Globalization, and the culture that accompanies it, means progress for most of the world's population, yet "without a sense of home and belonging," life could become "barren and rootless."[21]

This is precisely the dilemma faced by the world's great religious traditions as they encounter one another in this age of globalization, for the merging of cultures could obscure religious differences. A vague amalgam of religious ideas could take the place of once vibrant and distinct religious traditions. We could be witnessing the homogenization of religion. Yet confronted with religious beliefs and practices very different from one's own, there is also the instinct to hold on to and defend one's own tradition. Fundamentalism is a modern phenomenon inasmuch as it is a reaction to certain secularizing tendencies in modern society. A similar reaction to religious pluralism could arise as religious communities encounter one another with ever greater frequency and immediacy. Some people will no doubt be attracted to what is different in another religion, but others will instinctively reject and recoil from it. What is needed is a new paradigm for religious encounter, one that respects religious difference yet allows for communication at a deep spiritual level. And that is exactly what Merton and Nhat Hanh brought to their historic meeting.

The New Spiritual Paradigm

Engaged spirituality as a paradigm for religious encounter consists of three basic elements: contemplative practice, social action, and interreligious dialogue. None of these elements is tradition-specific, that is to say, confined to a specific religious tradition. Every major religion has its contemplative practices. These practices are different, yet in the current situation of global encounter, we are finding that adherents of a particular religion, say, Christianity, can share meaningfully in the practices of another religion such as Buddhism. When they do, they often discover that many of their practices are quite similar, that Buddhist meditation, for instance, is not very different from certain forms of Christian prayer. By sharing in each other's practices adherents are better able to understand and appreciate each other's religion.

They may even end up appropriating some of these practices for themselves, thus expanding their contemplative repertoire. Merton, for instance, was curious about Nhat Hanh's training as a Zen monk and eager to report what he learned to his fellow Trappists. He had been pursuing the study of Zen for more than a decade when they met, so he was not ignorant of the teachings of Buddhists, but he wanted to know more about their practices. Later, when he traveled to Asia and met with Tibetan monks, he tried to learn as much as he could about the Buddhist practice of meditation and even considered returning at a later time to study with one of the lamas he met there. In the period since his death, many Catholic priests, nuns, and monks have followed his example, studying with Buddhist teachers and adopting some of their meditative practices—without feeling they had to abandon their own faith in order to do so.

Interreligious dialogue can facilitate the dissemination of contemplative practices across religious traditions by bringing practitioners into closer contact with one another. Contemplative practice, especially the kind pursued by Merton and Nhat Hanh, can in turn facilitate interreligious dialogue. It does so by creating an inner space, free of preconceptions and dogmatic convictions, the kind of psychic space in which true listening can take place. A few years ago I attended a workshop conducted by Robert Kennedy, a Catholic priest and approved Zen teacher, in which he explained what Zen meant to him. "Zen meditation," he said, "is a solvent." It dissolves prejudices and misconceptions, and sometimes beliefs as well. It allows one to be more open to experience, less constrained by previous interpretations of experience, and better able to hear what others have to say. It can also be unsettling because it invites the questioning of received opinion, including received beliefs. This does not mean that one must give up one's beliefs, only that one must take more responsibility for them. The practice of meditation, I have found, allows me to see things more clearly, make more creative choices, and ground my beliefs more fully in my personal experience. All of these factors, I am convinced, make for more effective dialogue.

Social action is another area in which practitioners of different religions are finding their interests converging. Thich Nhat Hanh discovered during the Vietnam War that Christians and Buddhists who had previously been antagonistic to one another could work together for peace. Not only were some of them at least united in their desire to end the war, but they could see a need to prepare their country for life after the war. Young people in particular were drawn to the voluntary service program he started to build schools in poor villages, teach peasants modern methods of farming, and introduce uneducated Vietnamese to the rudiments of sanitation and health care. Buddhists and Christians under the conditions of war found that they shared a vision of peace, even if they expressed it in different ways. Christians might speak of doing the will of God, and Buddhists of realizing their Buddha nature, but the practical objective was the same: to relieve suffering and restore wholeness.

In his personal tribute to his Buddhist brother, Merton observed that both he and Nhat Hanh deplored war "for the same reasons: human reasons, reasons of sanity, justice and love." He did not feel it necessary to appeal to the specific teachings of either religion in order to justify ending the war or relieving human suffering. It was enough that Buddhists and Christians shared a common humanity, that their ethical teachings expressed genuine compassion for others and a universal sense of justice. It might be argued that Christians are more experienced than Buddhists in applying ethical principles to social problems. In this respect, Buddhists could probably learn from them, and the Dalai Lama has said as much. Yet it is not as though there are no resources within Buddhism for addressing social issues. Buddhist social teachings are as profound in their way as Christian social teachings. What is needed are creative ways to apply these teachings to the exigencies of the present day, and for this to happen the two religions must work together.

Genuine dialogue, in which there is a free and open exchange of ideas, can contribute to the resolution of even the most intractable problems. That is something we have learned in other contexts. Now we are in a situation in which the most serious problems are global. They affect people in all parts of the world in ways that cannot be treated in isolation. We are coming to realize just how interdependent we are and just how important it is to have everyone's input. Buddhists and Christians, Muslims and Jews, Hindus and Sikhs, need to bring their unique religious histories and perspectives to bear on problems that are worldwide in scope, rather than be drawn into petty territorial disputes or endless discussions of internal differences. Problems such as global warming, an aging world population, or the spread of infectious diseases will require the combined efforts of the wisest people we can find, and religion has traditionally been one of the major repositories of human wisdom.

Yet if interreligious dialogue can contribute to the solution of social problems, it is also the case that attention to social problems can contribute to interreligious dialogue. We sometimes think of dialogue simply as communication between two persons, as the word "dialogue" would seem to imply. But my teacher Richard Niebuhr used to say that true dialogue has a triadic structure. It requires a third shared point of reference, something the two parties have in common that they can discourse about or act on together. This "common third" is what creates community. The community may be no larger than the family or it may encompass a whole nation or ethnic group, but what holds it together, what makes it more than a mere collection of individuals, is something beyond itself—a cause or an ideal, a shared purpose or reason for being. According to Niebuhr, there is a logic implicit in the idea of responsibility that moves inexorably toward "universal community" as the locus of social responsibility.[22] Buddhism and Christianity are both universal religions; we should therefore expect this logic to be particularly operative within their communities. As the world becomes more interconnected and the religions more involved with global issues, we should expect to see greater movement toward a universal community of responsibility based on shared social values and fueled by cross-cultural and interreligious dialogue.

When we speak of dialogue, however, it is important to realize that we are not merely talking about the sharing of ideas in some abstract or impersonal sense. True dialogue involves self-disclosure, openness, vulnerability, risk, and the willingness to change. Dialogue in this sense does not exist for the purpose of converting others to one's own point of view while remaining unaffected oneself. It is a transaction in which both parties should expect to change. But that is also true of contemplative practice and social action. People of all faiths report being deeply affected by their participation in these two forms of contemporary spirituality. Engaged spirituality, along with interreligious dialogue, could turn out to be one of the most powerful forces for religious renewal of all time.

Thomas Merton and Thich Nhat Hanh have been pioneers in the development of what has come to be known as engaged spirituality, though at the time they began their spiritual journeys they could not have known this was where they were headed. For the most part, they made it up as they went along. They drew on their own religious traditions and learned from others outside their traditions, but they also synthesized what they learned in unique and powerful ways. Although they did not have any clear models to go on, they became models for others. They proceeded, for the most part, independently of one another, starting from different places and taking different routes, yet they managed somehow to meet at the same place—or at least at a place of mutual recognition. In the succeeding chapters of this book, I will trace the spiritual development of these two remarkable individuals and show how they arrived at this common meeting place. I will then show how their influence has extended to others. The meeting of Thomas Merton and Thich Nhat Hanh is a sign of the times. It has, I believe, symbolic as well as historic significance.

2

Thomas Merton: Christian Contemplative

T HOMAS MERTON has said that he knew his autobiography would be popular. He did not know if he had written a good book, but he knew somehow that it would strike a resonant chord with readers. *The Seven Storey Mountain*, published in 1948, became an instant best-seller—and it continued to attract readers long after its author had moved on with his life. Reflecting on changes he recognized in himself five years later, Merton concluded that the author of this popular book was "dead."[1] He could no longer identify with the monk who emerges at the end of the book as the product of a classic religious conversion. The story of Merton's "conversion," as it turns out, did not end with his entrance into a monastery, but continued throughout his life. If there is one consistent theme to his story, it is his willingness to undergo profound personal change in order to realize the elusive goal of the contemplative life. By following the development of his thought through the phase of his life that begins with the publication of his autobiography and culminates in his meeting with Nhat Hanh, we can best understand what the contemplative life came to mean to him.

The Making of a Contemplative

A recent convert to Catholicism, Merton left a comfortable teaching position to enter a monastery with a reputation for being especially austere. He certainly was not one to do things by half measure.

Gethsemani was a Trappist monastery in rural Kentucky with a strict rule of silence and very little contact with the outside world. It is hard to imagine a more radical act of renunciation and separation from the world than his decision to join this order and take up permanent residence with this particular community. But for him it was no sacrifice because he saw his vocation as that of a contemplative. In the tradition of the Catholic Church going back to the fourth century, the contemplative life was clearly distinguished from the active life. If you were serious, the place to pursue such a life was the monastery, an institution specifically designed for this purpose. Separated from the demands and temptations of ordinary life, a person taking up residence in a monastery could expect to concentrate on cultivating a truly spiritual life. Work, study, and prayer were the main occupations of monks, with primary emphasis on prayer. In mid-twentieth-century America such a life would have seemed anachronistic to most people, yet it was precisely what Merton needed in order to pursue what he had come to see as his special calling.

Given present-day assumptions, it is easy to dismiss the monastic ideal as socially irresponsible, as an escape from the responsibilities of a democratic society. We need to remember, however, that more than any other institution the monastery was responsible for the preservation of learning during a time in history when civilization was under siege. Over a period of several hundred years, monks living in monasteries throughout Europe preserved manuscripts that would otherwise have been destroyed and developed methods of scholarly inquiry that would later be adopted by universities in Europe and elsewhere. By retreating to the monastery, Merton was escaping the ravages of the modern world as he saw it; but he was also entering an institution with a history of preserving the best of the spiritual tradition to which he owed allegiance. That included the contemplative tradition, which was now in danger of being lost. Since the seventeenth century, this aspect of Christianity had been, for all practical purposes, relegated to the monastery. If it was to be found anywhere, it would be in places like Gethsemani. To be a part of such a community, Merton was prepared to give up everything—even a career as a writer, something for which he had been seriously preparing himself.

One way to look at this move is to see it as an exercise in retrieval. Merton spent his first ten years in the monastery not only assimilating the spiritual practices of the community—the daily round of liturgy and prayer—but also exploring the literature of spirituality that had been compiled and preserved by the community over many centuries. He was an avid reader, and though the daily routine of the monastery did not provide much free time, he managed to explore broadly what is sometimes called the mystical tradition, beginning with the Desert Fathers of the fourth century and extending through the medieval German, Spanish, and English mystics. His considerable linguistic skills were a great advantage to him in this undertaking. Born in France and having lived there for a time, he was fluent in the language. He also had a sound education in the classics, including Latin and Greek, and was conversant in several other modern languages, particularly Spanish. He was at this time especially attracted to St. John of the Cross, a sixteenth-century Spanish mystic whose writings were highly regarded by the church but were not generally well known even within the monastic community. According to Merton, there was a time early in his training when his spiritual director thought he was spending too much time on St. John of the Cross and advised him to take a break from this kind of reading. He dutifully obeyed, but then a year later got permission to return to this course of study. He was intent on mastering this tradition, on appropriating it for himself.

It is important to recognize that Merton's purpose from the outset was not simply to acquire a scholarly understanding of the contemplative tradition; he wanted above all to *become* a contemplative. As a first step in that process, he needed to learn all he could from those who had gone before. There was probably no one in the monastery at that time who could have instructed him in the type of contemplative practice he sought, because the more advanced forms of contemplative prayer were not generally practiced even in monasteries at this time. So he looked to the writings of the masters for guidance. He also experimented with various forms of practice in order to discover for himself what worked best. To him the monastery was not simply a repository of tradition, a resource upon which to draw for an understanding of the contemplative tradition; it was also a laboratory in which to practice what the tradition had to teach and, if necessary, to invent a practice suitable to his own personality and time. Eventually Merton would contribute to the literature of contemplation as a writer and a contemplative in his own right. He could do so with authenticity, because what he wrote about he also lived.

For the initial readers of *The Seven Storey Mountain*, it must have seemed that the major crisis in his life had been resolved when he entered the monastery at Gethsemani. He seemed to have found his true vocation at last. But as his next piece of autobiographical writing was to reveal, he had simply taken the crisis to another level. *The Sign of Jonas*, published in 1953, is a fascinating book, written as he later observed "out of necessity."[2] Extracted from personal journals extending over a period of five years—from the completion of his autobiography through his ordination to his appointment as Novice Master—it recounts a continuing struggle with his vocation. He did not question his calling to the contemplative life, yet he was deeply conflicted over what it meant for him personally. Should he continue to write? He had given up his earlier ambition to be a professional writer in order to enter the monastery. Was he compromising his newfound vocation as a contemplative by continuing to write while living in the monastery? His abbot, Frederic Dunne, had ordered him to write, so he could rationalize that by telling himself it was a matter of obedience. But he was not entirely convinced, especially when it became apparent that his book was going to be a commercial success. "Look out," he told himself. "Maybe this business is going to turn your whole life upside down."[3]

There was also the question of whether he could be a true contemplative within this particular religious order. Prior to joining the Trappists, Merton had applied to the Franciscans (an order known more for the active life of service than for contemplation) and had been turned down. After describing his wild life as a college student (presumably including getting a woman pregnant), he was told that he was not suited to the religious life. But even after being accepted by the Trappists, a more contemplative order, he had doubts about whether this community was right for him. Because he felt his vocation was to the contemplative life, he was not sure that he belonged in an order that did not make pure contemplation the primary goal of the religious life. In particular, he wondered if he should not transfer to the Carthusians, a community of hermits who gathered occasionally but for the most part lived alone, each in his own hermitage. Merton felt particularly drawn to a life of solitude, which he thought might only be possible if he lived apart from others. So for a number of years he pestered his abbot and others in authority with requests to transfer to another order, and if this was not possible, for permission to live as a hermit while remaining affiliated with Gethsemani. He was consistently rebuffed. Out of respect for those in authority, he acknowledged that he might not have a purely contemplative vocation, but he could not believe that was so. "Everything in me," he wrote, "cries out for solitude and for God alone."[4]

Then there was his ordination to the priesthood, which occurred one year after the publication of his autobiography. He was convinced that the priesthood was "the one great secret for which I was born."[5] Yet he was concerned about how it might affect his vocation as a contemplative. "What is the Mass going to do to my interior life?" he asked himself, remembering that as a novice he found acts, thoughts, desires, and words all to be inadequate. "Resting in God, sleeping, so to speak, in His silence, remaining in His darkness, has fed me and made me grow for seven years." Now, he thought, "that too is likely to become inadequate."[6] The actual ordination event, extending over three days, proved to be one of the high points of his life, a "gigantic development" that he was "powerless to grasp or explain."[7] Yet how did it square with his thinking about solitude? Was it a contradiction or was it a fulfillment of his vocation as a contemplative that he did not yet understand? Merton does not question his decision to take ordination, any more than he seriously questioned his vocation as a contemplative. But he struggled to understand the meaning of his vocation in light of this and other events in his life. He was never satisfied that the issue had been resolved once and for all.

In the meantime, he had begun to write about contemplation. It was typical of Merton that he did not wait until he had resolved all his personal questions before he began to share what he had learned with others. His first attempt to explain contemplation was in response to a letter from a student at a Catholic women's college who had read his poems and wanted to know something about the practice of contemplation. His answer took the form of a treatise, later published as a booklet under the title *What Is Contemplation?* In this work he presents the traditional Catholic view of contemplation as a special gift of God for the purpose of sanctifying the life of baptized Christians. He insists that this gift is not limited to monks, that it is available, at least in principle, to everyone within the Christian community. But he also wants it understood that anyone pursuing this path must be prepared to pay the price, and that price is the renunciation of worldly interests, ambitions, anxieties, pleasures, and fears.

Following these introductory remarks, Merton proceeds to distinguish two types of contemplation: active and infused. The distinction is a familiar one, taken from traditional Catholic theology, and one that clearly favors the monastic life. Active contemplation, according to his definition, "makes use of all the resources of theology and philosophy and art and music in order to focus a simple affective gaze on God."[8] Liturgy is a prime example of active contemplation, "deeply affecting to any soul that has not had its tastes perverted by the artistic fashions of a degenerate age."[9] Active contemplation can prepare one for passive or infused contemplation, though most people are so disposed toward the active life that they never get beyond active contemplation. "Their vocation does not allow them to find the solitude and silence and leisure in which to empty their minds entirely of created things and to lose themselves in God alone."[10] Merton does not discount the active life, especially as pursued by persons dedicated to the service of God in others. Their way is definitely superior to that of "surface Christians," who are only concerned with adhering to the requirements of external religious observance. Yet he insists that contemplation in the strict sense of the word must be reserved for the "supernatural love and knowledge of God" directly infused into the soul by God—an obscure, yet real, personal experience of God.[11]

To love God with pure and disinterested love is, according to Merton, "perfect joy and the greatest of all rewards." This is not to say, however, that the life of one who takes this path is all sweetness and light. The presence of God in contemplation can be counted on to bring inner peace and strength, "but sometimes that peace is almost buried under pain and darkness and aridity."[12] The light of God directed toward the soul may not at first illuminate the mind. It may have the effect of darkening it, contradicting received ideas of God and removing even the consolations of prayer. Infused contemplation "sooner or later brings with it a terrible interior revolution."[13] The true contemplative does not flee from this internal upheaval, but rather seeks the presence of God in it. Eventually there will come an awakening in which the soul enters "a new world, a world of rich experience that transcends the level of all natural knowledge and all natural love."[14] From then on everything is different. Problems and even suffering may continue, but the love of God will have so taken possession of the soul that nothing can dislodge it. The contemplative at that point "has entered into the maturity of the spiritual life, the illuminative way, and is being drawn on towards complete union with God, in which sanctity and true Christian perfection are found."[15]

The treatise concludes with some practical advice for those wishing to follow the contemplative way. They are told, for instance, to avoid anything that might bring unnecessary complications into their lives, to do the tasks assigned to them with disinterested love and peace, and to seek solitude and silence as much as possible. They are encouraged not to be anxious about their progress along the way, because they are traveling by a path that "cannot be charted and measured."[16] As a reminder that he has not totally abandoned action for contemplation, Merton warns against the heresy of *quietism*, which he says "encloses a man within himself in an entirely selfish solitude which excludes not only other men but even God Himself." The quietist pursues "a false ideal of absolute 'annihilation' of his own soul, seeks to empty himself of all love and all knowledge and remain inert in a kind of spiritual vacuum in which there is no motion, no thought, no apprehension, no act of love, no passive receptivity but a mere blank without light or warmth or breath of interior life."[17] It is not clear that quietism was ever a serious temptation to Merton, but introducing it as a wrong turn on the contemplative path provided an occasion for him to make a connection between contemplation and action. Because Christian contemplation represents the perfection of love, he argues, it must sooner or later bring forth works of love. Yet he also advises the would-be contemplative not to be "anxious or solicitous to perform great works" for God, but to wait and be led by God to undertake "the works He has planned for you and by which He will use you to communicate the fire of His love to other men."[18]

In the course of this essay Merton quotes several important thinkers from the Christian theological tradition, including Thomas Aquinas, Bernard of Clairvaux, and John of the Cross. It is apparent that he has reflected deeply upon this tradition and incorporated it into his own thinking. It is not so evident that he has experienced all that he writes about. There is a sense that he is speaking as much to himself as to the reader when he warns that the path ahead will be difficult and may be devoid of the usual spiritual consolations. What is clear, however, is that he had chosen for himself the "dark path," the so-called apophatic approach to contemplation.[19] Within the contemplative tradition a distinction is made between the *kataphatic* approach, which uses scripture reading, visual symbols, and liturgical practices to elicit an affective response to God, and the *apophatic* approach, in which a person enters through meditation into a state of consciousness beyond words and images. The latter approach would not at that time have been considered a real option for someone not pursuing a religious vocation. In addressing his remarks to all baptized Christians,

Merton implies that it should be possible for anyone to follow this path, even though most will not choose it. For those who elect to follow this course, he lets them know what to expect. In particular, he prepares them for the likelihood that it will not offer the usual assurances of God's presence. The dark path, as he describes it, is fraught with existential dread.

From Merton's journals, and particularly the passages selected for inclusion in *The Sign of Jonas*, we learn that he experienced an existential crisis of his own around this time. The crisis focused on his writing. He had set himself the ambitious task of writing a theology of contemplation that would be nothing less than a grand synthesis of scripture and tradition. He researched the subject, compiling hundreds of pages of notes; yet unlike most of his other writing, he was unable to make progress with this particular project. Soon after his ordination, undoubtedly one of the defining moments of his life, he collapsed while celebrating the Mass and had to be hospitalized and for a time gave up writing; even his journals were a patchy affair. Then, "in the depth of this abysmal testing and disintegration of my spirit," he later observed, "I suddenly discovered completely new moral resources, a spring of new life, a peace and happiness I had never known before and which subsisted in the face of nameless, interior terror."[20] Eventually he returned to the project that had so frustrated him and saw the book through to completion in 1951. Yet he was never very happy with it, regarding it as one of his least successful efforts, and most critics would agree with that assessment. In spite of some felicitous observations, examples, and analogies, *The Ascent to Truth*, as it came to be titled, has a rather dry, academic feel to it. The author of this work is reporting on the contemplative tradition with the objectivity of a scholar, rather than speaking as one who tried to live it on a daily basis.

Reflections on the Contemplative Experience

Prior to completing this scholarly project, Merton wrote another, quite different book on the subject of contemplation, one that proved to have wide popular appeal. *Seeds of Contemplation* first appeared in 1949, shortly after the publication of *What Is Contemplation?* In a journal entry from the previous summer, he speaks of writing this book "during the week," giving the impression that it might have been something dashed off in haste.[21] Actually the book had been in process for some time and was to undergo further revision within a year of publication. Then, in 1962, he brought out another version, greatly revised and expanded, entitled *New Seeds of Contemplation*. Both books have sold well, and together they have been translated into more than a dozen languages. None of Merton's other writings so clearly reveal the development of his thought on the subject of contemplation as these two books do, one written soon after the publication of his autobiography and the other shortly before the start of his social criticism. Unlike *Ascent to Truth*, which he had such difficulty writing, *Seeds of Contemplation* is designed to evoke the experience of contemplation rather than just talk about it. It is written in a language that is sometimes didactic, but more often poetic. More than any of his writings to this time, it captures the spirit and tone of the contemplative life as he lived it.

There is no mistaking the monastic setting of these reflections. Merton occasionally addresses his remarks specifically to monks, as when he criticizes them for developing "an attachment to prayer or fasting, or to a pious practice or devotion, or to a certain external penance, or to a book or a system of spirituality, or to a method of meditation or even to contemplation itself."[22] Yet it is clear from the outset that he did not write this book simply for monks. He wrote *as* a monk for a much wider audience. In the opening lines of the book, he boldly asserts that "every moment and every event of every man's life on earth plants something in his soul." Most of these "seeds of contemplation" perish and are lost, because most men are not prepared to receive them. They only grow, he believes, in "the good soil of liberty and desire."[23] Merton's primary purpose in writing this book, as he makes clear near the end, was to share what he had learned from the practice of contemplation and to do so in a way that would give guidance to those who freely desired to take up this path, whether monk or lay. "The highest vocation in the Kingdom of God," he writes, "is that of sharing one's contemplation with others and bringing other men to the experimental knowledge of God that is given to those who love Him perfectly."[24]

One of the necessary conditions for contemplative practice, as he understood it, is the experience of solitude. Merton initially sought solitude for himself by entering a monastery. Though not entirely alone as a member of a monastic community, he was at least removed from the secular world with all its distractions. During the early years of his training, his order did not permit him to read magazines or newspapers, listen to the radio, or converse with fellow monks. Bound by the rule of silence, he could only communicate by sign language. There are places in *Seeds of Contemplation* where Merton implies that anyone who is at all serious about contemplative practice should try to approximate this form of life. "Do everything you can to avoid the amusements and the noise and the business of men. Keep as far away as you can from the places where they gather to cheat and insult one another, to exploit one another, to laugh at one another, or to mock one another with their false gestures of friendship." He even suggests not reading the newspaper.[25] Yet he does not equate solitude with world denial. He recognizes that those who try to escape the world merely by leaving it and "hiding in solitude" will end up taking it with them into solitude. Although he continues to insist that "physical solitude, exterior silence and real recollection are morally necessary for anyone who wants to lead a contemplative life," he acknowledges that the "truest solitude is not something outside you, not an absence of men or of sound around you: it is an abyss opening up in the center of your own soul."[26] His reflections on his own contemplative experience are meant to point the way into that abyss.

Merton begins his reflections where his own spiritual journey began—with the all too familiar human longing to find oneself. Other creatures, he observes, are given their identity along with their nature; they simply are what they are. Human beings create an identity for themselves through the choices they make, but these choices are often self-defeating. Rather than lay claim to our true identity, we create a false one, which in turn imprisons us. We may think we are free, but we are actually captive to our own selfish desires and egotistical illusions. We are unable to find true happiness, because we do not know who we truly are. The true self, Merton contends, can only be found in God—and then only as God finds us. The contemplative quest, as he experienced it and wrote about it, is at once a search for God and for oneself.

To engage seriously in this quest is to commit oneself to honest and thorough self-examination. Merton models this self-critical approach in his journals, where he openly questions himself, his motives, and his resolve. But it also comes out in this work, if somewhat more indirectly, as when he speaks of the "disease of spiritual pride."

Here is a man who has done many things that were hard for his flesh to accept. He has come through difficult trials and done a lot of work, and by God's grace he has come to possess a habit of fortitude and self-sacrifice in which, at last, labor and suffering become easy. It is reasonable that his conscience should be at peace. But before he realizes it, the clean peace of a will united to God becomes the complacency of a will that loves its own excellence.[27]

Merton valued integrity and humility equally. In fact, he saw them as virtually indistinguishable. To be truly humble is to be the person you actually are before God. But that, as he found out, is no easy task. It takes "heroic humility to be yourself and to be nobody else but the man, or the artist, that God intended you to be." Besides, he acknowledged, "you can never be sure whether you are being true to your true self or only building up a defense for the false personality that is the creature of your own appetite for esteem."[28] That is why contemplative practice is so important. It is a way to break down these egoistic defenses and prepare oneself for genuine "self-emptying."

In spite of the obvious importance that contemplative practice had in Merton's life at this time, he says surprisingly little about it in this book. In the section "Mental Prayer," he says that "true contemplation" begins with the "direct intervention of God" and goes on to say that before this can happen "we ordinarily have to labor to prepare ourselves" through meditation and active forms of prayer. We might expect him, at this point, to give some specific directions for meditation or mental prayer based on his own experience, but he does not. He notes that there are "all kinds of techniques and methods of meditation and mental prayer" but declines to comment on any of them, except to say that they are fine "for those who can use them."[29] The trouble with all these methods, he feels, is that people tend to rely on them instead of thinking for themselves. To suppose that you are obliged to follow the author of one of these books on meditation to a particular conclusion would be a mistake, he warns. It may be that this approach does not apply to you. "God may want you to end up somewhere else."[30] But then Merton goes on to speak of where the practice of meditation might eventually lead—and the reference to his own practice is unmistakable. If your practice should take you "beyond the level of your understanding and your imagination" to a place of darkness where you can no longer think of God, you may be led into a "completely simple form of affective prayer," with few words or none, or to a "simple contemplative gaze" in which your attention is directed to God in faith, without assurances of any kind. We are now clearly beyond "meditation" as a process involving active thought and into the sphere of true contemplation.[31]

Though reluctant to talk about his own contemplative practice, Merton speaks eloquently of the *experience* of contemplation, an important characteristic of which is a sense of emptiness. This is not the emptiness of meaninglessness or despair such as we find in much existentialist literature, but rather of freedom from the limitations of self. According to Merton, an "abyss of freedom" opens up within us whose function is to "draw us utterly out of our own selfhood" and into an "immensity of liberty and joy." If there is any sorrow associated with this process, he says, it is that we retain a sense of "separate existence."[32] Reflecting on the process, he concludes that he is the same person he has always been. If anything, he is more himself than ever. But he has discovered a depth of freedom in himself that he had not known previously. Experiencing his own emptiness, he has had a taste of the Infinite.

In the depths of this freedom, which he describes as not so much a place as an activity, Merton encounters Love. It forms a kind of inner "citadel," which nothing from the outside can penetrate. He describes the experience as follows:

> There is a whole sphere of your own activity that is excluded from that beautiful airy night. The five senses, the imagination, the discoursing mind, the hunger of desire do not belong in that starless sky. . . . You find that you can rest in this darkness and this unfathomable peace without trouble and without anxiety, *even when the imagination and the mind remain in some way active* outside the doors of it. . . . Within the simplicity of this armed and walled and undivided peace is an infinite unction which, as soon as it is grasped, loses its savor. You must not try to reach out and possess it altogether. You must not touch it, or try to seize it. You must not try to make it sweeter or try to keep it from wasting away.[33] (Italics added).

Those who have practiced deep meditation will have no trouble recognizing this experience, even if they would describe it somewhat differently, for it is a familiar one. The mind remains active, thoughts and images continue to appear, but they are no longer distracting. They do not capture our attention as they would ordinarily. Yet wonderful as this experience is, we should not try to hold on to it. According to Merton, "the moment we demand anything for ourselves or even trust in any action of our own to procure a deeper intensification of this pure and serene rest in God, we defile and dissipate the perfect gift that He desires to communicate to us in the silence and repose of our own powers." Merton clearly sees our own activity as "an obstacle to the infusion of this peaceful and pacifying light."[34] At this point in the development of his thought, there is a rather deep divide between contemplation and action.

There might also seem to be a separation between the experience of contemplation and the teachings of the church. After all, the contemplative path offers a person direct access to God and appeals to personal experience rather than church doctrine for its authority. It is little wonder that contemplative teachings have been regarded with suspicion throughout much of church history or that practitioners of the contemplative way such as Origen and Eckhart have sometimes been considered heretics. Merton, however, does not see it that way. He thinks that the great contemplatives of the past, the saints as he calls them, arrived at their deepest and most vital, their most individual and personal, knowledge of God, "precisely because of the Church's teaching authority, precisely through the tradition that is guarded and fostered by that authority." He even goes so far as to dismiss any claim to contemplative knowledge of God that is not sanctioned by the Catholic Church. Outside of the teaching authority of the church, guided by the Holy Spirit, he asserts, one finds "only the void of nirvana or the feeble intellectual light of Platonic idealism, or the sensual dreams of the Sufis."[35] He makes it clear that these other traditions do not measure up. *Seeds of Contemplation* is a work firmly anchored in the Christian tradition—even to the exclusion of other religions.

Hearing this book read aloud to his fellow monks soon after publication, Merton notes in his journal that he is glad it has been written and read. But then he adds: "Surely I have said enough about the business of darkness and about the 'experimental contact with God in obscurity' to be able to shut up about it and go onto something else for a change."[36] He could not have known at that time just how great a shift was about to occur in his thinking. When the revised version came out twelve years later under the title *New Seeds of Contemplation*, it was a very different book, and he was in many respects a different person. The changes that he underwent during this period of his life are intimated in some of the journal observations in *The Sign of Jonas*. He acknowledges, for instance, that he had come to accept writing as a part of his contemplative vocation rather than a divergence. "Sometimes I feel that I would like to stop writing, precisely as a gesture of defiance. . . . And yet it seems to me that writing, far from being an obstacle to spiritual perfection in my own life, has become one of the conditions on which my perfection will depend."[37] He had decided to live the life of a monk to the best of his ability and at the same time to write about it. The challenge would be "to put myself down on paper, in such a situation, with the most complete simplicity and integrity, masking nothing, confusing no issues." He knew it would be difficult, "because I am all mixed up in illusions and attachments." He determines nevertheless to "put it all down," confusions and all, without exaggeration or special pleading, in the interests of "a complete and holy transparency." He wonders if this way of losing himself might not, after all, be his way into solitude.[38]

As Merton's sense of vocation expands, so also does his understanding of solitude. When he first began to receive letters from readers of his autobiography, he thought they might disrupt his solitude. He was prepared to accept the letters as a penance but found them instead to be a blessing. "People write to me with great simplicity as though it were the most natural thing in the world . . . it is beautiful to see how genuine people can be . . . it is beautiful to see God's grace working in people." And then he makes an observation that anticipates the future direction of his thought. "The most beautiful thing about it," he says, "is to see how the desires of the soul, inspired by God, so fit in and harmonize with grace that holy things seem *natural* to the soul, seem to be part of its very self."[39] He is beginning to revise his understanding of contemplation to bring it more in touch with the world and the lives of ordinary people.

In 1951, he was given a new assignment within the monastic community. He was appointed Master of scholastics, with the responsibility of preparing fellow monks for ordination and solemn vows. (Four years later he was given even greater pastoral responsibility as Master of novices, with oversight of the spiritual formation of all new monks.) He thought at first that this job might interfere with his solitude but found instead that it led him further into solitude. It became for him a "new desert," and the name of this desert was compassion.[40] He came in time to see in his students "something of the depths of solitude which are in every human person, but which most men do not know how to lay open either to themselves or to others or to God."[41] During this period, he was coming to know experientially what he had previously only known intellectually, namely his solidarity with others in their solitude.

Something else was happening at this time, the full significance of which would only come to light much later. Merton was beginning to take an interest in other religions. He had considered the Eastern religions briefly during his period as a student at Columbia University but found them confusing and unpromising. His comments about other religions in the first edition of *Seeds of Contemplation* were unsympathetic, if not disparaging. Yet in *The Sign of Jonas* there is evidence of an awakening interest in Buddhism. The Archbishop of Nanking had visited Gethsemani and talked about China, the contemplative life, and Buddhist monasticism. Merton notes without objection "the reproach that Buddhists fling at us, that is, we are all very fine at building hospitals but we have no contemplatives."[42] When a Hindu writes to him about yoga, Merton replies immediately, asking him to send some books. Even a chemist hired to help with some paint jobs is invited to speak to the community when it is learned that he is a postulant in a Zen Buddhist monastery in Hawaii.

We know that Merton was reading about Zen during this time, because in 1958 he wrote to D. T. Suzuki, the most well-known Japanese interpreter of Zen to the West, inviting him to write an introduction to a collection of sayings of the Desert Fathers that he was preparing for publication. In that letter he speaks of his growing fascination with Zen. "Time after time, as I read your pages, something in me says, 'That's it!' Don't ask me what. I have no desire to explain it to anybody, or to justify it to anybody, or to analyze it for myself. I have my own way to walk, and for some reason or other Zen is right in the middle of it wherever I go. . . . If I could not breathe Zen I would probably die of spiritual asphyxiation."[43] Even before he undertook a major revision of *Seeds of Contemplation* in 1961, Merton was having misgivings about his earlier judgments of other religions. In the seventh printing of *Seeds*, which came out less than a year after the first edition, he made a number of revisions that affected the general tone of the book but did not greatly alter its substance. One of those changes, however, was quite significant. That was his decision to remove all the pejorative references to other religions.

An Enlarged Vision of the Contemplative Life

In the preface to *New Seeds of Contemplation*, Merton explains that it is "not merely a new edition of an old book," but is in many ways "a completely new book."[44] Some of the more problematic passages in the earlier book are omitted or modified, especially those reflecting an attitude of intense world renunciation, while additions are made that give the later version a more inclusive and nonsectarian feel. Among the additions is a whole new introductory section that addresses the question, "What is contemplation?" This is the same question he considered earlier in response to a student's inquiry, but now his approach is quite different. The traditional distinction between active and infused contemplation is gone, along with his many appeals to the authoritative teachings of the church fathers. In the new work, Merton places contemplation squarely within the context of ordinary life and appeals directly to experience. The opening lines of the book set the tone for what is to follow:

> Contemplation is the highest expression of man's intellectual and spiritual life. It is that life itself, fully awake, fully active, fully aware that it is alive. It is spiritual wonder. It is spontaneous awe at the sacredness of life, of being. It is gratitude for life, for awareness and for being. It is a vivid realization of the fact that life and being in us proceed from an invisible, transcendent and infinitely abundant Source. Contemplation is, above all, awareness of the reality of that Source.[45]

Merton has not abandoned the dark path. He continues to insist that the knowledge that comes through contemplation is "too deep to be grasped in images, in words or even in clear concepts." It can only be suggested by words and symbols, and even then "the contemplative mind takes back what it has said, and denies what it has affirmed." While this form of "knowing" is beyond us, beyond ordinary knowing and unknowing, it is nevertheless integral to who we are. And it puts us in touch with what is most real in the world around us. Contemplation, he concludes, is an "awakening to all that is Real within the real."[46]

From the opening section of the book, one might conclude that Merton had abandoned traditional Christian teaching in favor of something more general and inclusive. But that is not altogether the case. The material added to *Seeds of Contemplation* to create *New Seeds of Contemplation* contains much that is explicitly Christian. For instance, he expands his treatment of Christ and adds to what he had previously written about the Virgin Mary (including comments that show he has a non-Catholic audience in mind). In several places he adds pastoral advice reflecting his experience as a mentor to the young monks at

Gethsemani, for by now he holds the title of Master of novices with responsibility for the theological education and spiritual formation of all initiates. The tone of the book is less severe and more reassuring than the previous work, more understanding and accepting of the "habits and diversions of ordinary people."[47] Merton does not give up his earlier insistence that the contemplative life requires a measure of "ascetic self-discipline," but he is more realistic and shows greater appreciation for the situation of his readers.

One new element in the book that contributes to this change of tone is his introduction of themes from the wisdom tradition. This is a strand of Christian thought that emphasizes the goodness of creation and the values inherent in ordinary life. The true spiritual life, Merton observes, "is a life neither of dionysian orgy nor of appollonian clarity: it transcends both. It is a life of wisdom, a life of sophianic love."[48] This theme is expressed in many places in his journals from this period, but it is particularly evident in his response to nature. Merton responded with Zen-like immediacy to the natural beauty of his surroundings—to the woods at various seasons of the year, to the birds whose flight and sounds invariably evoked a sense of wonder, and to the other creatures he encountered on his frequent walks in the woods. The concluding section of *New Seeds* is especially lyrical in this regard, speaking of creation as a "garden of delight" and of God's presence in creation as a "cosmic dance." It would be fair to say that *New Seeds* retains the substance of the earlier book, yet set within a framework that not only changes the tone but greatly expands the scope and vision of the work.

Merton also brings to this revised version a philosophical dimension that was not present in the earlier work. It comes out most clearly in his discussion of the self, the subject of contemplative experience. This is not a new topic for him, as we have seen. In the previous book he spoke at length about discovering oneself and realizing one's true identity in God. What he lacked at that time was an adequate language for differentiating the self of ordinary experience from the self disclosed through contemplation. Initially he employed a true/false dichotomy based on the concept of Original Sin to make this distinction. "To say that I was born in sin is to say I came into the world with a false self," he writes. What is this false self? we may ask. It is one that "wants to exist outside the radius of God's will and God's love." It is the egocentric self that tries to build itself up at the expense of others and in defiance of the reality that its existence is totally dependent upon God. Such a self, he thinks, can only be an illusion, whereas the truth about the self is "hidden in the love and mercy of God."[49] From the contemplative perspective, life is "a series of choices between the fiction of our false self, whom we feed with the illusions of passion and selfish appetite, and our true identity in the peace of God."[50] In these passages from his earlier work, Merton seems to espouse a kind of moral and religious dualism.

Yet it is more complicated than that. Even in the earlier *Seeds*, Merton was groping for a way to distinguish the self of contemplation from the self of ordinary experience beyond simply pointing to the distortion introduced by sin. "One of the greatest paradoxes of the mystical life," he writes, "is this: *that a man cannot enter into the deepest center of himself and pass through that center into God, unless he is able to pass entirely out of himself and empty himself and give himself to other people in the purity of a selfless love.*"[51] But if one passes entirely out of oneself and empties oneself, what becomes of the true-self/false-self distinction discussed earlier? It would appear that it is no longer relevant. In the concluding section of *Seeds*, Merton observes that however much we may feel we have experienced God's love, as long as there is any sense of separation, any awareness of distance and difference between ourselves and God, "we have not yet entered into the fullness of contemplation." We have yet to pass through the abyss that separates us from God. Once we make this transition, however, we realize there was no abyss after all. "What happens is that the separate entity that was *you* suddenly disappears and nothing is left but a pure freedom indistinguishable from infinite Freedom, love identified with Love." You as the subject of this experience, if we may call it an experience, no longer exists as a separate and distinct subject capable of self-judgment or self-reflection. Thus, he concludes, "where contemplation becomes what it is really meant to be, it is no longer something poured out of God into the created subject, so much as God living in God and identifying a created life with His own Life so that there is nothing left of any significance but God living in God."[52]

In *New Seeds*, Merton carries this line of thought further. In the opening section of the book where he discusses the meaning of contemplation, he introduces a new concept: the transcendent self. He distinguishes this self from the self of ordinary experience, which he variously calls the external, empirical, or superficial self. Although he sometimes speaks of this transcendent self as the true self, he does not do so in contradistinction to what he previously called the false self. The external self, as he understands it, is not inherently sinful, as the false self is. It is simply the self that "works in the world, thinks about itself, observes its own reactions and talks about itself." Whenever we use the personal pronoun "I" in ordinary discourse, we are referring to this self. By comparison, the transcendent self is "mysterious and unknown," by its very nature "hidden, unnamed, unidentified in the society where men talk about themselves and about one another."[53] It belongs to a wholly different plane than the empirical self. It is *this* self, Merton says, that is "united to God in Christ." And what has all that to do with contemplation? Contemplation is our awakening to this mysterious and elusive self, this unknown "I" beyond observation and reflection. The contemplative, he asserts, does not arrive at a true insight into the nature of the self by way of observation or deduction, but rather by an "intuitive awakening in which our free and personal reality becomes fully alive to its own existential depths, which open out into the mystery of God."[54]

Some years later Merton wrote an essay specifically addressing the question "Who is it that has a transcendent experience?" He notes in this essay that various metaphorical expressions have been used to speak of transcendent or mystical experience but insists that none of these expressions is really adequate. They point to a problem: "the problem of a self that is 'no-self,' that is by no means an 'alienated self' but on the contrary a transcendent Self." Transcendent experience, he had come to see, is not experience in the ordinary sense of the word, any more than the subject of the experience is a self in the ordinary sense of that word. To put it in Christian terms, the subject of transcendent experience is "metaphysically distinct from the Self of God and yet perfectly identified with that Self by love and freedom, so that there appears to be but one Self." Transcendent experience is an illumination of this relationship of identity and love. It is not a typical "religious or spiritual experience," in which the subject of the experience remains "more or less conscious of himself as subject" and may even have the awareness of subjectivity "heightened and purified," but rather an experience in which, according to Merton, "there is a radical and revolutionary change in the subject."[55]

In the so-called higher religions such as Christianity and Buddhism, the path of the mystic is sometimes spoken of as one of "self-emptying" or "self-naughting" rather than self-affirmation or self-fulfillment. That is not because those who follow this path are thought to have

lost their metaphysical status as discrete selves—regressed, as it
were, into nonentities—but because they have come to recognize their
true status as quite other than what it would appear to be empirically.
If we are to make any sense of mystical experience, Merton observes,
it is important that we *"become detached from our everyday conception
of ourselves as potential subjects for special and unique experiences,
or as candidates for realization, attainment and fulfillment."*[56] He
concludes his essay with the observation that this whole question is
"a matter of crucial importance for the dialogue between Eastern and
Western religion."[57] We will return to this subject later, but for now
it is worth noting that Merton's deeper understanding of the self
developed in the context of his study of Zen.

Merton's Turn toward the World

Along with his discovery of Buddhism, another development was
taking place in the author of *New Seeds of Contemplation* that would
profoundly affect his sense of vocation. He had begun a "turn toward
the world" that would place him at the forefront of some of the most
controversial social and political issues confronting America in the
1960s. Without leaving the monastery, he became known during this
period as a radical social critic and prominent antiwar activist. There
is scarcely a hint of this development in *Seeds*. But in *New Seeds*,
published in 1962, Merton signals a change. He does so by the way
he expands the chapter "The Root of War Is Fear."

   In the earlier book his comments on war are fairly brief and rather
general, while in the later book they are much more developed and
include specific references to the political climate of that time. For
instance, he contends that "everyone is becoming more and more
aware of the widening gulf between good purposes and bad results,
between efforts to make peace and the likelihood of war."[58] He goes
on to speak even more pointedly, asking "What is the use of post-
marking our mail with exhortations to 'pray for peace' and then spending billions of dollars on atomic submarines, thermonuclear weapons,
and ballistic missiles?" It is not that he thinks there is no value in
prayer accompanied by action. But he is struck by the "disproportion
between our piety and the enormous act of murderous destruction
which we at the same time countenance without compunction and

without shame!" As a Christian people we apparently see no contradiction between "praying to the God of peace" and simultaneously "planning to annihilate not thousands but millions of civilians and soldiers, men, women and children without discrimination, even with the almost infallible certainty of inviting the same annihilation for ourselves!"[59] He clearly has in mind the nuclear arms race and the much-discussed possibility that the Cold War might lead to an all-out war between the United States and the Soviet Union.

Even before *New Seeds* was in print, Merton submitted the chapter on war as a separate article to the *Catholic Worker*, a publication with a reputation for taking radical positions on political issues. So that there would be no mistaking his intent, he attached some additional paragraphs specifically addressing what he called "the present war crisis." In these introductory paragraphs, he asserts that the world is headed toward a nuclear holocaust, "plunging headlong into frightful destruction, and doing so *with the purpose of avoiding war and preserving peace!*" To illustrate the insanity of nuclear war, he cites those who would build bomb shelters "where they will simply bake instead of burning up quickly" and who would defend their shelters with machine guns "to prevent their neighbor from entering." The only sane response in this situation, he contends, is to work for the total abolition of war. We must set ourselves to this task "both as individuals and in our political and religious groups." Otherwise we will "by our passivity and fatalism" cooperate with the "destructive forces that are leading inexorably to war." No longer is Merton advising the would-be contemplative to refrain from reading the newspaper; he is sounding a call for social action. "Christians must become active in every possible way, mobilizing all of their resources for the fight against war." They may not succeed in this undertaking, but it is their duty to do whatever they can to advance the cause of peace. "It is the great Christian task of our time."[60]

Merton followed this article a few months later with one in *Commonweal*, a Catholic journal with a much wider audience. "Nuclear War and Christian Responsibility" lays out the basic argument he will advance in all subsequent writings on the subject of nuclear war.[61] First, he asserts that the mere existence of nuclear weapons is a serious threat to peace. In a world where another Hitler is always possible, these weapons pose the possibility of mass destruction on a scale never before imagined. Even our own democratically elected leaders, he felt, were prepared to use them if necessary. They say that nuclear weapons would only be used as a last resort but do not categorically rule out the possibility of a first strike. Previous experience has shown, according to Merton, a tendency toward escalation in any war. Self-imposed ethical restraint tends to give way to expediency and a general desire to put an end to the war by whatever means available. Second, he questioned the policy of intimidation practiced by the American government. By threatening the use of nuclear weapons, he believed, we make their actual use seem more plausible. In time we may even come to think of nuclear war as ethically justifiable. Yet for Merton, there can be *no* ethical justification for nuclear war. He was convinced that the theory of the "just war" advanced by theologians in the past to justify limited war under conditions of self-defense simply did not apply to nuclear war. He cites the statements of recent popes to support this view, while acknowledging that they nowhere specifically condemn the use of nuclear weapons. The logic of their statements, he thought, leads to that conclusion, especially what they say about the "uncontrolled effects" of weapons of mass destruction. Nuclear war by its very nature represents a unique situation in human history inasmuch as it puts the very survival of humanity at risk.

What is the responsibility of the Christian in this situation? According to Merton, Christ did not come to bring peace to the world "as a kind of spiritual tranquilizer." Rather he gave to his disciples "a vocation and a task, to struggle in the world of violence to establish his peace not only in their own hearts but in society itself."[62] Merton is particularly concerned about what he considers the pervasive condition of "moral passivity" and "demonic activism" in the modern world. There is, on the one hand, a general attitude of submission to a determinism that renders people completely irresponsible, and on the other hand a frenzy of technological improvisation and proliferation that is increasingly out of control. We need to slow down the production of arms and move toward disarmament. But equally important, and perhaps more difficult, we must find a way to restore a sense of moral responsibility within the general population. We cannot wait until the world is on the brink of war. For it would be folly to suppose that persons who have been till then "passive, inert, morally indifferent and irresponsible" will suddenly recover "their sense of obligation and their awareness of their own power." We must begin now to form the nation's conscience in respect to this unprecedented threat to human survival. We cannot leave it to our leaders to do our thinking for us. "We have to make ourselves heard."[63]

Because *Commonweal* reached a larger audience, this article attracted more notice than the previous one. Merton came under attack for his views and also for speaking out on a subject that was not considered the proper province of a monk. He had submitted the article in advance to the censors of his religious order and received approval for publication. Yet now that the article had proven controversial, it would be more difficult for him to get approval for this kind of writing. In fact, within three months of the publication of "Nuclear War and Christian Responsibility," he was informed by the abbot general in France that he was forbidden to publish any more articles on the subject of war and peace. He was determined, however, to speak out and make himself heard on the subject. So he adopted various tactics to circumvent the ban, including publishing in little-known journals, writing under a pseudonym, distributing mimeographed letters among a network of friends, and editing a book of essays on peace without identifying himself as the editor.

In the meantime, he had begun to speak out on other social issues, notably race relations. In 1963, Merton first published his "Letters to a White Liberal." What makes these essays so remarkable in the context of the time is that they do not unequivocally endorse the civil rights movement led by Martin Luther King. Merton is clearly in support of what King is doing, especially his use of nonviolent protest as an instrument of social change. But he is critical of white liberals who suppose that they can correct the injustice of segregation without acknowledging their own complicity in racial injustice. As long as they retain control of the power structure and do not give up any of their advantages, they have not addressed the root cause of black dissent. "American society *has to change* before the race problem can be solved," he writes.[64] That change will not come about peacefully unless whites freely give up their position of presumed superiority, listen to what blacks have to say, and work with them as equals in the cause of social justice. The only alternative to a radical change in the prevailing attitude of the white power structure, Merton believed, was violent protest on the part of blacks.

As the Vietnam War continued to escalate, he wrote on that subject as well. He saw American policy, which claimed to be realistic, as largely a product of myth and completely out of touch with the needs of the Vietnamese people. "Our external violence in Vietnam is rooted in an inner violence which simply ignores the human reality of those we claim to be helping."[65] He saw a connection between the violence in Southeast Asia and the violence in American cities. "In Vietnam, the U.S. has officially adopted the policy that the best way to get across an idea is by fire and dynamite. Is it surprising that the Negro has caught on, and decided that he will try a little bit of the same?"[66] The various crises confronting the nation, including domestic violence, racial conflict, and nuclear armament, were, according to Merton, all rooted in ourselves. The basic problem, as he saw it, is not merely political or economic or legal (and never really was). "It is a spiritual and psychological problem of a society which has developed too fast and too far for the psychic capacities of its members, who can no longer cope with their inner hostilities and destructiveness. They can no longer really manage their lives in a fully reasonable and human way—only by resort to extreme and possibly destructive maneuvers."[67]

So what is the solution? In an essay on the Christian roots of non-violence, he recommends that we seriously examine our own "delusionary thinking," while at the same time endeavoring to learn from our adversaries. "The dread of being open to the ideas of others generally comes from our hidden insecurity about our own convictions." We fear that we will be dislodged from our deepest convictions. Yet if we are mature and open-minded, "we may find that in viewing things from a basically different perspective—that of our adversary—we discover our own truth in a new light and are able to understand our own ideals more realistically."[68] We should then be in a position to approach problems in a more humane and constructive way.

Wise as this counsel may be, one might wonder what it has to do with contemplation. Has Merton given up contemplative practice for social action? How does he reconcile his life of relative solitude as a Cistercian monk with his new role as social critic and peace activist? To answer this question, we must first go back to *Seeds of Contemplation* and consider what he says there about action. In that earlier work (as well as in *New Seeds*), he speaks of contemplation and action as intrinsically related. "*Far from being essentially opposed to each other, interior contemplation and external activity are two aspects of the same love of God,*" he writes. Then he adds, as a corollary, "*the activity of a contemplative must be born of his contemplation and must resemble it.*"[69] (Italics added.) This last statement might seem to imply that contemplation is primary and that action, properly conceived, derives from it, thus tending to resemble it. Although this interpretation may accurately reflect Merton's view at the time, it is not the only possible interpretation, particularly in light of what he has to say later about the self. The statement could mean that action and contemplation naturally exhibit many of the same qualities, because both derive ultimately from personal union with God. At the deepest level of selfhood, what he later came to call the "transcendent Self," there is no real distinction between contemplation and action. Both express the will of God; both are manifestations of the gracious love of God.

Merton's Opening to Others

Still we may ask: Why did Merton's action at his time take the form of social action, active engagement with problems of the larger society? He offers a partial explanation in the preface to *New Seeds of Contemplation*, where he notes that it had been twelve years since the publication of the earlier version of this book.

> When the book was first written, the author had no experience in confronting the needs and problems of other men. The book was written in a kind of isolation, in which the author was alone with his own experience of the contemplative life. And such a book can be written best, perhaps only, in solitude. The second writing has been no less solitary than the first: but the author's solitude has been modified by contact with other solitudes; with the loneliness, the simplicity, the perplexity of novices and scholastics of his monastic community; with the loneliness of people outside any monastery; with the loneliness of people outside the Church.[70]

During this time Merton expanded his experience of other people and in the process gained a greater appreciation for their suffering. Through the many letters he received from persons of diverse backgrounds and commitments from outside of the monastery, as well as by teaching and counseling the cadre of young men who were coming into the monastery at this time, he widened and deepened his vision of the world.

This change did not take place all at once. Merton notes in his writings two times when he had occasion to spend a day in nearby Louisville and realized that a profound shift had occurred in his perception of people. The first incident occurred in August 1948, nearly seven years after he entered the monastery, when he was asked to accompany a foreign visitor on a trip to the city. Looking back on it some years later, Merton says that he wondered at the time "how I would react at meeting once again, face to face, the wicked world." To his surprise he found it "no longer so wicked after all." He speculates that "perhaps the things I had resented about the world when I left it were defects of my own that I had projected upon it. Now, on the contrary, I found that everything stirred me with a deep and mute sense of compassion." He makes several observations about the people he passed on the street that day, but does not pursue this line of thought, because, as he says, "I seemed to have lost an eye for merely exterior detail and to have discovered, instead, a deep sense of respect and love and pity for the souls that such details never fully reveal."[71] From this account it would appear that a shift had already begun in his perception of others, even before he began to broaden his experience of the world through his teaching and correspondence. To what are we to attribute this shift if not to his contemplative practice? Assuming that he was following the dark path during this period of his life and not just writing about it, we would expect to see just the sort of change described here.

But before pursuing this idea further, we need to consider a second incident in which Merton reports a radical shift in his perception. This is the famous "epiphany" at the corner of Fourth and Walnut reported in *Conjectures of a Guilty Bystander*. It occurred in March 1958, nearly ten years after the previous incident, when he was once again in Louisville on monastery business. Here is how he described it in his journal the following day:

> Yesterday, in Louisville, at the corner of 4th and Walnut, suddenly realized that I loved all the people and that none of them were, or, could be totally alien to me. As if waking from a dream—the dream of my separateness, of the "special" vocation to be different. My vocation does not really make me different from the rest of men or put me in a special category except artificially, juridically. I am still a member of the human race—and what more glorious destiny is there for man, since the Word was made flesh and became, too, a member of the Human Race![72]

Reflecting on this experience some years later, he says "it was as if I suddenly saw the secret beauty of their hearts, the depths of their hearts where neither sin nor desire nor self-knowledge can reach, the core of their reality, the person that each one is in God's eyes." If only they could see each other in this way, he laments. "There would be "no more war, no more hatred, no more cruelty, no more greed." But then, he concludes, "this cannot be *seen*, only believed and 'understood' by a peculiar gift."[73]

Would it be too much to say that in these moments of intense illumination Merton realized the fruits of his contemplative practice? In his earliest writing on the subject, the booklet entitled *What Is Contemplation?* he had said that contemplation, if pursued far enough, would bring about an "interior revolution," that it would eventually give way to an "awakening" in which a person would experience the world in a new way, transcending "all natural knowledge and all natural love." This would seem to be what happened in both of these incidents. In the first, he was able to see beyond exterior detail and to experience a deep respect, love, and pity for others that external observation alone could not elicit. In the second incident, the illusion of a separate existence and special vocation as a contemplative dissolved. He realized that he loved all of these people and that none of them could be totally alien to him. It was as though he saw into the depths of their being, saw them with God's eyes. He concludes his later reflections on a philosophical note with the observation that there is at the center of our being "a point of nothingness which is untouched by sin and by illusion, a point of pure truth, a point or spark which belongs entirely to God, which is never at our disposal, from which God disposes of our lives, which is inaccessible to the fantasies of our own mind or the brutalities of our own will."[74] This must surely be the transcendent Self of which he speaks so insightfully in his later Zen writings. But it is also the self "hidden in God," to which his contemplative practice had been directed all along.

He had always said that in finding God we would find ourselves and other people. In the original version of *Seeds*, he considered the possibility that one might become a hermit in order to escape from others but rejected this idea. "Go into the desert not to escape other men but in order to find them in God," he exhorted.[75] He believed even then that union with God implied solidarity with others, yet this remained a rather abstract idea until he experienced it for himself. In the two Louisville accounts, he describes what I would call "compassionate seeing." It is not the seeing of ordinary experience, but rather a seeing in depth, free of the illusion of separateness and superiority. It is the sort of perception that results from the dissolution of prejudice, suspicion, and the many other forms of defensiveness that typically cloud our vision of other people. Merton's contemplative practice over a period of many years had prepared him for this experience. It had helped open him to the experience of unconditional love. But other things that were happening in his life at that time also contributed to this inner transformation. His work as a writer, teacher, spiritual counselor, and priest undoubtedly affected his inner development. From his journals and other writings, we know that he was deeply engaged in this work. It was, moreover, the kind of work that brought him into relationship with others at a deep and personal level, so it could hardly have failed to have a profound effect upon him.

Action, along with contemplation, contributed significantly to Merton's spiritual development during this important phase of his life. Far from being contradictory, these two ways of being in relation to others actually proved complementary. In contemplation he was brought to a deep place within himself, where identification with others could occur; whereas his work on behalf of others took him outside of himself, yet also brought him into relationship with others, albeit in a different way. Action put him in touch with the particularity of others—their specific needs, fears, and aspirations. Through action on their behalf, he was able to connect with them in a more concrete and existential way than through contemplation alone. He was no less himself in his action, inasmuch as the action proceeded from that same deep place within himself; yet it was a more public self, a more available self, that emerged. He might not have been able to act as freely for others if it had not been for his contemplative practice. Conversely, he might have succumbed to quietism had he not remained within the community and accepted the responsibilities given him by his abbot. Contemplative practice helped to dissolve the artificial barriers between himself and others, the projections and illusions that separated him from others, thus preparing the way for action on their behalf. Responsible action within the religious community brought him into concrete relationship with others, eliciting a compassionate response to their needs and aspirations, thus enabling him to realize the fruits of his contemplative practice.

Contemplative as Prophet

Once having made this "turn toward the world," Merton gave himself fully to his enlarged sense of vocation. He embraced responsibility for the world with the same passion and commitment that he had brought to his earlier renunciation of the world. No longer did he simply receive and acknowledge letters from readers; in 1958 he initiated an active correspondence with a wide range of individuals in all parts of the world. He developed over time an international network of correspondents that included Boris Pasternak, D. T. Suzuki, Erich Fromm, Abraham Heschel, Dorothy Day, Rosemary Reuther, Daniel Berrigan, and Abdul Aziz among others. He published widely in many different venues, frequently recycling the same article in a slightly modified form in order to address the largest possible audience. In addition to writing articles on controversial subjects such as nuclear disarmament, race relations, and the Vietnam War, he reviewed a broad array of books by novelists, poets, and other leading intellectuals. He translated several Latin American writers from Spanish into English and even did an interpretive translation of a Chinese religious classic (despite not knowing Chinese). He also edited anthologies of his own work, selections from the writings of Gandhi, and a collection of essays on peace (including one of his own). During the period of the early to mid-1960s, Merton was a prolific writer with a growing international reputation.

Although his interests at this time were wide-ranging, Merton tended to focus on the subject of peace. Even before he went public with his social criticism, he had noted in his journal that "the thought of trying to do something positive and evident for peace is overwhelming."[76] He was particularly intent on advancing the cause of nonviolent resistance in the face of escalating violence at home and abroad. This should come as no surprise if we recall what he said earlier about the "activity of the contemplative," that it must be "born of contemplation and must resemble it." Nonviolent resistance epitomizes this kind of action. It presupposes honest self-examination and a sincere commitment to truth. What Merton said of Gandhi would apply to anyone pursuing the path of nonviolence: "his *nonviolence* was effective insofar as it began first within himself, as obedience to the deepest truth in himself."[77] True nonviolence also entails compassion. Merton was impressed with the leadership of Martin Luther King in large measure because King did not seek structural change in society solely for the sake of his own oppressed people, but also for the sake of their white oppressors. The purpose of his nonviolent protest movement on behalf of civil rights "in its deepest and most spiritual dimensions," Merton wrote, was "to awaken the conscience of the white man to the awful reality of his injustice" so there could be genuine repentance and true reconciliation of the races.[78] To the argument that nonviolence as a strategy is not always effective, he replied that it is more important to be true to oneself and compassionate toward one's adversary than to succeed in achieving a desired outcome. Anyone who would follow the path of nonviolent resistance for whatever reason or cause, he felt, must be prepared to act with humility, patience, and love—and leave the outcome to God.

Before leaving the subject of nonviolent resistance, I want to emphasize that in Merton's view the primary rationale for this approach to resolving social problems is religious and metaphysical, not political or ethical. The practice of nonviolent resistance, as he saw it, derives from faith in the underlying unity of all beings in God. He realized that this faith is expressed differently by Hindus than by Christians. Where a Hindu would tend to speak of Atman or Brahman as providing the basis for unity, a Christian would most likely appeal to "the Gospel message of salvation for *all*" or "the Kingdom of God to which *all* are summoned." His point is that the religious divisions that produce conflict and lead to violence are not ultimate. Christians especially are called to witness to this underlying unity through their actions. "The great historical event, the coming of the Kingdom," he writes, "is made clear and is 'realized' in proportion as Christians themselves live the life of the Kingdom in the circumstances of their own place and time."[79] This will not happen, however, if Christians are bent on destroying their adversaries in the interests of peace, justice, and love. The objective of nonviolent resistance, he was convinced, is not to defeat the enemy in order to impose our own solutions, but to create conditions for greater openness and communication among all parties to the conflict. Thus, he was deeply troubled by the turn toward violence in the latter stages of the antiwar movement. In particular, he saw protest and resistance against the Selective Service Act as "oriented to the affirmation of the rightness, the determination and conviction of the protesters, and not to the injustice of the law itself."[80]

Given his intense interest in social issues during these years, it is a wonder that Merton remained in the monastery. There were certainly those who thought he should leave. They included people who thought a monk should not get involved in worldly affairs as well as those who thought he would be more effective working for social change outside the monastery. Yet he did not leave. He believed it was his calling as a contemplative monk to speak out on social issues. He no longer saw his position in the monastery as one that separated him from the world, but rather as one that gave him a unique perspective on the world, one that he could share with others. William Shannon, in his biography of Merton, identifies the historical moment when he first articulated this view. In a letter to Pope John XXIII on the occasion of his election to the papacy, Merton writes that he has "come to think in terms of a contemplative grasp of the political, intellectual, artistic and social movements in this world." He was at this time only thinking of offering sympathy and understanding to the "honest aspirations of so many intellectuals everywhere in the world and the terrible problems they face."[81] But he was convinced that this kind of support could make a difference.

In time, his vision widened and he became more of a social prophet. His perception of the dynamics of war and the irrelevance of the traditional theory of the just war in a nuclear age, his penetrating critique of the white liberal response to racial injustice, and his persistent objection to the tendency of capitalism to produce moral passivity and spiritual atrophy all conform to the traditional role of the prophet. Merton's contemplative practice together with his monastic location gave him a unique perspective from which to mount this kind of social critique. He made this very point in the talk he gave to the monks at Gethsemani on the day following his meeting with Nhat Hanh. Commenting on the Buddhist monk's opposition to the war in Vietnam, he said that it is "good for a monk to say things like this," because he is not associated with any particular political party or program. "He can stand up and speak as a detached, free man. He can say, 'In the name of peace, this thing is wrong.'" If Merton had allowed himself to be totally caught up in social action without the benefit of a contemplative perspective, he would not have been nearly as effective a social critic and visionary.

There is then, as he shows, a distinct contribution that contemplation can make to social action. It can help form a person for action by providing a unique perspective toward the situation in which the person is called to act. Merton would have been uncomfortable, however, with a merely pragmatic justification for contemplative practice. He was convinced that contemplation was valuable in and of itself as an expression of our essential humanity. It was, in any case, his calling, independent of any contribution it might make to the solution of social problems. He makes this point forcefully and eloquently in a letter to his friend Daniel Berrigan, the well-known poet, priest, and peace activist, at a time when the protest movement encompassing both civil rights and the war was just beginning.

> There is an absolute need for the solitary, bare, dark, beyond-concept, beyond-thought, beyond-feeling type of prayer. Not of course for everybody. But unless that dimension is there in the Church somewhere, the whole caboodle lacks life and light and intelligence. It is a kind of hidden, secret, unknown stabilizer, and a compass too. About this I have no hesitations and no doubts, because it is my vocation.[82]

Merton never gave up his contemplative practice or abandoned the dark path to which he felt especially called. Even at the height of his involvement in world affairs when he was no longer constrained by the censors of his religious order or by an abbot who would not let him leave the monastery, he continued to pursue the solitary life and to seek an ever-deeper experience of the mystery of God. His contemplative quest eventually took him to Asia and a transforming personal encounter with Buddhism—but that is another story.

3

Thich Nhat Hanh: Engaged Buddhist

THICH NHAT HANH first emerged on the world scene in the spring
of 1966 when he embarked on a speaking tour to promote the
cause of peace in Vietnam. Feelings about the war were beginning to polarize, but most people in the United States at that time
supported the war based on the Cold War ideology of unremitting
opposition to communist expansion anywhere in the world. Neither
he nor the cause he represented was well known, and as a result his
efforts on behalf of peace were largely misunderstood, even by those
who opposed the war. As he traveled around this country he was
shocked by the intense hostility expressed by Americans on both
sides of the issue. In one of the places where he spoke, he was asked
during the question-and-answer period why, if he cared so much about
his people, he was in the United States rather than Vietnam. He
breathed deeply and replied that he was here because this was where
the *roots* of the war were.

This answer is typical of Nhat Hanh. He is the kind of person who
tries to get at the roots of a conflict, even though such an approach
is not generally well understood or much appreciated by those involved. He is also an activist, which does not fit the Western stereotype
of Buddhists as world-denying ascetics. He was therefore an enigma
to most Americans at that time. He is better known now, but not
necessarily better understood. We need to go back to *his* roots if we
are to understand and appreciate how he became the spiritual leader
he is today.

Preparation for Leadership

Born in 1926 in a small village in central Vietnam, Nhat Hanh was attracted to the religious life at an early age, though the nature of this attraction did not portend his later role as a social activist. He compares his decision to become a monk with "falling in love." At the age of nine, he was touched by an image of Buddha sitting peacefully on the grass that he saw in a magazine, and he knew then that he wanted to be "peaceful like that." Some time later his class took a field trip to a nearby mountain where he was told a hermit lived. Nhat Hanh wanted to meet him, because he had heard that a hermit was "someone dedicated to becoming peaceful and happy like a Buddha." When he found out that the hermit was not there, he struck out on his own in search of him. What he found instead was a deep, clear well where he could see "every pebble and every leaf" all of the way to the bottom. He drank from its sparkling water and felt completely fulfilled. It was, he later said, "as if I were meeting the hermit face to face."[1] A seed had been planted (what Merton would call the seed of contemplation) and it continued to grow, until four years later he took his vows as a monk at Tu Hieu pagoda outside of the city of Hue in central Vietnam.

The monastery where Nhat Hanh trained belonged to the Lam Te sect of Vietnamese Buddhism. This is the same tradition of Zen Buddhism that D. T. Suzuki trained in (called Rinzai in Japanese), though his training would have been somewhat different because the Vietnamese version was influenced by Vietnamese culture. The most notable feature of Nhat Hanh's novitiate was the use of *gathas*, short verses designed to focus a person's mind on the activity of the moment. In the beginning, Nhat Hanh was given a practice manual containing fifty of these gathas and told to memorize it. There was one for virtually every activity a monk might engage in during the course of a day, including washing hands and going to the toilet. Before entering the monastery, Nhat Hanh had received some Western education (French) and had the impression that the monasteries were rather old-fashioned. He was not particularly pleased to be given a book of sayings to memorize and practice without any theoretical explanation or justification. When he voiced his concerns to a fellow novice, he was told this is the way it was done there. If he wanted to learn Zen, he would have to accept it. So he resigned himself to beginning his training "in the traditional way," and eventually came to appreciate it. At the time he thought the manual was "written for young people and those just beginning the practice of Zen," but later concluded that it is "the very essence of Zen Buddhism."[2]

With the possible exception of the emphasis on gathas, Nhat Hanh's early monastic training was typical of the training of most Zen monks at that time. It included studying the classical texts of Buddhism in Chinese, meditating with the aid of a *kung-an* (koan in Japanese), and devoting many hours to formal sitting practice. "Sitting meditation," he has written, "is a great joy. The lotus or half-lotus position makes it easier to breathe freely, to concentrate deeply, and to return to the state of mindfulness." Yet he has also said that sitting is not the whole of Zen. "We can practice as well while walking, eating, talking, working and in all positions and activities" as long as we are mindful of what we are doing.[3] This is an important observation, because it explains the relatively minor role of sitting meditation in his later writings. By the time he had established his own religious community, some forty years after beginning his training as a monk, he had concluded that "mindfulness is the key." It is "the energy that sheds light on all things and all activities, producing the power of concentration, bringing forth deep insight and awakening."[4]

Judging by his later observations, Nhat Hanh was not disappointed in the training he received as a monk, at least in regard to preparation for the contemplative life. But he was critical of other aspects of his education. As a student, he wanted a curriculum with more emphasis on philosophy, literature, and foreign languages. When authorities at the Buddhist Institute in Hue, where he was then studying, were not responsive to his suggestions, he and several other students left and took up residence in a small temple on the outskirts of Saigon, where they could pursue studies in Western philosophy and science. They were convinced that these subjects would help them "infuse life into the practice of Buddhism" in Vietnam.[5] By making this move, they declared themselves part of a reform movement within Vietnamese Buddhism that had begun in the 1930s. Inspired by a similar reform effort in China, it promoted a general renewal of native culture and a revival of Buddhist institutions. It was responsible, among other things, for the creation of a dynamic youth organization and a publication directed primarily to young people. Concerning this movement, Nhat Hanh has written: "The Buddha's teachings were presented in a new light by a young generation of Western-educated intellectuals, and this helped enormously in the task of bringing Buddhism to the young."[6] As one of the young people attracted to this movement, he was preparing even then to make his own contribution.

Nhat Hanh's role in this reform effort initially took the form of writing and teaching about Buddhism. By the age of 24, he had already published several books and was gaining a reputation as an excellent teacher. His writings included a short work in Vietnamese, later translated into French as *Aujourd'hui le Bouddhisme* (Buddhism Today) and cited by Thomas Merton in his book *Mystics and Zen Masters*.[7] It gives some indication of Nhat Hanh's views at that time. The thesis of the book is that Buddhism, as a living religion, must continually change if it is to retain its vitality. For this to happen, it is not enough for Buddhists to study the classical texts of their religion. They must enter into the experience that gave birth to the religion. While this might be said of any religion, it has a specific connotation for Buddhists. It means entering into the experience of *suffering*, and not just suffering in general but the specific form intrinsic to their own time. Buddhists are committed to relieving suffering—their own as well as others'—but in order to do so effectively they must be prepared to confront the illusions of their age and be willing to look deeply into the causes of suffering. This deep looking can only occur if there are practices in place that cultivate it. Traditionally one would go to a monastery to learn them, but not everyone, he thought, could take the time to enter a monastery and train with a master. So a form of practice would have to be found that is suitable for persons living in the world. Buddhism, he concluded, will only retain its vitality in the modern age if it adapts to the conditions of that age.

For Nhat Hanh those conditions included war. In the background of most of his early work was the French–Indochina War, a war for national independence, begun in 1947 when the French sent troops to Vietnam to regain control over their former colony following a communist takeover the previous year. It was a bitter conflict, culminating in the defeat of the French forces at Dien Bien Phu and ending with the Geneva Peace Accords in 1954. The terms of the peace agreement included the temporary partitioning of the country at the seventeenth parallel to be followed by national elections. But the elections were never held, and a period of great confusion resulted. Hordes of people migrated from north to south to escape communist control, while in the south the government of Ngo Dinh Diem, with support from the United States, presented itself as a bulwark against communism. United in their opposition to French colonialism, the

Vietnamese Buddhists supported the struggle for national independence, though not a communist takeover. They were therefore in a position to be a force for national unity.

Yet the period immediately following the Peace Accords was a time of great uncertainty for the Buddhist religious establishment, which was hesitant to act. For Nhat Hanh it was a period of great opportunity. He was invited by a daily newspaper to write a series of articles on Buddhism that would address some of the problems people had with the religion. The response to his articles was quite positive; for many it was the first time Buddhism had been presented "as something very refreshing and relevant." Nhat Hanh was also invited by a Buddhist institute in Saigon, which earlier he had helped found, to propose a new curriculum. In response, he convened a series of meetings involving hundreds of young monks, nuns, and others who shared his vision for the country. From these meetings came a proposal for a curriculum that would include not only the basic teachings of Buddhism, but also Western philosophy, languages, science, and other subjects that he said "could help us understand our society and the contemporary world."[8] In other words, it would be the curriculum that he wanted when he was a student. During this time he also started a magazine called *The First Lotus Flowers of the Season*, dedicated specifically to the young monks and nuns who were endeavoring with great difficulty to give expression to a new vision of Buddhism.

By 1956, the All-Vietnam Buddhist Association was publishing its own official journal with Nhat Hanh as editor. The journal sought to promote unity among Buddhists by emphasizing their nationalist and humanist aspirations, but it also criticized the Diem government for its repressive methods. According to Nhat Hanh, President Diem could have had wide popular support in the country at that time if he had been willing to share power with other noncommunist nationalists in his government. But that was not the approach he took. "From the moment of his assumption of power, Diem spared no effort to eliminate every form of opposition to his regime and had no faith in anyone except members of his own family and his own church."[9] Buddhists in particular were subject to persecution, not only for their opposition to the government but simply because of their religion. Nhat Hanh attributes this policy to the influence of President Diem's brother, an archbishop in the Catholic Church. As early as 1957, the government had tried to do away with Wesak, the celebration of Buddha's birth, as a national holiday. Under pressure from Buddhists throughout the country, the government was forced to reverse this decision, but then six years later reinstated it, setting in motion a sequence of events that led eventually to the downfall of the regime and the assassination of President Diem and his brother.

In the meantime, Nhat Hanh was beginning to meet resistance to his reform efforts from the religious establishment. The journal he edited was discontinued, officially for financial reasons but in his opinion because the hierarchy did not approve of his articles. According to Cao Ngoc Phuong, a young woman who was one of his students at the time and who later was given the religious name Chan Khong (True Emptiness), "all the young monks were fond of him and wholeheartedly supported his efforts to renew the teachings and practice, but the more conservative elders were not supportive of his innovations."[10] So in the fall of 1957, in the face of growing opposition from within his own religious order, Nhat Hanh withdrew to the mountains near Saigon, where he helped found an experimental community with a small band of friends. They named the community Phuong Boi (Fragrant Palm Leaves) and viewed it as a place of healing. He told one of his friends at the time: "We have lost our last anchor. Perhaps our practice isn't strong enough. We need a hermitage where we can devote ourselves to practice."[11] The setting they chose was quiet and peaceful, a forested area "sheltered from the harshness of worldly affairs," a place where they could "put down roots."[12] It was also a place where they could practice meditation while continuing to study and write about the "new Buddhism" taking shape at that time.

During his residence at Phuong Boi, Nhat Hanh made trips to various temples where he would sometimes offer a series of talks on Buddhism. It was on one of these trips that he met Sister Chan Khong, and during this time he gathered about him a cohort of young activists whom he called his "thirteen cedars."[13] In early 1961, while on a teaching mission in Dalat, he learned that his name had been removed from the membership list of An Quang Pagoda. Because he had helped found this temple in the early 1950s and had been teaching there since 1954, this was a particularly painful rejection. It is evidence of just how intense the resistance to his reform efforts had become within the religion. But he also faced growing opposition from the government on account of his writings. Even Phuong Boi was no longer a safe haven, and most of the community had moved away by then. In the fall of 1961, Nhat Hanh was offered a fellowship to study comparative religion at Princeton University. His friends encouraged

him to accept it, saying that there was nothing more he could do at
that time to help the situation in Vietnam. So he left the field of
action and withdrew to the ivory tower for a period of sustained study
and personal reflection at one of the world's leading research
universities.

From Reflection to Action

Nhat Hanh has written scarcely anything about his time at Princeton,
but he has published selections from his journals for the period 1962
to 1966, which show that the academic year 1962–1963 marked an
important turning point in his life. In the fall of that year, he took a
teaching position at Columbia University. He maintained his connection with Princeton but moved to New York, where he shared an
apartment with an American student. With the war escalating and
the situation back home becoming increasingly tense, he felt a growing
sense of dread. "Our homeland is about to pass through a devastating
storm," he wrote. "The oppressive regime, relying on force to satisfy
its greed, has caused too many injustices." The storm could break at
any moment, he thought. "We must strengthen ourselves for the coming
test."[14] Then one autumn night he had two vivid and disturbing dreams.
In both he was confronted by scenes of death and destruction, situations in which his efforts to help only resulted in greater suffering
for the innocent. He awoke from these dreams unsure of their meaning
but convinced that they had something to do with the situation in his
homeland. "When the storm of destruction hits," he concluded, "I
only hope that I am at home to face it with my friends."[15]

This was the beginning of a very introspective time for Nhat Hanh.
In his journals, he laments how much we allow society to define who
we are and questions whether we any longer know our own true
aspirations. "We become a stranger to ourselves, molded entirely by
society." In language remarkably similar to what one finds in Merton's
writings at this time, Nhat Hanh says that he sometimes feels "caught
between two opposing selves—the 'false self' imposed by society and
what I would call my 'true self.'" Because it is easy to confuse the
two, he realizes it can be a battle to get back to one's true self. He
compares this experience to being caught in a storm. "I rarely hear
such a storm coming until it is already upon me," he writes. "I know
it must have been brewing a long time, simmering in my own thoughts

and mental formations, but when such a frenzied hurricane strikes, nothing outside can help. I am battered and torn apart, and I am also saved."[16] He tells of passing through such a storm beginning in October 1962.

It was an existential crisis that began in a very mundane way. He was in the university library looking for books that would help him in his research when he came upon a volume that had been there for seventy years but had only been checked out twice. He suddenly had an overwhelming desire to meet and hug the two people who had previously checked out this book, though he knew this was impossible. Holding the book in his hands, he had a flash of insight.

> I understood that I am empty of ideals, hopes, viewpoints, or alle-
> giances. . . . In that moment, the sense of myself as an entity among
> other entities disappeared. I knew that this insight did not arise from
> disappointment, despair, fear, desire, or ignorance. A veil lifted silently
> and effortlessly. . . . At that moment I had the deep feeling that I had
> *returned*.[17]

He then went into a period of intense withdrawal that lasted for several weeks. During this time he did not talk to anyone, even his roommate. "I became a battlefield," he says. "I couldn't know until the storm was over if I would survive, not in the sense of my physical life, but in the deeper sense of my core self."[18]

Emerging from this ordeal, he experienced "an almost thrilling sense of aloneness." He was sure no one would recognize him in this new manifestation, not even his friends. For typically our friends do not want us to change; they want to hold on to the image they have of us. But that is no way to live. It would be better, he thought, "if everyone cast me from their thoughts. I cannot be a human being and, at the same time, be an unchanging object of love or hatred, annoyance or devotion. I must continue to grow." He would, he says, wish the same for his friends. He would "incite chaos" if it would help them "break through the shells that confine them." For there is nothing more glorious, he writes, than "to witness a friend's *return*, not exactly a return, but an infinitely exquisite moment when he emerges from the chaos caused by the annihilation of his last refuge."[19] Following this experience Nhat Hanh felt reborn. "I am," he says, "like someone just recovered from a near-fatal illness who has stared death in the face."[20]

Yet even then the process of inner transformation was not over. One night, a short time later, he was reading Dietrich Bonhoeffer's account of his final days when, he says, "I felt a sudden surge of joy, accompanied by the faith that I could endure even greater suffering than I had thought possible." He expresses the impact of this seminal moment in a beautifully poetic way. Bonhoeffer, he writes, "was the drop that made my cup overflow, the last link in a long chain, the breeze that nudged the ripened fruit to fall." His heart was overflowing with love. He felt courage and strength well up within him. "All feelings, passions, and sufferings revealed themselves as wonders, yet I remained grounded in my body." He concludes that "life is miraculous, even in its suffering." Echoing one of the great insights of the Mahayana Buddhist tradition, he asserts that nothing is permanent, yet neither is there impermanence; no separate self exists, yet neither is there "no-self." Though one might regard this as a mystical way of experiencing reality, Nhat Hanh is reluctant to speak of it as even religious. What he felt, he says, "was totally and utterly human."[21]

These breakthrough experiences—whether one calls them religious or mystical or simply human—were undoubtedly profound and life-transforming for Nhat Hanh. He acknowledges that "such moments might only come once in a lifetime" and could "pass unnoticed" if one were not mindful. He likens attending to such moments to the work of the Zen Master who knows how to use the dazzling light of these instants "to illuminate the journey of return, the journey that begins from nowhere and has no destination."[22] What they offer, above all, is insight into the self. "Almost no one," he had said earlier, "listens to his or her true self."[23] We cling to the illusion of freedom, yet most of the time we act mindlessly out of fear, anger, or ambition. Only when we are free from the fallacy of the self as a separate entity, when we are able to see clearly into the interrelationship of all things, are we truly free. Only then are we free to be ourselves and to act on the basis of understanding rather than ignorance. Recalling his earlier discussion of the true-self/false-self distinction, we might say it is only when we are our true selves that our actions are truly our own and not simply a reflection of society. In any case, Nhat Hanh soon passed from this period of intense self-reflection with its moments of shattering personal insight and entered one of purposeful and productive action, a time in which he really did *come into his own* both as an original thinker and a courageous leader.

By the spring of 1963, opposition to the Diem regime in South Vietnam had intensified. It came to a head in April, when at the instigation of his brother, the Catholic archbishop, President Diem decreed that the Buddhists would not be permitted to display their religious flag on the traditional anniversary of Buddha's birth. There were demonstrations in protest of this action and confrontations with the police in which a number of people were killed or injured. There were also a great many arrests and reports of torture. The monks who led these demonstrations were accused by the government of being communists. Then, on June 11, 1963, a monk by the name of Thich Quang Duc burned himself to death in public, the first of many acts of self-immolation by Buddhist monks and nuns in protest of the government's actions. This protest set off more demonstrations until finally an agreement was reached with the government—one which would be broken only a short time later.

From his position in the United States, Nhat Hanh was soon drawn into the action. The period between June and October was a particularly difficult time for him. He was frequently called by newspapers and television stations for interviews about the situation in his country; he traveled to Washington, D.C., Chicago, and other major cities in an effort to generate support for the peace movement; and he helped lead a protest march in front of the White House that was organized by the Association of Overseas Vietnamese. Translating reports of human rights violations and presenting them to the United Nations, he was instrumental in persuading the UN to send a delegation to Vietnam to investigate charges of human-rights abuses. His most dramatic action, however, was a highly publicized five-day fast on behalf of the people of Vietnam, which he undertook in October of that year. In announcing the fast, he made the following statement:

> The people of Vietnam have already suffered too much. This is the moment we need the entire human family to pray and to act. Immediately after this press conference, I will enter into a silent meditation and fast in order to pray for my homeland. I implore all members of the human family, all who can feel the suffering of Vietnam, to join their prayers for the suffering to stop.[24]

He was not asking for pity. As he makes clear elsewhere in his journals, he was asking for the love and respect due the Vietnamese as human beings. But in order for there to be genuine love, he was convinced, there must be understanding.[25] He was doing all he could at this time to promote that understanding.

On November 1, 1963, a coup d'etat brought down the Diem government. Suddenly there was an opportunity for real change in the country, and as the focal point of protest the Buddhists were in a position to be major contributors to that change. Nhat Hanh had been invited to stay on at Columbia University and establish a department of Vietnamese studies, but after the fall of the Diem government he received an urgent appeal from the Buddhist leadership in Vietnam to return and help them reorganize. He saw this appeal as an opportunity to realize his dream for reform. On December 16, 1963, he left the United States for Vietnam. A few weeks later he submitted a three-point proposal to the executive council of the recently formed Unified Buddhist Church. He asked them first, to call for a cessation of hostilities in Vietnam; second, to establish an institute for the study and practice of Buddhism that would teach the country's leaders to act with a tolerant, open-minded spirit consistent with Buddhist practice; and third, to create a center for training social workers who could help bring about nonviolent social change based on the Buddha's teachings.[26] All the elements of Nhat Hanh's previous vision for a renewed, engaged Buddhism were present in this proposal. It seemed that his time had finally come.

The council, however, adopted only one of his proposals, that calling for an Institute of Buddhist Studies. The others were considered unrealistic. But Nhat Hanh was not deterred. The next two years proved to be among the most productive of his life as he moved ahead with his agenda for change, without the official approval of the Buddhist hierarchy, but with the support of many young people. The Institute for Higher Buddhist Studies, which eventually became Van Hanh University, was established in February 1964. At the same time he set up the first of several experimental villages, the purpose of which was to serve as "models for social change."[27] The villagers would be encouraged to assume responsibility for developing their own local economy and providing for their own education and health care. Young people would be trained to help them become more self-reliant by establishing schools and medical centers in the villages, teaching them modern farming methods, and showing them ways to improve public sanitation, but they would be expected to participate fully in the process. "We learn from the villagers," he wrote, "and try to test our ideas with their support."[28] It was the beginning of what later became known as the School of Youth for Social Service, undoubtedly, Nhat Hanh's greatest contribution during this period.

Founded in September 1965, the School of Youth for Social Service has been compared to the Peace Corps as a vehicle for the expression of youthful energy and idealism on behalf of humanity. It was one of the proposals that the executive council of the Unified Buddhist Church had turned down earlier. But based on the success of the experimental villages, Nhat Hanh went back to the council and asked for its support to launch a nationwide appeal for help with rural development and social change.[29] He received their endorsement but no financial assistance. He nevertheless announced the start of a program that would train young people to serve the poor in remote areas of the country. The response to this announcement was overwhelming, with more than a thousand applications for three hundred places in the program.

Because he could not pay anyone to teach in the program, Nhat Hanh went to the faculty at Saigon University and explained what he wanted to accomplish. On the basis of his appeal, many of them agreed to teach without pay. The facilities necessary for offices, classrooms, and dormitories were provided by several local Buddhist temples until such time as a permanent campus could be built.[30] Initially the school was affiliated with Van Hanh University, but this support was withdrawn when Nhat Hanh became too controversial for the Buddhist hierarchy. Yet by then the program had achieved a life of its own. It continued to function without official status from 1966 until 1973, when the Unified Buddhist Church agreed to establish the Buddhist Committee for Reconstruction and Social Development with the School of Youth for Social Service as its nucleus.[31] Throughout the war, the young people in this program, often at great personal risk, struggled to help Vietnamese peasants rebuild villages that were sometimes bombed out as many as three or four times, while also teaching them ways to improve their lives.

Another of his innovations during this period has proved to have long-lasting significance. On February 5, 1966, Nhat Hanh ordained six leaders of the School of Youth for Social Service as members of a new religious order, which he called Tiep Hien (Order of Interbeing). The order was conceived as neither a clerical nor a lay order. It was seen as an inclusive community of Buddhist practitioners—men and women, clergy and lay—committed to a common life of service. They would be united by their adherence to fourteen precepts, which Nhat

Hanh composed to take the place of several hundred precepts that had regulated the lives of Buddhist monks and nuns for more than 2,500 years.

These precepts, which are still in use, were meant to express the deep meaning of Buddha's teaching in a form appropriate to our own time. The first is: "Do not be idolatrous about or bound to any doctrine, theory, or ideology, even Buddhist ones. Buddhist systems of thought are guiding means; they are not absolute truth." This precept was formulated in response to the intolerance and fanaticism that Nhat Hanh saw all around him, though it is also in keeping with the traditional Buddhist principles of impermanence and nonattachment. Other precepts proceed along the same line. For instance, the second reads: "Do not think the knowledge you presently possess is change-less, absolute truth. Avoid being narrow-minded and bound to present views. . . . Do not force others, including children, by any means whatsoever, to adopt your views, whether by authority, threat, money, propaganda, or even education." In addition to promoting a spirit of tolerance, the fourteen precepts teach awareness of the suffering of others, simplicity of lifestyle, personal integrity, and the courage to oppose injustice. They embody the core ethical teachings that all Buddhists are expected to honor, along with teachings specifically designed to express the philosophy of engaged Buddhism.[32] Besides studying and practicing these precepts, members of the Order of Interbeing are expected to devote sixty days a year to the "practice of mindfulness" within a community of friends. In this way Nhat Hanh sought to adapt monastic practice to the requirements of an active life of service to others.

Activist in Exile

By the beginning of 1966, the war had escalated further. Buddhists were once again demonstrating, this time on behalf of free elections. When government officials finally agreed to hold elections, they sought to insure their own election by arresting many of the Buddhist leaders, including senior officers in the National Army.[33] It was a discouraging situation made worse by the increased fighting between North and South Vietnam. It was also a very dangerous time in which many monks were killed, nearly including Nhat Hanh himself. On one occasion, a grenade thrown into the temple he was staying at was deflected by a curtain and exploded next to the room in which he was sleeping. Yet he did not hesitate to go where the suffering was greatest. When a terrible flood ravaged a region where the fighting was most intense, he traveled there with a group of young social workers to provide support for the relief effort.[34] According to Chan Khong, his presence inspired many young Buddhists to join their cause.

Then, in March 1966, Nhat Hanh was invited to the United States to present a seminar on Vietnamese Buddhism at Cornell University. This noncontroversial public appearance was to be followed by a speaking tour, arranged by the Fellowship of Reconciliation, in which he would have an opportunity to present to the American people the viewpoint of those in his country who were neither communist nor anticommunist, but simply wanted an end to the war. Because he felt this sentiment had not been fairly represented and because the situation in Vietnam was becoming increasingly desperate, he accepted the invitation. On May 2, 1966, Nhat Hanh left for the United States thinking he would be gone for just a few weeks.

His meeting with Thomas Merton later that month was only one of many encounters with prominent Americans. He also met with Senator William Fulbright, a leading critic of the war, and Robert McNamara, Secretary of Defense and one of the war's staunchest defenders, among others. On June 1, he held a press conference in Washington, D.C., in which he presented a five-point peace proposal calling upon the United States government to do the following:

1. To issue a clear statement of its desire to help the Vietnamese people establish a government genuinely responsive to Vietnamese aspirations.
2. To end all bombing.
3. To limit its actions to a purely defensive role.
4. To convincingly demonstrate its intention to remove its troops over a specified period of months.
5. To offer reconstruction aid free of ideological and political strings.

That very day he was denounced by the South Vietnamese government as a traitor.[35] It soon became evident to the Buddhist leadership in Vietnam that it would not be safe for him to return to his homeland anytime soon. Though he did not realize it then, this event marked the beginning of an exile that continues to this day. By taking a clear position that favored neither side in the conflict, Nhat Hanh had made himself an enemy to both sides.

His position is eloquently set forth in an article he wrote for the *New York Review of Books* in June 1966. In this article—which we may assume contains the essence of the appeal for peace he was making throughout the country at that time—Nhat Hanh says that Buddhists who want an end to the war face an impossible dilemma. "If we openly call for peace, we are identified with the communists and the government will try to suppress us. If we criticize the communists, we find ourselves aligned with those Vietnamese who have been propagandists for the Americans for years and whose words against communism are soiled and discredited because they have been paid to say them. To be honorably anticommunist has been to remain silent, and, being silent, we have been labeled as innocent of the dangers of communism."[36] By imposing labels on others and insisting on a rigid dualism of communist or anticommunist, American policy had made peaceful political dissent in Vietnam very difficult. "Now the U.S. has become too afraid of the communists to allow a peaceful confrontation with them to take place, and when you are afraid you cannot win."[37] The policy of sending more American troops to Vietnam and bombing the countryside also had not achieved its purpose. It only made the communists stronger by intensifying the hatred of the Vietnamese people for Americans. "Only America," he concluded, "has the capability of stopping this war, which is destroying not only our lives, but our culture and everything of human value."[38] The American government, he lamented, will not stop the war as long as the American people are so blinded by ideology—not to mention fear, anger, ambition, and greed—that they cannot see the *reality* of what is going on.

In a book titled *Vietnam: Lotus in a Sea of Fire*, published originally in Vietnamese and translated into English shortly after he came to the United States, Nhat Hanh undertakes to explain what he sees as the reality of the situation in his country. He discusses the historical antecedents of the war, the relationship of the Buddhist religion to Vietnamese nationalism, the reform movement within Buddhism, and the need for an alternative to merely continuing the war or capitulating to the communists. In an introduction to the English edition, Thomas Merton notes that Nhat Hanh speaks for "a renewed and 'engaged' Buddhism that has taken up the challenge of modern and Western civilization in its often disastrous impact upon the East." He calls this book "the first really clear and articulate expression of this peculiarly Asian viewpoint."[39] What is most remarkable, he asserts, is the way the author is able to combine the impetus for renewal in Buddhism with the movement for reform in Vietnamese society. Nhat Hanh states this purpose most succinctly when he says that "the Buddhists of Vietnam desire to mobilize the potential force of their religion in order to rebuild their society, and consequently they have carried Buddhism into every domain of life: culture, economics, politics and social welfare."[40] But the war has frustrated their efforts, wreaked havoc upon the society, and caused immense suffering. The religious leadership has therefore had to focus its efforts on ending the war. Their approach, he believes, represents the best hope for peace; but it will require the support of others.

According to Nhat Hanh, if one looks deeply into the situation one will realize that "what has developed in Vietnam is an international, ideological war between the United States and the People's Republic of China."[41] These two great world powers are acting out of fear of one another, with each one accusing the other of exploiting the situation in order to extend its own power. There can be no satisfactory resolution of this conflict, he contends, short of a fundamental change of attitude on the part of the United States. It is for this reason that he has come to America. He has come with a view to arousing the conscience of the American people and changing their perception of the war. His is a spiritual mission arising out of a non-dualistic view of the world and a deep sense of compassion for the victims of the war. His message is meant to appeal to basic human values shared by Christians and Buddhists alike. "Within both of these great religions," he asserts, "there is occurring a revolution designed to make them more relevant to the problems of life."[42] So it should be possible for them to work together for peace and the creation of a better society.

In an analysis of the Buddhists' role in the Vietnam War, Buddhist scholar Sallie King has noted that their purpose was at first simply "to protect the practice of Buddhism," but they came in time to be identified with a more general struggle against political oppression and for an end to the war.[43] She reports that within the Buddhist Struggle Movement there were three identifiable factions. The "most visible, politically active group" was led by Thich Tri Quang, Thich Tam Chau, and Thich Thien Minh. They were able to stage mass demonstrations and even negotiate the withdrawal of government troops on several occasions. Although they were in principle committed to nonviolence, their tactics were provocative and sometimes bordered on violence. Thich Nhat Hanh represented a different group, one that took a more strictly pacifist approach. (As Thomas Merton observed, he was no "political operative.") He worked largely through the School of Youth for Social Service to minister to the victims of the war and aid in the reconstruction of homes and villages. A third, less-known group was allied with the National Liberation Front and may well have participated in overt acts of violence.[44]

Overall the Buddhist peace movement was exceptionally peaceful. It embodied, for the most part, the principles of nonviolent resistance made famous by Gandhi and strongly advocated by Merton. In one of his writings in exile, Nhat Hanh discusses the philosophy of nonviolence as practiced by the Buddhists in Vietnam. He calls it love in action.

> The essence of nonviolence is love. Out of love and the willingness to act selflessly, strategies, tactics, and techniques for a nonviolent struggle arise naturally. Nonviolence is not a dogma; it is a process. Other struggles may be fueled by greed, hatred, fear, or ignorance, but a nonviolent one cannot use such blind sources of energy, for they will destroy those involved and also the struggle itself. Nonviolent action, born of the awareness of suffering and nurtured by love, is the most effective way to confront adversity.[45]

By way of illustration, he cites some of the tactics used by nonviolent protesters in Vietnam to oppose government policies and resist government coercion. "In 1966, when the people of Hue and Danang learned that Field Marshall Nguyen Cao Ky was about to bring tanks and troops from Saigon to suppress the movement for peace, the people of those cities brought their family altars—the most sacred objects in their homes—onto the streets, relying on the culture and tradition to oppose the forces of destruction."[46] Fasting was another technique used by Buddhist leaders at the height of a crisis, and writers and artists contributed their talents to the protest movement in the form of antiwar books, articles, poems, and songs.

The self-immolation of Buddhist monks was undoubtedly the most controversial of the actions carried out in the name of peace by members of the movement. Whatever we may think of this form of protest, Nhat Hanh insists it was not done out of anger or despair.

"The Vietnamese monks, nuns, and lay people who burned themselves were saying with all their strength and determination that they were willing to endure the greatest of suffering in order to protect their people." They were acting out of love. Moreover, he contends, none of these protests, including the self-immolations, was part of an overall plan or strategy. "Confronting the situation and having compassion in our hearts, ways of acting came by themselves." And that, he believes, is how it should be. "If you are alert and creative, you will know what to do and what not to do. The basic requisite is that you have the essence, the substance of nonviolence and compassion in yourself."[47]

Nhat Hanh was not unrealistic; he knew how difficult it could be for anyone, himself included, to maintain an attitude of nonviolence, compassion, and love under the conditions of war. At a time late in the war when many of those who had remained in Vietnam to continue his work were growing weary of the struggle, he wrote "A Manual on Meditation for the Use of Young Activists" to assist them in their work. (This manual, which began as a long letter to a member of the staff of the School of Youth for Social Service, was later expanded into a book and translated into English with the title *The Miracle of Mindfulness*.) Nhat Hanh wrote it to remind his students of the discipline required to maintain a contemplative outlook in the midst of difficult circumstances. The discipline he advocated, he also practiced. He called it the practice of mindfulness. It entails "keeping one's consciousness alive to the present reality."[48] The practice, he said, is facilitated by "conscious breathing," which means attending to each breath with single-minded awareness. Mindfulness practice can accompany walking or any other activity as long as one is fully aware of what one is doing. He believed, in fact, that any action performed with full awareness could become a form of meditation, a lesson he first learned as a young monk through the use of gathas.

The practice of mindfulness, he writes, "is the miracle by which we master and restore ourselves."[49] It frees the mind, and when the mind is free the heart will naturally fill with compassion: "compassion for yourself, for having undergone countless sufferings because you were not able to relieve yourself of false views, hatred, ignorance, and anger; and compassion for others because they do not yet see and so are imprisoned by false views, hatred and ignorance and continue to create suffering for themselves and others."[50] Mindfulness allows us to look deeply into reality, to where there is no separation, no discrimination, even between oneself and one's enemies.

All beings, he says, are interdependent, contained within a universal web of relationship. To think of oneself as separate and distinct from others is the ultimate illusion, the root of all suffering. To realize oneness with others—what he calls non-discrimination mind—is the goal of all true practice and the basis for any effective action on behalf of others. Nhat Hanh concludes this manual, written in the waning days of the war, on a poignant note. "There are many people who have written about these things without having lived them, but I've only written about those things I have lived and experienced myself. I hope you and your friends will find these things at least a little helpful along the path of our seeking: *the path of our return*."[51] These last words are ironic, for although he clearly has in mind the spiritual path of return that brings us back to our true selves, his own deep desire to return to his homeland could not have been far from his thoughts at this time.

Nhat Hanh had planned to go back to Vietnam at the conclusion of his speaking tour, but he was strongly advised not to return by those who feared for his safety. He was asked instead to remain abroad and serve as an emissary for the peace movement. In 1968, formal peace talks between the United States and North Vietnam began in Paris and would continue for the next five years. At the instigation of the Overseas Vietnamese Buddhist Association, based in Paris, a Vietnamese Buddhist peace delegation was formed with Nhat Hanh as chair. It was not one of the four official delegations to the peace conference and had no real role in the actual negotiations, but it contributed nonetheless to the peace process. Nhat Hanh and his small staff were a conduit for information from Vietnam to the rest of the world and a source of humanitarian aid to Vietnamese orphans and others in distress.

Working out of a small, one-room office in one of the poorer sections of Paris, the Buddhist Peace Delegation sought to inform people about conditions and events in Vietnam that generally went unreported, such as widespread hunger, resistance to the draft, and the arrest and torture of Buddhist monks and nuns. Their principle means of communication was the mimeograph. They published a newsletter in three languages and corresponded personally with representatives of organizations and agencies sympathetic to their cause. Their most ambitious project, however, was finding sponsors for orphaned children, many of whom were cared for by Buddhist nuns in day-care centers throughout Vietnam. The sponsors were asked to contribute a small amount of money regularly to the support of a child. Their contributions were sent to the Unified Buddhist Church in Vietnam, which turned the funds over to the nuns to administer. Everyone on the delegation staff took turns translating applications and letters from Vietnamese families to sponsors in Europe and the United States. According to Chan Khong, by the end of the war there were nearly 20,000 people contributing to this relief effort.[52]

Yet it was a difficult time for Nhat Hanh. He was separated from his own people and increasingly alienated from the peace movement. Jim Forest, a young American peace activist and friend of both Merton and Nhat Hanh, visited him in the summer of 1972. He recorded his impressions in a booklet entitled *Only the Rice Loves You*.[53] The last time he had seen Nhat Hanh prior to this visit, the Buddhist monk had seemed full of hope in spite of the horrors of the war. But now much of that hope had faded. "There seemed an unspeakable sadness in him, as if he were a Hasidic rabbi at Auschwitz." Although his spirit lightened before the visit was over, this brief period of depression was symptomatic of the anguish Nhat Hanh was experiencing at that time. Two factors in particular contributed to his mood: the death of a close friend in Vietnam and some disturbing tendencies within the peace movement.

A month earlier Nhat Hanh had received word of the death of Thich Tanh Van, the Buddhist monk who replaced him as head of the School of Youth for Social Service. According to the official report, Tanh Van was returning from relief work in Suoi Hgne when his small car was hit by a U.S. Army truck. Refused admittance to a U.S. Army hospital, he died two days later. Thousands came to his funeral in recognition of the great contribution he had made to relieving the suffering of his people. Nhat Hanh was devastated. Tanh Van had been his most beloved student and friend, closer than a brother. "He cannot be replaced," Nhat Hanh told Forest, as he showed him pictures of the school and of his friend. This incident is emblematic of Nhat Hanh's predicament. In spite of the distance that separated him from his colleagues and students in Vietnam, he remained deeply committed to their work. Yet he could not be there to work alongside them or share in the hardship and danger they faced on a daily basis. Moreover, he could not be there to share their grief when one of their number disappeared or was killed. It was hard being an activist in exile.

But then it was also hard being a peace activist committed to nonviolence at a time when the peace movement was becoming increasingly caught up in the very violence it opposed. Earlier in the war, Forest observes, there had been considerable interest in the United States in the Buddhists' nonviolent struggle. Many Americans involved in the peace movement took heart from what the Buddhists were doing in Vietnam. But now they seemed to have lost interest in the Buddhists' struggle, "even though it continued as intensely as ever." Leaders of the peace movement, in the States and elsewhere, had by this time become "openly critical of the Buddhists for putting primary emphasis on a cease-fire, rather than the nature of the future government in South Vietnam." Forest notes that one peace periodical had gone so far as to connect the Buddhist movement to the American CIA. "There was even a time last year," he writes, "when a pacifist leader informed Nhat Hanh that his invitation to speak at a rally had been withdrawn because he was 'politically unacceptable.' " It is little wonder he was depressed.

Yet he never completely lost hope. Even in the darkest days of the war, Nhat Hanh looked forward to the time when he could return to Vietnam and resume the work he had begun years earlier. On the day in 1973 when the Peace Accords were signed, he was in Bangkok, meeting with leaders of the Unified Buddhist Church and making plans for Buddhist participation in the reconstruction and social development of Vietnam following the war.[54] For a time these plans succeeded beyond anyone's expectations. With the cooperation of monks and nuns in every province of the country, the development work of the School of Youth for Social Service was greatly expanded. Where there had been seventeen day-care centers in March 1973, by January 1975, there were more than 300.[55] But then the communist government of North Vietnam seized control of South Vietnam and made it clear that there would be no further role for the Buddhists in the rebuilding of their country. Nhat Hanh was refused permission even to enter Vietnam. So once again he was relegated to the role of activist in exile.

In December 1976, a year after the war finally ended with the withdrawal of American troops and the fall of Saigon, Nhat Hanh attended the World Conference on Religion and Peace in Singapore. While he was there he was approached by some Vietnamese women who told him about the plight of thousands of Vietnamese in refugee

camps in Thailand, Malaysia, Indonesia, Hong Kong, and Singapore—
refugees with no prospect of being accepted into any other country
because of immigration quotas. They were called boat people, because
they had fled in vessels that were often barely seaworthy. Singapore
had a tough policy against accepting boat people and would order
them to put back to the sea when they were caught trying to land.
Nhat Hanh actually witnessed one of these boats being pushed out
to sea. The next day he addressed the conference and made an
impassioned plea on behalf of the boat people. He said they were
drowning because they were not permitted to land in countries such
as Singapore and were not allowed to immigrate anywhere else. The
members of the conference were deeply moved by his testimony and
after lengthy discussion commissioned him to mount a rescue
operation.[56]

Within a few weeks he had raised more than $200,000, rented two
ships, and rescued more than 800 refugees from the high seas. His
plan was to transport them to Australia and Guam, where he would
challenge the immigration quotas imposed by Australia and the United
States on refugees from this part of the world. When word of his plan
got out, refugees in Thailand and Malaysia began leaving camps where
some of them had been living since 1975, in the hope of joining his
rescue operation. This development greatly angered the United Nations High Commissioner on Refugees who ordered them to stay and
publicly questioned the wisdom of the project. Though it was not his
intent to encourage more refugees to leave, Nhat Hanh could not
prevent those who chose to leave from seizing this opportunity to get
away. In the face of growing opposition to the project, even the
secretary general of the World Conference on Religion and Peace
withdrew his support. Less than three months after the project began,
Nhat Hanh was forced to abandon his efforts on behalf of the boat
people.[57]

A Community of Resistance

Deeply disappointed that he could not continue the work he had
begun in his homeland, Nhat Hanh withdrew for a time from any kind
of public role. He no longer held press conferences or met with world
leaders. He even ceased traveling and attending conferences, devoting

himself almost exclusively to private activities such as writing, meditation, gardening, and printing. A few years earlier, he had purchased a small plot of land with a dilapidated farmhouse and stable not far from Paris. While continuing to live in the city, he spent most of his weekends fixing up the house in the country with the help of friends. It became his retreat during the long ordeal of the peace talks. Those who worked on the house with him were mostly his colleagues in the peace movement. They did not just work together; they meditated and took tea together during these weekend retreats. Nhat Hanh sometimes used the stable adjacent to the farmhouse as a hermitage, but for the most part it was a place of community.

By 1975, the farmhouse was sufficiently rebuilt to serve as a year-round residence. So a group of them, eleven in all, decided to move there. On the weekends, their Vietnamese friends from Paris would join them. In that way they were able to continue their life together. Explaining their decision to leave the city and establish a residence in the country, Chan Khong notes that "the war had ended, and we were cut off from Vietnam with no way to help." They needed a place of healing, and this was such a place. It was in a beautiful, natural setting, undisturbed by painful reminders of Vietnam. It allowed them to return to the simple life they had left behind. Here they could raise their own vegetables, enjoy the seasons, practice meditation, and deepen their spiritual understanding. They named their little community *Les Patates Douces* (Sweet Potatoes), because in Vietnam people ate sweet potatoes when they could not get rice. "It is the poorest food, and we knew we needed some way to stay in touch with the poorest of our country," Chan Khong remembers.[58]

During the period from 1975 to 1982, Nhat Hanh maintained his connection with the wider world mainly through his writings, publishing *The Miracle of Mindfulness* at this time. The English translation was done by a young American named Mobi Warren, who learned Vietnamese from him while working as a volunteer for the Buddhist peace delegation. She observes in the introduction that "the fighting is over at last. Our hearts can rest a little, but now the more difficult task is at hand: the task of healing. It is not possible for most of us to be in Vietnam working with our own hands. . . . For people in our community here, healing must be the constant remembrance and transformation of the sufferings the people in Vietnam and we ourselves have been through."[59] It would be difficult to overstate the importance of this community to Nhat Hanh at this time in his life—

just because it was a place of healing. Although he has not written much about this period of his life, he has talked about community in ways that indicate what it must have meant to him.

In a conversation with Daniel Berrigan in the spring of 1974, he discussed what he then called "communities of resistance." By resistance he does not mean simply resistance to war, but resistance to "all kinds of things that are like war." There are many features of modern society, he says, that assault one's integrity and rob one of the capacity to be oneself. So resistance in our time must mean "opposition to being invaded, occupied, assaulted, and destroyed by the system." The initial purpose of resistance, he insists, should be "to seek the healing of yourself in order to be able to see clearly." He acknowledges that this definition may be unacceptable to some because it does not call for any "positive act of resistance" on the part of the community. Yet he believes it is the place to begin. "I think that communities of resistance should be places where people can return to themselves more easily, where the conditions are such that they can heal themselves and recover their wholeness."[60]

He recalls how he and several friends set out to form such a community in Vietnam in the late 1950s. He is referring, of course, to Phuong Boi. This community was successful, he believed, "because it grew out of the [religious] tradition, because most who came to the community had undergone some training in monasteries." Yet it was different from the traditional monastic community because there were no rules and no central authority. Also, it was open to non-monks— writers and artists—to stay for various lengths of time. This arrangement worked, he says, "because the people who came there had the same kind of need."[61] They came seeking healing, and the community provided a place of healing, what he has elsewhere called a "spiritual homeland."[62] We know from Chan Khong's account that Nhat Hanh turned to this community for personal healing at the time of his expulsion from An Quang Pagoda.[63] Asked what had become of the members of this community, he said they had scattered. Because of the war, they could not return to Phuong Boi. Still, he believed the community accomplished its purpose. Wounds that were very deep were healed and relationships developed that persisted throughout the war. In spite of the separations imposed by the war and its aftermath, members of the community, he observed, continued to feel "the presence of each other."[64]

Nhat Hanh goes on to speak of what he looks for in a community of resistance. It should be "beautiful, healing, refreshing both in surroundings and in substance." In such a community you should expect to meet "people who symbolize a kind of freshness; their look, their smile, their understanding, should be able to help." He thinks that the surroundings should be pleasant if possible, but there must be at least one person there who can create a friendly atmosphere. "The place should be identified with such a person. So even if that person is not there, when people come near the place, they would like to drop in."[65] This is, of course, a good description of the community he was helping to form at that time. The surroundings were truly magnificent, with flowers blooming year-round. "The air at Sweet Potato was very fresh," according to Chan Khong, "and practicing walking meditation along the hills surrounding the house was a joy."[66] Sweet Potato was a joyful, meditative community. Although it was too painful for the members to sing traditional Vietnamese songs, they were able to compose their own songs inspired by the contemplation of nature. When they received word of terrible injustices being committed by the government of Vietnam, they were naturally distressed. The entire group would then go out on the hills for long walking meditations, sometimes for several hours. If they could do nothing for the victims under these circumstances, they could at least restore calm in themselves. And sometimes they were able to help. They were often the only reliable source of information concerning violations of human rights within their country.

So they were a community of resistance, these friends of Nhat Hanh living together in a converted farmhouse on a small plot of land a few hours from Paris. They were a community of resistance in the sense that they actively opposed injustice whenever they could; but primarily they represented a place of healing and wholeness in the midst of suffering and alienation. "It is our task," Nhat Hanh told his friend Berrigan, "to try to set up communities which are expressing life, reality, and are doing active resistance work."[67] Although he never entirely abandoned active resistance work—collecting and disseminating information on human rights abuses in Vietnam, for instance—his emphasis at this time in his life was on creating a community that would express a certain quality of life, that would demonstrate that "life is possible, a future is possible."[68] He was, of course, the central figure in this community, the one who set the tone for all the rest. One of the examples he has used in his talks and writings to illustrate the importance of such an individual to the community is taken from his experience with the boat people. It concerns a boat that is caught in a storm and the passengers are on the verge of panic, but one person is calm. That one person is able to bring calm to everyone else simply by being there and being at peace with himself.[69] Nhat Hanh was that kind of presence for this little community struggling to find a mission at a time when the future was dark and uncertain.

A New Global Mission

Even though Nhat Hanh did not travel much during this time and only occasionally saw visitors, the community attracted a growing number of people who were looking for a different quality of life than could be found in the city. By 1982, it was clear that Sweet Potato was much too small to accommodate all the people who wanted to come there for retreats. So Nhat Hanh and Chan Khong went looking for other property, preferring the south of France where the climate would be more like that in Vietnam. They found what they were looking for near Bordeaux. Initially they purchased twenty acres surrounded by rocky, forested hills and including three old stone buildings. When a Vietnamese family indicated a desire to join them, they acquired a second property nearby that would be suitable for farming. They called these two tracts of land Upper Hamlet and Lower Hamlet respectively; the entire community was given the name Plum Village.[70]

The inspiration for the name came from a vision they once had of establishing a retreat center in Vietnam where they would train social workers. In 1973, a piece of land in the forested highlands of Vietnam was actually acquired for this purpose by the man who was then director of the School of Youth for Social Service. They thought they would plant persimmon trees on this land and sell the fruit to support the center, so they named it Persimmon Village. But the director died a year later, and by 1975 it was apparent that neither Nhat Hanh nor Chan Khong would be returning to Vietnam anytime soon. Plum Village was an attempt to rekindle that earlier dream. Instead of persimmons, they would raise plums and use the proceeds to support relief work for children in Vietnam and other Third World countries. They eventually planted more than 1,200 plum trees, many of them purchased from donations by children, and by 1992 the trees were producing six tons of fruit annually.[71]

The main reason for establishing this community, however, was to provide a retreat center for social workers and others seeking spiritual renewal. During the first summer at Plum Village, the community took in a hundred people, the following year twice that number. By 1991, they were receiving more than a thousand guests from all over the world, and Plum Village has continued to expand its facilities to accommodate this growing interest. In 1987, the Vietnamese refugees who had tried to make a living by farming the Lower Hamlet gave up the effort and moved out. This land was converted into a residential community for Vietnamese monks and nuns as well as some Westerners and lay practitioners who wanted to train with Nhat Hanh. He subsequently developed a four-year training program that would prepare teachers to be "agents of transformation" in their own countries.[72] As interest in the community and its work continued to grow, other facilities were added, and now there are five separate hamlets that constitute Plum Village. There is also a much larger contingent of monastics living there year-round.

In February 1998, my wife and I visited Plum Village. We spent two weeks as guests of the community, participating fully in the events of the winter retreat, which included a delightful celebration of Tet, the Vietnamese New Year, on the evening before we left. I can personally attest to the contemplative spirit that pervades the community. The day typically begins with sitting meditation an hour before sunrise and concludes with a ceremony of some sort. For instance, one evening we took part in a ceremony for three retreatants who were planning to leave soon and wanted to make a formal commitment to the practice. Everything at Plum Village is done mindfully, including eating meals, carrying out work assignments, and walking together as a group once a day. (We were told by one of the leaders, "If you have been to Plum Village and have not taken part in walking meditation, you have not been to Plum Village.") Twice a week during the retreat there were dharma talks by Nhat Hanh, which everyone attended, and once a week there was a dharma discussion, in which we met in small groups and shared our experiences with one another. Although I was unable to have a private meeting with Nhat Hanh, I benefited greatly from hearing his talks and sharing in the life of the community.

One reason that interest in the community has grown in recent years is that Nhat Hanh has taken on a more public role. In 1982, he accepted an invitation to attend the Reverence for Life Conference in New York. While there he met some of the leading Buddhist practitioners in America and learned of the growing interest in meditation in this country. He agreed to return the following year and lead retreats on Buddhism and peace work.[73] The response to his talks was so positive that he has come back to the United States nearly every year since. He has also led retreats and workshops in South America, Europe, Australia, the Middle East, and Asia. While most of his presentations are addressed to a general audience, he has conducted retreats for specific groups such as American veterans of the Vietnam War, environmentalists, and psychotherapists. Throughout this period he has continued to write. His publications in English now number more than 30. They include *Being Peace*, based on talks he gave during his 1985 American tour; *Cultivating the Mind of Love*, a series of talks originally presented to visitors at Plum Village in the summer of 1992; and *Living Buddha, Living Christ*, a major contribution to the Buddhist-Christian dialogue, published in 1995. With this kind of public presence, it is little wonder that the community he helped to found has continued to grow.

Greater public visibility alone, however, cannot account for the extraordinary growth of interest in his work. Nhat Hanh has clearly made a deep spiritual connection with people throughout the world. If his ministry was initially directed to the Vietnamese people in their struggle for national independence and subsequently to the American people in the hope that they could influence their leaders to put an end to the war in Vietnam, his current ministry has an even larger audience and carries what many would consider a more universal message. In *Being Peace*, he says: "Engaged Buddhism does not only mean to use Buddhism to solve social and political problems, protesting against bombs, and protesting against social injustice. First of all we have to bring Buddhism into our daily lives."[74] His ministry was, of course, always about transforming lives and actualizing Buddhism in the present time. That was the main point of his early book *Aujourd'hui le Bouddhisme* and a central theme of his manual on meditation for young activists, written during the war. But in the absence of war and far removed from the social crisis in his homeland, he has focused most of his attention in recent years on the ordinary lives of people and in the process has given his message a more universal form.

The universalization of Nhat Hanh's message is particularly evident in the increased importance given to love in his later writings. It is the major theme of two of his most recent books, *Cultivating the Mind of Love* (1996) and *Teachings on Love* (1997). While love, in the way he talks about it, has not always been a conspicuous theme in Buddhism, it is certainly not absent from traditional Buddhist teachings. Nhat Hanh notes that Shakyamuni, the historical founder of the religion, predicted that the next Buddha would be named Maitreya, the Buddha of Love, implying that love would have greater prominence in the future.[75] He may think that the time is right for an emphasis on love because of the pervasive condition of alienation in contemporary society. In a personal conversation with Chan Khong, I was told that Nhat Hanh has been deeply affected by the suffering "within relationships" of those he has encountered in his travels. That this theme resonates with traditional Christian teachings on love could also be a factor in his decision to give greater emphasis to it. Whatever the reason, I believe this shift of emphasis has contributed to the universality of his appeal.

Along with a refocusing of his message in recent years, another shift in emphasis was noted by those who work closely with him. In Plum Village especially, Nhat Hanh has been observed giving greater attention to the training of monks and nuns. The proportion of monastics within the community has grown considerably in the past few years, so they naturally require more of his attention. But there is also a sense that he feels he must train them to carry on his work, that without them his work will not go forward. One of his recent books, *Stepping Into Freedom*, is given over almost entirely to the translation of historic Buddhist texts having to do with monastic life. There is no question that he is focused as never before on what Merton called monastic formation. Moreover, he is deliberately reintroducing the Vietnamese monks and nuns under his care to their own heritage. During the two weeks that I was at Plum Village, he was concluding a series of talks on the subject of anger, but he was also lecturing on the early history of Buddhism in Vietnam. On more than one occasion, he met separately with the monastic members of the community for special instruction. It is as though without this anchor in tradition, the universal message of Buddhism might be lost.

Contemplative as Activist

It is important to remember that Thich Nhat Hanh did not set out to
be a social activist. He was drawn initially to the contemplative life,
which for him, as for Merton, meant entering a monastery and training
to be a monk. In this respect the Buddhist and Christian traditions
are not so different. Their practices, however, are. The Zen monastery
where Nhat Hanh trained required monks to attend closely to all their
actions—working, eating, brushing teeth, closing doors—to insure
that they were done in a mindful way. The gathas of which he speaks
so often in his writings were devices to help focus a person's attention
on whatever action he or she was doing at the moment. They were
not meant to take the person beyond action into some higher state of
consciousness, but rather to bring full awareness to bear on the present
moment. Instead of being distracted by thoughts about the past or
the future, a monk is taught to be fully attentive to what he is doing
here and now. Sitting meditation is important to this practice, but in
Nhat Hanh's view it does not enjoy a privileged status. It is one of
the ways of practicing mindfulness, but not the only way. For him,
mindfulness is the essence of the practice, and it applies to everything
a person does in or out of the monastery.

In *Zen Keys*, one of his most analytical works, Thich Nhat Hanh
reflects on the nature of mindfulness. It is, he says, a form of "direct
experience," free of concepts and images, a form of understanding in
which there is "no distinction between subject and object, no evalua-
tion, and no discrimination."[76] Our language does not permit us to
say much about this unique form of understanding, because language
itself tends to be dualistic, evaluative, and discriminatory. But he
offers an example in the hope it will evoke some recognition on our
part. Suppose, he says, that I invite you to join me for a cup of
tea. Often when we drink tea with someone we are so engrossed in
conversation that we are not aware of what we are doing. But if you
drink the tea mindfully, he is confident you will have a direct experience of the tea. Later, in reflecting on the experience, you may have
occasion to evaluate it and compare it with other such experiences,
but by then the experience is gone. What remains is only the idea
of the experience. In the actual moment, there is no idea of the
experience—just the experience. There is also no differentiation between subject and object. When you are fully absorbed in the act of
drinking tea, "the tea is you and you are the tea." And so it is with

mindfulness practice. To act mindfully, he contends, is to enter into "direct communion" with reality.[77]

For Nhat Hanh and the tradition he represents, there is no intrinsic separation between contemplation (considered as mindfulness) and action (considered as anything a person does with full awareness). The challenge, as he saw it in the early 1950s, was to take this practice out of a monastic setting and bring it to bear on the conditions of modern life. Only in that way could Buddhism hope to survive as a living religion. He did not focus his attention at that time on the practice as much as on the reforms that would be needed in order to make the practice relevant to the time. He wanted young people to have an education that included Western philosophy and science, because he was convinced that these subjects would infuse new life into the practice of Buddhism in his country. "You have to speak the language of your time," he later wrote, "to express the Buddha's teachings in ways people can understand." He also wanted Buddhist monks and nuns to confront the social problems of their day and not simply chant sutras or sit quietly in meditation. He saw many ways in which they could contribute to the relief of human suffering and the general betterment of human life. He envisioned them operating schools, establishing health centers, training farmers in modern agricultural methods, and in general "practicing meditation while doing the work of helping people."[78] But he knew that they would have to leave the monastery and take their practice out into the world in order for this transformation to take place.

How are we to account for this secular, social activist strand in Nhat Hanh's thought? Although there was already a reform movement within Vietnamese Buddhism at the time he began his religious training, he took the movement further in the direction of social action than those who preceded him. Engagement with social issues was implied in his message from the outset, and it has continued to be a central component of his teaching to the present day. He clearly does not see a conflict between his contemplative practice and social action. That is because, in his experience, *mindfulness elicits compassion and compassion has no limits.* "If while we practice we are not aware that the world is suffering, that children are dying of hunger, that social injustice is going on everywhere," he has written, "we are not practicing mindfulness." The practice of mindfulness begins with attention to whatever is going on in the present moment. If practiced consistently it will eventually lead us, he thinks, to look deep within ourselves

and our situation. When that happens "compassion arises in us naturally," and we see what we have to do to help.[79]

Mindfulness, as Nhat Hanh came to understand it, is not just a
matter of acting with full awareness of what one is doing at the moment;
it entails looking into oneself and one's situation for a basis on
which to act. Over time this practice can lead to remarkable self-
understanding and profound self-transformation. We saw an example
of just such a transformation in Nhat Hanh's identity crisis of 1962
while he was teaching at Columbia University. Events in his own
country may have precipitated the crisis, yet there can be no question
that his practice prepared him for it. Nhat Hanh experienced, in an
intensely personal way, his own emptiness. His inherent sense of
himself as "an entity among others" disappeared and a veil was lifted,
"silently and effortlessly," so that he was able to see things in a new
way. So great was the change that he was not sure his friends would
even recognize him. Yet this dissolution of his socially constructed
identity was necessary if he was to assume a new role on the world
stage.

Experiences of this kind brought Thomas Merton closer to God. For
Nhat Hanh, it was more a matter of realizing the ultimate emptiness,
impermanence, and interdependence of all things. In true Zen fashion,
he is reluctant to make metaphysical claims for these ideas. He
certainly does not want to appear doctrinaire or absolutist in his
assertions about ultimate reality. He prefers to speak of concepts such
as emptiness and impermanence as "skillful means." They can help us
attain an experience of ultimacy, but they do not, in and of themselves,
constitute the experience. Other concepts might do just as well, though
there is one to which Nhat Hanh seems particularly committed, and
that is *interbeing*. He coined this term as a modern translation of a
Chinese expression found in one of the ancient texts of Buddhism
and has expressed the hope that it might some day become widely
accepted.[80] Every other concept he uses points to this one. The concept
of no-self, for instance, plays a central role in Buddhist thought. But
its primary use, according to him, has been to counter the tendency
to absolutize the self, not to deny the existence of the self altogether.
No-self, he thinks, is best understood to mean "no separate self,"
which in turn points to the interbeing of all things. "To see things in
their interbeing nature," he writes, "is to perceive their nature of
interdependence, [their] not having a separate, independent self."[81]

It should come as no surprise then that when Nhat Hanh started his own religious order in 1966, shortly before leaving Vietnam for the United States, he named it the Order of Interbeing. The fourteen precepts that constitute the core values of this order are "guidelines for living mindfully" in a world of interbeing. These guidelines include practicing nonattachment to your own views in order to be open to the views of others; helping others through "compassionate dialogue" to renounce fanaticism and narrowness; seeking creative ways of being with those who are suffering, thus awakening yourself and others to the reality of suffering in the world; living simply and sharing time, energy, and material resources with those who are in need; getting in touch with what is "wondrous, refreshing and healing" both inside and around you; making every effort to reconcile and resolve conflicts, however small; and having the courage to speak out about situations of injustice, even when doing so might threaten your own safety and well-being.[82] Seeing the world as an interdependent reality helps one to act in this way, though acting according to these precepts can also help one to see reality in this way.

To Nhat Hanh, seeing and doing are intrinsically related. What most interferes with responsible action on behalf of others is the distortion to our awareness caused by ego. This distortion is rooted in our sense of being a separate self, our failure to comprehend the interdependent nature of reality and include others in our self-understanding. Mindfulness practice helps to break down this sense of separation and put us in touch with our true self, which includes all beings. Nhat Hanh captures this experience eloquently in his poem entitled "Call Me by My True Names." Written at the time of his involvement with the boat people, it is so much at the heart of his teaching that it bears quoting in full.

Do not say that I'll depart tomorrow
because even today I still arrive.

Look deeply: I arrive in every second
to be a bud on a spring branch,
to be a tiny bird, with wings still fragile,
  learning to sing in my new nest,
to be a caterpillar in the heart of flower,
to be a jewel hiding itself in a stone.

I still arrive, in order to laugh and to cry,
  in order to fear and to hope,

the rhythm of my heart is the birth and
  death of all that are alive.

I am the mayfly metamorphosing on the
  surface of the river,
and I am the bird which, when spring comes,
  arrives in time to eat the mayfly.

I am the frog swimming happily in the
  clear water of a pond,
and I am also the grass-snake who,
  approaching in silence,
  feeds itself on the frog.

I am the child in Uganda, all skin and bones,
  my legs as thin as bamboo sticks,
and I am the arms merchant, selling deadly
  weapons to Uganda.

I am the 12-year-old girl, refugee
  on a small boat,
who throws herself into the ocean after
  being raped by a sea pirate,
and I am the pirate, my heart not yet capable
  of seeing and loving.

I am a member of the politburo, with
  plenty of power in my hands,
and I am the man who has to pay his
  "debt of blood" to my people,
dying slowly in a forced labor camp.

My joy is like spring, so warm it makes
  flowers bloom in all walks of life.
My pain is like a river of tears, so full it
  fills up the four oceans.

Please call me by my true names,
so I can hear all my cries and my laughs
  at once,
so I can see that my joy and pain are one.

Please call me by my true names,
  so I can wake up,
and so the door of my heart can be left open,
the door of compassion.[83]

In realizing our true self, he is saying, we awaken to the reality of interbeing and find our heart open to all beings without regard to their apparent moral worth.

Nhat Hanh's social activism is grounded in personal transformation. Mere activism, in his view, lacks the inner resources necessary to be an effective force for good. He saw this most clearly during the war, when the so-called peace activists—with their intense hostility towards the United States government and their insistence on nothing short of a communist takeover in Vietnam—only served to exacerbate the situation and prolong the war. Possibly for this reason, among others, the emphasis of his teaching has shifted since the war from direct involvement in social causes to training in the practice of mindfulness. In books, lectures, and workshops, he endeavors to teach persons of all nationalities and religions how to live mindfully. He continues to be an advocate for social justice, peace, and reconciliation, but he does not believe any of these conditions are attainable apart from personal transformation. So that is where he has chosen to place the emphasis of his engaged Buddhism.

Thomas Merton, circa 1965. Photograph by John Howard Griffin, used with permission of the Merton Legacy Trust and the Estate of John Howard Griffin.

The material on the following facing pages is the program for a meeting sponsored by the Fellowship of Reconciliation at New York's Town Hall on June 9, 1966. This copy of the program includes a personal inscription by Nhat Hanh to Merton: "To my brother Thomas Merton in fond remembrance and appreciation."

NHAT HANH IS MY BROTHER
by Thomas Merton

This is not a political statement. It has no ulterior motive, it seeks to provoke no immediate reaction "for" or "against" this or that side in the Vietnam war. It is on the contrary a human and personal statement and an anguished plea for Thich Nhat Hanh who is my brother. He is more my brother than many who are nearer to me by race and nationality, because he and I see things exactly the same way. He and I deplore the war that is ravaging his country. We deplore it for exactly the same reasons: human reasons, reasons of sanity, justice and love. We deplore the needless destruction, the fantastic and callous ravaging of human life, the rape of the culture and spirit of an exhausted people. It is surely evident that this carnage serves no purpose that can be discerned and indeed contradicts the very purpose of the mighty nation that has constituted itself the "defender" of the people it is destroying.

Certainly this statement cannot help being a plea for peace. But it is also a plea for my Brother Nhat Hanh. He represents the least "political" of all the movements in Vietnam. He is not directly associated with the Buddhists who are trying to use political manipulation in order to save their country. He is by no means a Communist. The Vietcong is deeply hostile to him. He refuses to be identified with the established government which hates and distrusts him. He represents the young, the defenseless, the new ranks of youth who find themselves with every hand turned against them except those of the peasants and the poor, with whom they are working. Nhat Hanh speaks truly for the people of Vietnam, if there can be said to be a "people" still left in Vietnam.

Nhat Hanh has left his country and has come to us in order to present a picture which is not given us in our newspapers and magazines. He has been well received — and that speaks well for those who have received him. His visit to the United States has shown that we are a people who still desire the truth when we can find it, and still decide in favor of *man* against the political machine when we get a fair chance to do so. But when Nhat Hanh goes home, what will happen to him? He is not in favor with the government which has suppressed his writings. The Vietcong will view with disfavor his American contacts. To have pleaded for an end to the fighting will make him a traitor in the eyes of those who stand to gain personally as long as the war goes on, as long as their countrymen are being killed, as long as they can do business with our military. Nhat Hanh may be returning to imprisonment, torture, even death. We cannot let him go back to Saigon to be destroyed while we sit here, cherishing the warm humanitarian glow of good intentions and worthy sentiments about the ongoing war. We who have met and heard Nhat Hanh, or who have read about him, must also raise our voices to demand that his life and freedom be respected when he returns to his country. Furthermore, we demand this not in terms of any conceivable political advantage, but purely in the name of those values of freedom and humanity in favor of which our armed forces declare they are fighting the Vietnam war. Nhat Hanh is a free man who has acted as a free man in favor of his brothers and moved by the spiritual dynamic of a tradition of religious compassion. He has come among us as many others have, from time to time, bearing witness to the spirit of Zen. More than any other he has shown us that Zen is not an esoteric and world denying cult of inner illumination, but that it has its rare and unique sense of responsibility in the modern world. Wherever he goes he will walk in the strength of his spirit and in the solitude of the Zen monk who sees beyond life and death. It is for our own honor as much as for his safety that we must raise our voices to demand that his life and personal integrity be fully respected when he returns to his smashed and gutted country, there to continue his work with the students and peasants, hoping for the day when reconstruction can begin.

I have said Nhat Hanh is my brother, and it is true. We are both monks, and we have lived the monastic life about the same number of years. We are both poets, both existentialists. I have far more in common with Nhat Hanh than I have with many Americans, and I do not hesitate to say it. It is vitally important that such bonds be admitted. They are the bonds of a new solidarity and a new brotherhood which is beginning to be evident on all the five continents and which cuts across all political, religious and cultural lines to unite young men and women in every country in something that is more concrete than an ideal and more alive than a program. This unity of the young is the only hope of the world. In its name I appeal for Nhat Hanh. Do what you can for him. If I mean something to you, then let me put it this way: do for Nhat Hanh whatever you would do for me if I were in his position. In many ways I wish I were.

"I must speak out for peace. I have come to America to describe to you the aspirations and the agony of the voiceless masses of the Vietnamese people of all faiths who have no means to speak for themselves."

THICH NHAT HANH

Vietnam and the American Conscience   June 9, 1966

Moderator:

ALFRED HASSLER
Executive Secretary of the Fellowship of Reconciliation and the International Committee of Conscience on Vietnam

Tributes By:

DANIEL BERRIGAN, S.J.
Associate editor, *Jesuit Missions*, lecturer, author, poet, vice-chairman, Fellowship of Reconciliation

ABRAHAM J. HESCHEL
Professor of Jewish Ethics and Mysticism, Jewish Theological Seminary of America, philosopher-theologian, co-chairman, Clergy Concerned About Vietnam

ROBERT LOWELL
Poet, author, translator. Recipient of Bollingen, Guggenheim and Pulitzer awards in poetry.

ARTHUR MILLER
World-renowned playright, author *Death of a Salesman, The Crucible, View from the Bridge*, etc. International President, P. E. N.

JOHN OLIVER NELSON
Chairman, Executive Committee, Fellowship of Reconciliation; member, American Committee, International Committee of Conscience on Vietnam; Director, Kirkridge Retreat Center

[handwritten note:] To my brother Thomas Merton in fond remembrance and appreciation Thich nhat hanh

A Reading of Thich Nhat Hanh Poems

A MESSAGE TO THE AMERICAN PEOPLE: THICH NHAT HANH

The meeting will be closed with a Buddhist prayer for peace chanted in Vietnamese by Thich Nhat Hanh.

About the honored speaker THICH NHAT HANH:

One of the founders of Van Hanh, the Buddhist University in Saigon
Director of Youth for Social Service
Author of 10 published volumes including "Oriental Logic" and "Engaged Buddhism," a volume of suppressed "peace poetry."
Editor of *Thien My,* a leading Buddhist weekly
Director of the Institute for Social Studies
Professor of Philosophy of Religion

The International Committee of Conscience on Vietnam is a committee of the Fellowship of Reconcilation, with headquarters at Nyack, New York and in Copenhagen. Close to 10,000 leaders of most of the world's principal faiths, in more than 35 countries, have affiliated themselves with its statement, "They Are Our Brothers Whom We Kill," copies of which are available at the literature table this evening. Thich Nhat Hanh, an early signer of the statement, is a member of both the ICCV and the FOR. Arrangements for his trip in this country have been made by the Fellowship and by the Inter-Universities Committee for Debate on Foreign Policy.

Thich Nhat Hanh, summer of 1972. Photograph by James Forest.

4

Entering into Dialogue

A S WE BEGIN THE twenty-first century, it is becoming increasingly
evident that the world's leading religions must find a way to
engage in serious and meaningful dialogue with one another
if they are to avoid being drawn into more destructive forms of engagement. Thomas Merton saw the need for what he called interfaith
dialogue, and he also saw that the contemplative tradition had something unique to contribute to that dialogue. In a book published in
1967, a year before his death, he wrote:

> One of the most important aspects of the interfaith dialogue has also so
> far been one of the least discussed: it is the special contribution that the
> contemplative life can bring to the dialogue, not only among Christians,
> but also between Christians and the ancient religions of the East, perhaps
> even between Christians and Marxists.[1]

Merton could see the possibility of a contemplative contribution to
interreligious dialogue at this time in his life, because he had by then
achieved a deep, personal understanding of the contemplative path
and had begun his own dialogue with other religions. In subsequent
years, Nhat Hanh would also emerge as a leading contributor to
interreligious dialogue, though, as we shall see, he came to it by a
different route.

The Merton-Suzuki Dialogue

At a time when he was immersed in the Christian mystics, writing
about St. John of the Cross and lecturing to novices about a wide

range of Christian contemplative thinkers, Thomas Merton, as we have noted, was also reading the works of a Zen Buddhist thinker, D. T. Suzuki. He was so intrigued by what he perceived as similarities between Christian mysticism and Zen that he initiated a correspondence with Suzuki by asking him to write an introduction to a selection of writings from the Desert Fathers that he was preparing for publication. It is a sign of the times that the Church censors would not permit him to publish a book on Christian monasticism with an introduction by a Zen Buddhist. Eventually Suzuki's rejected introduction, together with a subsequent exchange of views between these two religious thinkers, was published as a part of a more comprehensive assessment of Zen by Merton, but by then his views had developed considerably. His internal dialogue with Zen, as well as with other religions, had progressed to the point where he was no longer limited to noting similarities and differences of beliefs and ideas; he was beginning to discern an inner spiritual connection between these two religions that went beyond words and concepts.

Merton's correspondence with Suzuki began in 1959. He had recently completed a translation of stories and sayings by the Desert Fathers, the original Christian monks of the fourth and fifth centuries, and was struck by how they resonated with the stories of famous Chinese and Japanese Zen masters. Suzuki agreed to write an introduction for this book, but it turned out to be very different from what Merton expected. Rather than commenting on the wisdom of these early Christian monks, the distinguished authority on Zen took this occasion to write a tightly constructed essay comparing Buddhism and Christianity on the theme of innocence and knowledge. He took as the starting point for his discussion a question addressed to him at a conference of philosophers: What is the Zen concept of morality? In responding to this question, he sought a point of agreement between Christians and Buddhists and thought he found it—not in the sayings of the Desert Fathers (whom he scarcely mentions), but in the writings of a fourteenth-century German mystic, Meister Eckhart.

Suzuki contends that for both Christians and Buddhists the true basis of moral action resides in "purity of heart," which in turn derives from the ultimate emptiness or poverty of the self. It is out of this "zero" that good actions arise and evil actions are avoided. So radical is this notion of emptiness that all attempts to describe the experience inevitably result in distortion and misunderstanding. It is for this reason, he says, that the Zen Master typically advises his students to transcend or cast away the experience. Devoid of the trappings of our self-constructed identities, relying on nothing and going beyond the receiving of an impulse of any sort: this is the goal of Zen training according to Suzuki. Yet when we reach this point of ultimate emptiness, paradoxically, we find ourselves back where we started, as "the ordinary Toms, Dicks and Harrys we had been all along."[2] Buddhist and Christian monks, he thinks, have had a clearly defined way of pursuing this goal. It involved a life of poverty, simplicity, tribulation, obedience, humility, meditation, silence, and other virtues. Yet to the question of how we are to realize this emptiness in our own time "in the midst of industrialization and the universal propagandism of the 'easy life,' " Suzuki has no answer. He is frankly skeptical of the monastic solution, concluding his essay with the poignant observation that the "day of the Desert Fathers is gone; we are waiting for a new sun to rise above the horizon of egotism and sordidness in every sense."[3]

Merton was obviously moved by this essay and challenged by it. Without knowing that the censors would turn it down as an introduction to the *Wisdom of the Desert,* he immediately proposed to write another piece to go with it "to explain and integrate your own study in the whole plan." He felt that most readers would not otherwise grasp its real intent. He told Suzuki: "I will absolutely have to bring to light some clear Christian texts which show conclusively that what you are saying really belongs to the authentic Christian tradition; it is not merely something that you, as a Buddhist, have read into it through Eckhart."[4] More than likely Merton relished the opportunity to engage in serious dialogue this seminal thinker, whose works he had been reading for years (possibly as early as his graduate study at Columbia). The result, however, is somewhat disappointing—a rather dry, academic argument in which he quotes Dostoyevsky, invokes Augustine, and attempts to buttress the position of the Desert Fathers with citations from the sixth-century monk John Cassian.

Merton's chief criticism of Buddhism is that it seems to treat emptiness as a complete negation of personality, "whereas Christianity finds in purity of heart and 'unity of spirit' a supreme and transcendent fulfillment of personality." He qualifies this claim by observing that Christians have a tendency to identify personality with the illusory and exterior ego-self, "which is certainly not the true Christian 'person,' " while Suzuki with his comment about returning to the ordinary Tom, Dick, and Harry at the conclusion of the process of self-emptying

shows that personality as a value is "not absent from Buddhist practice."[5] Merton makes a further distinction between Christianity and
Buddhism. Following a suggestion of Cassian's, he argues that the
monastic life has a twofold purpose, the intermediate end being purity
of heart and the ultimate end being the Kingdom of God. Purity of heart,
Merton thinks, corresponds roughly to Suzuki's term "emptiness," but
there is no Buddhist equivalent of the Kingdom of God. "This is the
real dimension of Christianity, the eschatological dimension, which
is peculiar to it, and which has no parallel in Buddhism."[6]

In his reply, Suzuki has no difficulty disposing of Merton's arguments. "Father Merton's emptiness, when he uses this term, does not
go far enough and deep enough," he writes. It is "still on the level
of God as Creator and does not go up to the Godhead," a less anthropo-
morphic concept for the transcendent, which Suzuki associates with
Eckhart. The same is true of what he says about the "ultimate end
of the monkish life." Here too Merton does not go far enough. "Zen
emptiness," according to Suzuki, "is not the emptiness of nothingness,
but the emptiness of fullness in which there is 'no gain, no loss, no
increase, no decrease.'" As for Christian eschatology, he offers a
distinctly Zen-like interpretation. He contends that the Kingdom of
God is "something never realizable and yet realized in every moment
of our lives. We see it always ahead of us though in reality we are
always in it."[7]

In his concluding remarks, Merton struggles to reply. Uncomfortable
with Suzuki's reliance on Eckhart, who has a reputation in some
circles as a heretic, he abandons Cassian and calls on another Christian mystic, John Ruysbroeck, to lend support to his position. On the
subject of eschatology, he acknowledges that Suzuki's intuition is
sound and "much more deeply Christian than perhaps he himself
imagines." Merton basically concedes that Suzuki has gotten the better
of the argument, concluding their dialogue with the observation that
"thanks to his penetrating intuitions into Western mystical thought,
we can so easily and agreeably communicate with one another on the
deepest and most important level."[8] Looking back on this dialogue
ten years later, Merton is somewhat embarrassed by his contribution.
It is not that what he said was wrong in the sense of being false or
erroneous, but "any attempt to handle Zen in theological language,"
he has decided, "is bound to miss the point."[9] By then his attempt to
appropriate Eastern thought and assimilate it to his own contemplative
vision had progressed considerably.

Merton's interest in Zen clearly influenced his revision of *Seeds of Contemplation*, most of which took place following his correspondence with Suzuki, but it shows up in other ways as well. In 1965, he produced a most remarkable work entitled *The Way of Chuang Tzu*. This book consists of his personal rendering of the stories and sayings of a Chinese Taoist from the third century before Christ. It cannot be called a translation, because he did not know Chinese (as he did French, Spanish, and German). Utilizing four translations in three languages, including a literal version prepared especially for his use by the Chinese scholar John Wu, he puts forth his own poetic reading of this classic text, not a faithful reproduction but a "personal and spiritual interpretation."[10] The result is a lively, engaging, and sometimes haunting work. Merton shows in his reading of Chuang Tzu the same intuitive grasp of Eastern mystical thought that he attributed to Suzuki in respect to Western mystical thought. Because he was not dealing in this work with a systematic or analytical thinker but with one who was primarily intuitive, Merton could trust his own intuition. As he says in the preface, "Chuang Tzu is not concerned with words and formulas about reality, but with the direct existential grasp of reality in itself."[11] In this Chinese sage, Merton found someone with whom he had a natural affinity, someone to whom he could relate on a deep spiritual level beyond abstract ideas and doctrinal formulations.

It is a small step from there to what is probably his best essay on Zen, an introduction he wrote for a book entitled *The Golden Age of Zen* by his friend John Wu. In it, Merton asserts that the "great obstacle to mutual understanding between Christianity and Buddhism lies in the Western tendency to focus not on the Buddhist *experience*, which is essential, but on the *explanation*, which is accidental and which indeed Zen often regards as completely trivial and even misleading." Christianity, because it begins with "revelation," has always been profoundly concerned with statements and formulations, yet this "obsession with doctrinal formulas, juridical order and ritual exactitude has often made people forget that the heart of Catholicism, too, is a *living experience* of unity in Christ which far transcends all conceptual formulations."[12] He is at pains to insist that he does not want to throw out fundamental beliefs or dispense with theology altogether. Neither is he maintaining that all religions at the experiential level, stripped of doctrines, explanations, and creeds, are identical or even alike. He is also fully aware of how difficult it can be to access the experience of others, especially when all we have to go on are texts, some of them many hundreds of years old and from cultures very different from our own. Nevertheless he wants to hold out for a kind of "intuitive affinity" that permits mutual understanding and a deep level of communication across cultures and among persons of different religious traditions.[13]

Merton's Asian Journey

In order to test this conviction, Merton needed to get beyond the mere study of texts and communicate directly with persons who were themselves living embodiments of the religions they professed. That chance came unexpectedly in 1968 when he was invited to participate in a conference of his religious order in Bangkok. He did not expect to be allowed by his abbot to attend; but when permission was granted, he seized the opportunity to expand his trip to include other sites in Asia and meetings with representatives of other religions. He kept a journal of the trip, which he no doubt intended to edit for publication, that was published only posthumously. As he departs from San Francisco on the first leg of the journey, he writes in his journal:

> The moment of take-off was ecstatic. The dewy wing was suddenly covered with rivers of cold sweat running backward. The window wept jagged shining courses of tears. Joy. We left the ground—I with Christian mantras and a great sense of destiny, of being at last on my true way after years of waiting and wondering and fooling around.[14]

As this passage indicates, Merton was clearly prepared to take his engagement with other religions, and Buddhism in particular, to a new level.

This trip was the culmination of a lifetime of spiritual searching. Merton went with a prepared mind and a ready heart, not knowing what lay ahead but open to whatever might come. In a paper prepared in advance of the trip, he describes himself as "a pilgrim who is anxious to obtain not just information, not just 'facts' about other monastic traditions, but to drink from the ancient sources of monastic vision and experience."[15] In a period of less than two months, he attended two conferences (the one in Bangkok for members of his own religious order and another in Calcutta for representatives of various religions), met with several Tibetan lamas (including the Dalai

Lama), and visited historic religious sites in India, Thailand, and Ceylon (now Sri Lanka). He planned to go on to Japan and to meet with some well-known Zen teachers. But before he could complete the trip he had planned, he died suddenly and somewhat mysteriously in Bangkok just as the conference to which he had been originally invited was beginning. By then, however, he had accomplished what he came for.

Early in the trip Merton attended a conference in Calcutta sponsored by the Temple of Understanding, an organization established "to foster education, communication and understanding among the world religions."[16] There he heard presentations by representatives of various religions, including a rabbi from New York and one from Jerusalem and a Chinese scholar from Taiwan. Rather than read his prepared paper, he gave a more informal talk that captures in a succinct and prophetic way what his trip to Asia, as well as the search that preceded it, was all about. He began his talk by identifying himself as a monk speaking for monks, "a very strange kind of person, a marginal person, because the monk in the modern world is no longer an established person with an established place in society." He is someone "who withdraws deliberately to the margin of society with a view to deepening fundamental human experience." Merton goes on to say what this deepening of experience might entail.

> The marginal man accepts the basic irrelevance of the human condition, an irrelevance which is manifested above all in the fact of death. . . . He struggles with the fact of death because there is something deeper than death, and the office of the monk or the marginal person, the meditative person or the poet is to go beyond death even in this life, to go beyond the dichotomy of life and death and to be, therefore, a witness to life.

Along the way he must be prepared to confront doubt and to struggle with it in order to break through to "a certitude which is very, very deep because it is not his own personal certitude, it is the certitude of God Himself, in us." God has called us, Merton believes, "to pierce through the irrelevance of our life, while accepting and admitting that our life is totally irrelevant, in order to find relevance in Him." This relevance is not something we can grasp or possess; it can only be received as a gift. "Consequently," he says, "the kind of life I represent is a life that is openness to gift; gift from God and gift from others."[17]

Merton ended his talk with what he called "a small message of hope." It bears quoting in full since it goes to the heart of what he thought contemplatives could contribute to the dialogue among religions.

> [T]here are always people who dare to seek on the margin of society, who are not dependent on social acceptance, not dependent on social routine, and prefer a kind of free-floating existence under a state of risk. And among these people, if they are faithful to their calling, to their vocation, and to their message from God, communication on the deepest level is possible. And the deepest level of communication is not communication, but communion. It is wordless. It is beyond words, and it is beyond speech, and it is beyond concept. Not that we discover a new unity. We discover an older unity. My dear brothers, we are already one. But we imagine that we are not. And what we have to recover is our original unity. What we have to be is what we are.[18]

The remainder of his Asian journey was the working out of the implications of this statement, the living out of this extraordinary message of hope.

In the days and weeks preceding his death, Merton had a number of memorable meetings, mostly with Tibetan Buddhists. It is interesting that his encounters with living representatives of Buddhism in the waning days of his life should have been almost exclusively with Tibetan Buddhists. Until that time he had been preoccupied with Zen Buddhism, a very different form of the religion. Of the two, Zen is much more austere and less given to the use of images, more in the apophatic than the kataphatic tradition of spirituality. Yet Merton responded well to the Tibetans he met, establishing an immediate rapport with them. He observed in his journal that they are "the only ones who, at present, have a really large number of people who have attained to extraordinary heights in meditation and contemplation," and that was what he was looking for. He felt at home with them, "even though much that appears in books about them seems bizarre if not sinister."[19]

At the conclusion of a meeting with one of the Tibetan lamas at his remote hermitage in the mountains near Darjeeling, the lama expressed surprise that they should have gotten on so well, in as much as one of them was a Buddhist and the other a Christian. "There must be something wrong here," he joked. Although Merton could appreciate the humor in this remark, he did not take these sessions lightly. He asked probing questions and listened intently to what these advanced spiritual practitioners had to say about their religion.

With the Tibetans, he typically asked about their practice of meditation and not just their religious beliefs, though invariably the conversation came back to experience.

Of all the Buddhists he met on this phase of his trip, Merton was most impressed with Chatral Rimpoche. Writing in his journal about their meeting, he said that they talked for two hours or more, "covering all sorts of ground, mostly around the idea of *dzogchen* [the most advanced form of meditative practice in Tibetan Buddhism], but also taking in some points of Christian doctrine compared with Buddhist: *dharmakaya* [the transcendent body of Buddha], the Risen Christ, suffering, compassion for all creatures, motives for 'helping others'— but all leading back to *dzogchen*, the ultimate emptiness, the unity of *sunyata* [void] and *karuna* [love], going 'beyond the *dharmakaya*' and 'beyond God' to the ultimate perfect emptiness." They agreed that neither of them had experienced perfect emptiness. Yet, according to Merton, the "unspoken or half-spoken message of the talk was our complete understanding of each other as people who were somehow on the edge of a great realization and knew it and were trying, somehow or other, to go out and get lost in it—and that it was a grace for us to meet one another."[20]

Historically the most significant meeting of the trip was with the Dalai Lama. Merton did not think at first that he wanted to meet with the spiritual and political leader of the Tibetan Buddhists in exile. "I've seen enough pontiffs," he told Hal Talbott, the American who arranged his meetings with the lamas.[21] But when the time came he agreed to the meeting, and it went so well for both of them that two additional sessions were scheduled.[22] The conversations between Merton and the Dalai Lama were wide-ranging. From Merton's notes, one gets the impression that they went from a somewhat academic discussion of topics relating to epistemology and metaphysics to a more personal exchange focusing on questions of monastic life and religious practice. The Dalai Lama, he observed, was initially concerned with correcting "partial and distorted Western views of Tibetan mysticism" but later wanted to know more about Western monasticism—religious vows, the rule of silence, and even whether monks watched movies. Merton enjoyed the conversations and was particularly impressed with the "solidity" of the lama's ideas, although he found communication through a translator sometimes difficult. At one point he wanted to talk about "freedom and grace" but gave up because the translator had difficulty getting his meaning. He eventually got around to asking for the Buddhist's views on monasticism and Marxism, the topic which he had chosen for his lecture at the upcoming conference in Bangkok, and received a thoughtful response from his holiness. Overall the meetings were warm and cordial. Merton left with a feeling of great respect, even fondness for the Dalai Lama and with the conviction that there was a "real spiritual bond" between them.[23]

The Dalai Lama was equally impressed. In his recollections some fifteen years later, he recalls that even though he knew very little about Merton prior to their meeting a mutual understanding quickly developed between them. His initial impression was of someone with a "deep interest in Eastern philosophy, mainly Buddhism, and especially meditation." (Talbott remembers him getting down on the floor to demonstrate Buddhist meditative posture and breathing technique for his Christian guest.) As the conversation progressed, he was struck by Merton's considerable knowledge of Buddhism and also by his open-mindedness. "Such a person," he observes, "was very useful in this period, when the West and East were just coming to know each other." As a result of the meeting, the Dalai Lama felt his understanding and respect for the Christian religion had been enhanced. "Because of meeting with him I found many common practices between Christian monks and Buddhist monks, the way of living, mainly, the simplicity and contentment and great devotion to one's spiritual development."[24]

The meeting was not entirely serious. The Dalai Lama recalls a humorous exchange having to do with belts. Merton's was thick and practical, whereas his was only a cord that did not prevent his robes from slipping. He later acquired a belt similar to Merton's for himself, symbolic perhaps of his willingness to learn from the West. On a more serious note, he says his most lasting impression was that of Merton as a "holy man." Though he is not sure how this term would be interpreted in the West, from a Buddhist perspective it means "one who sincerely implements what he knows."[25] In subsequent years, the Dalai Lama has continued to acknowledge Merton's influence. As previously noted, an important conference of Buddhists and Christian monks, convened at Gethsemani in the summer of 1996, was held largely at his urging to honor Merton and further the work that he had begun.

In all his meetings with Buddhists, Merton made no effort to obscure or gloss over fundamental differences among the religions. Sonam Kazi, a lay monk who accompanied him on several of his visits (including the one to the Dalai Lama), said at one point that he was opposed to "mixing traditions," even Tibetan traditions, and Merton did not disagree. In fact, Merton went to some length in the paper he prepared for the Temple of Understanding Conference (but did not actually deliver) to record his opposition to what he called "facile syncretism, a mishmash of semireligious verbiage and pieties, a devotionalism that admits everything and therefore takes nothing with full seriousness." He calls instead for "scrupulous respect for important differences, and where one no longer understands or agrees, this must be kept clear—without useless debate."[26] Merton was nonetheless fascinated by the similarities and analogies he found within and among the various traditions. He plays with some of these analogies in notes to himself recorded in his journal. For instance, he composed a meditation on the metaphor of *door*, with Christ as the door that is not a door—an apparent allusion to the metaphor of the "gateless gate" in Buddhism. He is not saying that Christ is the Buddha or that Christ represents emptiness in the Buddhist sense. He uses Buddhist concepts and images to shed light on Christian texts and doctrines, to disclose a deeper meaning wherever possible but not to replace Christian terms with Buddhist ones or to meld Christian and Buddhist concepts into a new religious synthesis.

Near the close of the Indian portion of his trip, Merton made a critical assessment of his Asian journey to that point. He concluded that his meetings with the Dalai Lama and various other Tibetans had been the most significant thing so far, "especially in the way we were able to communicate with one another and share an essentially spiritual experience of 'Buddhism' which is also somehow in harmony with Christianity."[27] In addition, he recorded a dream that in retrospect may be seen as symbolic of his Asian experience. In the dream he saw a mountain that he recognized as Kanchenjunga, the awesome Himalayan mountain that he could see from his window in Darjeeling on days when the weather was clear. It was all white, pure white, yet he realized something about it was different. Then he heard a voice say, "There is another side to the mountain." And he realized that he was not viewing the mountain in the way that he did from his hotel window. In his dream the mountain was turned around so that he was seeing it from the Tibetan side.[28] That is an appropriate symbol for what had happened to him during this phase of his trip. Merton had been viewing Buddhism not from a Western perspective but empathetically from a Tibetan perspective. What he had hoped to realize on this trip, "communication at the deepest possible level," had occurred, even if much of what was communicated could not be expressed in words.

The Epiphany at Polonnaruwa

There was, as it turned out, another experience of "communication beyond words" awaiting Merton, one that did not require the presence of another person. Before returning to Bangkok for the conference that had brought him to Asia in the first place, Merton took an excursion to Sri Lanka and to Polonnaruwa where he visited the site of some of the most famous stone images of Buddha to be found anywhere in the world. To his companion, a Roman Catholic vicar, these images simply represented "paganism," but for Merton they were the occasion of a spiritual, even "mystical" experience. So moved was he by the sight that he could not write about it for several days. Yet when he does record his impressions, it is with such a sense of immediacy that you feel you are there with him. To have discovered this passage in his journal following his death must have been a stunning experience. Even for someone who has read it many times, it is still quite moving, so much so that it bears quoting in full.

> I am able to approach the Buddhas barefoot and undisturbed, my feet in wet grass, wet sand. Then the silence of the extraordinary faces. The great smiles. Huge and yet subtle. Filled with every possibility, questioning nothing, knowing everything, rejecting nothing, the peace not of emotional resignation but of Madhyamika, of sunyata, that has seen through every question without trying to discredit anyone or anything—*without refutation*—without establishing some other argument. For the doctrinaire, the mind that needs well-established positions, such peace, such silence, can be frightening. I was knocked over with a rush of relief and thankfulness at the *obvious* clarity of the figures, the clarity and fluidity of shape and line, the design of the monumental bodies composed into the rock shape and landscape, figure, rock and tree. And the sweep of bare rock sloping away on the other side of the hollow, where you can go back and see different aspects of the figures.
>
> Looking at these figures I was suddenly, almost forcibly, jerked clean out of the habitual, half-tied vision of things, and an inner clearness, clarity, as if exploding from the rocks themselves, became evident and obvious. The queer *evidence* of the reclining figure, the smile, the sad

smile of Ananda standing with arms folded (much more "imperative" than Da Vinci's Mona Lisa because completely simple and straightforward). The thing about all this is that there is no puzzle, no problem, and really no "mystery." All problems are resolved and everything is clear, simply because what matters is clear. The rock, all matter, all life, is charged with dharmakaya . . . everything is emptiness and everything is compassion. I don't know when in my life I have ever had such a sense of beauty and spiritual validity running together in one aesthetic illumination. Surely, with Mahabalipuram and Polonnaruwa my Asian pilgrimage has come clear and purified itself. I mean, I know and have seen what I was obscurely looking for. I don't know what else remains but I have now seen and have pierced through the surface and have got beyond the shadow and the disguise.[29]

It has been said that what happened at Polonnaruwa was not unique, that Merton reports similar experiences of a mystical sort in other places in his writings. But that is to miss the particular significance of this experience coming as it did at this particular time in his life. For Merton this was a realization, an actualization, of what he had been seeking in all his encounters with other religions, namely, an experience of the ineffable essence of the religion.

If we read the account closely, we see that it contains all of the elements basic to interfaith dialogue as Merton conceived it. In this encounter with what was, for him, an authentic expression of Buddhist faith, every question is "seen through" without a need to discredit anyone or anything. He is not disposed to mount an argument, much less a refutation of Buddhism. He is satisfied to see clearly into its essence. This "seeing," moreover, is from within and not simply from without, a truly empathetic understanding of the religion. In this contemplative moment, Merton experiences a deep inner peace, beyond all doubt. He realizes that to the "doctrinaire mind" such peace can be frightening, because it lacks the external, institutional support usually associated with religion. Yet without that support, in the immediacy of the moment, he experiences neither doubt nor fear. There is also great clarity. "All problems are resolved and everything is clear, simply because what matters is clear."

If there is one thing that the contemplative life should provide, it is clarification by way of simplification. Through the practice of meditation, one undertakes to see things just as they are without the overlay of thought or reflection. It is indicative of how far Merton had come in his own practice and in his attempt to penetrate the apparent differences between Christianity and Buddhism through dialogue that he could now experience this quintessentially Buddhist art form with such utter simplicity and immediacy. No wonder everything suddenly became clear for him. His dialogue with Buddhism, starting with Suzuki and extending through his meetings with the Tibetans, had finally borne fruit. He had reached the essence of another religion and had done so experientially.

All that remained was for him to return to Bangkok for the conference that had brought him to Asia in the first place, and make his presentation to fellow members of his religious order from around the world. Yet in the context of all that had happened since his arrival nearly two months earlier, it must have seemed anti-climactic. The title of his talk, "Marxism and Monastic Perspectives," reflects his interests prior to the trip and in particular his encounter with student radicals at a conference in Santa Barbara shortly before he left for Asia. He recalls one of the students saying to him, "We are monks also." Merton interpreted this remark to mean that these students considered themselves the "true monks" of their day. He took their claim as a challenge to think seriously about what the monastic life might have to offer the rest of society in a time of revolution. He addressed this challenge in his Bangkok talk, but his heart was not in it. He had to remind himself at a couple of points in the talk that his subject was Marxism. What he really wanted to talk about was Buddhism and the challenge it posed to Christian monasticism.

About halfway through the speech, he recounts some of his impressions from meetings with Buddhists in India and elsewhere. Gradually this interest takes over and the theme of the speech becomes how to achieve a better understanding of the monastic vocation as one of "total inner transformation." He concludes with these observations:

I believe that our renewal consists precisely in deepening this understanding and this grasp of that which is most real. And I believe that by openness to Buddhism, to Hinduism, and to these great Asian traditions, we stand a wonderful chance of learning more about the potentiality of our own traditions, because they have gone, from the natural point of view, so much deeper into this than we have. The combination of the natural techniques and graces and the other things that have been manifested in Asia and the Christian liberty of the gospel should bring us all at last to that full and transcendent liberty which is beyond mere cultural differences and mere externals—and mere this or that.[30]

It had only been a week since the epiphany at Polonnaruwa, and Merton was no doubt still trying to absorb the meaning of that experience. Yet he was also struggling to draw from it a direction for action. It is important to note that he has not abandoned the Christian religion. As he says, the historic encounter of East and West provides a wonderful opportunity to learn more about "the potentiality of our own traditions." He is not looking to the Asian religions to replace Christianity, but rather to assist in its inner renewal, just as his own encounter with these religions had assisted in his inner renewal and spiritual transformation.

Nhat Hanh's Engagement with Christianity

For Thich Nhat Hanh, the meeting of religions and the path of religious convergence took a different form than for Thomas Merton. Having grown up under the conditions of colonialism, Christianity held no initial appeal for him. The colonization of Vietnam by the French was closely allied with the efforts of missionaries to convert the population to Christianity. Many French missionaries took the position that the Vietnamese people could only be saved by giving up their ancestral traditions, which caused a great deal of ill will, particularly among Buddhists. The climate of mistrust was further exacerbated by the tendency of the French government to favor Catholics. It was a popular belief among Buddhists that Christianity was introduced to facilitate the conquest of Vietnam and that the only reason a person would convert to Catholicism was to gain some political advantage. This mistrust persisted even after the French withdrew in the mid-1950s. The archbishop of the Catholic Church for Vietnam at that time was, as we have noted, the brother of the President of Vietnam, and it was widely thought that he used his political connections to further the interests of Christians at the expense of Buddhists. Reflecting on this situation many years later, Nhat Hanh commented sardonically that "in such an atmosphere of discrimination and injustice against non-Christians, it was difficult for me to discover the beauty of Jesus' teachings."[31]

His attitude began to change when some Catholics who were not a part of the official hierarchy became involved in the peace movement. By then military conflict had resumed and the Americans had replaced the French as the driving force behind the effort to defeat communism.

The American government at first only sent military advisors to Vietnam, but before long they were dispatching troops and engaging in a massive bombing campaign directed at the communist insurgents. Because it was virtually impossible in this situation to distinguish communists from noncommunists, many innocent people were killed. In some cases whole villages were destroyed. By 1965, the war had reached "such a state of tragic absurdity," according to Nhat Hanh, that "no religious conscience" could fail "to speak out against it."[32] On the first of January, 1966, eleven Catholic priests made a public appeal for peace. They met resistance from the government and criticism from church officials, but their action was applauded by the Buddhists, whose patriarch had made a similar statement on behalf of peace a few days earlier. Opposition to the war had crossed religious lines and now included Catholics as well as Buddhists.

As a recognized leader of the peace movement, Nhat Hanh was glad for any support he could get. Buddhists, he wrote, "are willing to cooperate with other religious groups—Cao Daiist, Hoa Haoist, and especially Catholics—in order to realize peace and reconstruction for Vietnam."[33] It helped that important changes were taking place within both Vietnamese Buddhism and Catholicism at this time. Buddhists in Vietnam had begun even before the war to take a more engaged approach to political and social issues, and the war accelerated that process. The Catholic Church, as we have seen, was beginning to reassess its relationship to the non-Catholic world, largely as a result of the Second Vatican Council. Progressive Catholics were calling for greater appreciation of other cultures and a better understanding of other religions.

There was also a movement within the church away from hierarchical solutions to problems and toward a closer identification with the aspirations of indigenous people. Nhat Hanh felt that if church leaders were more closely identified with the aspirations of the Vietnamese people they would take a more critical stance toward the government. He was convinced that anyone who went into the villages as he did and worked among the peasants would recognize that what they wanted was not victory for either side but an end to the killing. So, following his trip to the United States in 1966, he met with Pope Paul VI in Rome and appealed to him to "speak to our Vietnamese Catholic brothers, advising them to cooperate with the other religious groups in Vietnam in order to put an end to this atrocious war."[34] He realized that without the cooperation of the two major religions of Vietnam it would be difficult, if not impossible, to change the course of the war.

Can there be any doubt that Nhat Hanh's ideas concerning the value of interreligious dialogue and the need for cooperation among religions were forged in the furnace of war? Ironically, the conflict that so deeply divided the Vietnamese people had brought Buddhists and Catholics closer together. The younger generation of Buddhists and Catholics especially sought ways to work cooperatively to end the war and rebuild their country. In the process they came to know one another better. The "determination to work for peace and a democratic society," Nhat Hanh has written, "can serve to unite the various elements that have sometimes been divided, and lead them to an acceptance of each other based on this common interest." He could see this most clearly in the case of his own country where common action directed at the solution of a common problem enabled them to "overcome the obstacles and lay aside the ghosts that had haunted them for so many centuries."[35] Had it not been for the war—and the peace movement it spawned—there probably would not have been this coming together of Buddhists and Catholics in Vietnam.

Yet early in the war there was a series of incidents that threatened to divide the peace movement. Buddhist activists had been putting pressure on the Diem government to correct perceived injustices against their people, and the government had responded with further repressive measures. In June 1963, a Buddhist monk burned himself to death in a dramatic act of protest; public reaction, as we have noted, was immediate and intense. Demonstrations and other acts of resistance spread throughout the country. On the day of the monk's funeral the government reached an agreement with the Buddhist leadership, but the agreement did not last. Other burnings by Buddhist monks followed, until the Diem regime finally fell in a bloody coup that took the lives of both the president and his brother. The self-immolations no doubt helped bring down the Diem regime, but they also posed a serious ethical dilemma for many who were opposed to the war on religious grounds. They were characterized in news reports as suicides, and for most Christians, especially Catholics, suicide is a sin, so these acts were considered morally repugnant. But setting aside the question of whether they constituted suicide, many who opposed the war were troubled by such extreme acts of violence. How could Buddhists, who are generally regarded as pacifists, countenance such a thing? Did it not serve to discredit their cause in the eyes of the world? If nothing else, it pointed to a need for dialogue.

In June 1965, a group of prominent Vietnamese writers, including Thich Nhat Hanh, attempted to open a dialogue in behalf of peace with some of the world's leading humanists by writing open letters and publishing them in French and English. Nhat Hanh addressed his letter to Martin Luther King and took the occasion to discuss the self-immolations. He began by acknowledging that the "self-burning of Vietnamese Buddhist monks is somehow difficult for the Western Christian conscience to understand." He denied that these acts were suicides, saying he did not even regard them as protests in the usual sense. They were, in his eyes, acts of extreme self-sacrifice aimed at "moving the hearts of the oppressors, and calling the attention of the world to the suffering endured by the Vietnamese." But why burn oneself to make such a statement? Because, he said, it proves that what one has to say is of utmost importance. After all, nothing is more painful than a burn.

He then goes on to make an explicit connection to Buddhist religious practice. During the ceremony of ordination for monks within the Mahayana tradition, he writes, a person about to take his vows intentionally burns himself in several places on his body to show the seriousness of his commitment. "The Vietnamese monk, by burning himself, says with all his strength and determination that he can endure the greatest sufferings to protect his people." Still, it might be asked, why burn oneself to death? According to Nhat Hanh, it is only a matter of degree. The monk's intention is not to destroy himself but to express the depth of his compassion. He does not want to die, but he is willing to die if necessary for the sake of others. Those who commit acts of self-immolation in this context do not wish to destroy their oppressors; they simply want a change of policy. The real enemy, he contends, "is not man, but intolerance, fanaticism, dictatorship, cupidity, hatred, and discrimination which lie within the heart of man."[36]

Nhat Hanh concludes with an appeal for King's support in the struggle to end the war. "I am sure since you have been engaged in one of the hardest struggles for equality and human rights," he wrote, "you are among those who understand fully, and share with all their hearts, the indescribable suffering of the Vietnamese people."[37] A year later, on his speaking tour in the United States, he had an opportunity to meet King personally and to make his appeal directly.

It was a major breakthrough for the peace movement when Martin Luther King, with Nhat Hanh at his side, publicly announced his decision to oppose the war.

In the meantime there were more self-immolations, not only of Buddhist monks but also of several young Americans. One of the most highly publicized was that of Roger LaPorte, who set fire to himself in front of the United Nations building on November 8, 1965. LaPorte was a member of the Catholic Peace Fellowship and on the staff of the *Catholic Worker*. When Thomas Merton heard the news, he immediately sent telegrams to Jim Forest of the Catholic Peace Fellowship and Dorothy Day of the *Catholic Worker* expressing his profound distress at "current developments in the peace movement" and asking that his name be removed from the list of sponsors of the peace fellowship. "The whole thing," he wrote in a follow-up letter to Forest, "gives off a very different smell from the Gandhian movement, the non-violent movement in France and the non-violence of Martin Luther King."[38] He did not hold the Catholic Peace Fellowship responsible for the actions of one of its members, but the incident revealed a certain "craziness" in the peace movement and in the country as whole from which he needed to separate himself. On further reflection, Merton rescinded his request to have his name taken off the list of CPF sponsors and, according to Forest, remained engaged with the fellowship for the remainder of his life; but the incident had made a deep impression on him. For one thing, it prompted him to write one of his most important essays on the subject of nonviolence.[39] It also pointed up the need for more dialogue.

One of the most thoughtful and penetrating discussions of the issue of self-immolation from both a Buddhist and a Christian perspective occurred some years later in a conversation between Nhat Hanh and Daniel Berrigan. It took place in the spring of 1974, in the Paris apartment where Nhat Hanh was then living. For a period of about a month, the two peace activists met in the evening after work and talked, often late into the night. Berrigan brought along a tape recorder and produced a transcript of the conversation, which he later edited into a book entitled *The Raft Is Not the Shore*. He opens the discussion of self-immolation with the observation that such an extreme action on the part of dedicated Christians and Buddhists in response to the war was a source of inspiration to some and a scandal to others. He was personally involved with the LaPorte incident, inasmuch as he was asked to speak at a memorial service for the young man. In his talk he raised the question of whether this act should be called a suicide. He did not think so and was subsequently criticized for taking this position. It was the official position of the Catholic Church at the time that the act was suicide and should not be called anything else. In Berrigan's view, suicide proceeds from despair and loss of hope, and he did not think from what he knew of LaPorte that he had died in that spirit. Nhat Hanh agreed: "I see in the act of self-immolation the willingness to take suffering on yourself, to make yourself suffer for the sake of purification, for the sake of communication."[40] He goes on to say that he did not think self-immolation was very different from fasting for a cause, since fasting too can lead to death.

In support of his position, Nhat Hanh cites the example of two Buddhists he knew personally who immolated themselves in the cause of peace. Both of them, he is convinced, loved life and wanted to live but could not bear the suffering of others. "They wanted to do something or be something for others." He then introduces a new perspective into the discussion. "I would say that Jesus knew the things that were to happen to him. Why didn't he try to avoid them? Why did he allow himself to be caught in that situation—to be judged, to be crucified, to die? I think he did so because of others."[41] Berrigan concurs in this interpretation, noting how appropriate it is that they should be having this discussion on Good Friday, the day set aside by Christians for the remembrance of Christ's death. According to the gospel accounts, he tells his friend, Jesus went to his death *freely*. His death should therefore be seen as a gift "given in view of the lives of others and their possibilities."[42] As a Catholic, Berrigan wonders if the church might not have lost touch with this meaning.

Nhat Hanh then recalls an incident of self-immolation involving a fellow worker in the School of Youth for Social Service and one of the original members of the Order of Interbeing. Her name was Nhat Chi Mai, and she burned herself to death in May 1967, while he was in the United States. She prepared for the act by first going away and spending a month with her parents. She returned to the community so beautifully dressed that many of the members thought she was about to be married. Before setting fire to herself, she placed in front of her "a statue of the Virgin Mary and a statue of a woman Bodhisattva, Quan Am, the Buddhist saint of compassion." She also placed beside her a poem that read: "Joining my hands, I kneel before Mother Mary and Bodhisattva Quan Am. Please help me to realize fully my vow."[43]

There could hardly have been a more powerful statement of the convergence of the two religions—Buddhist and Christian—in the cause of peace than the scene of this young woman kneeling before these two ancient symbols of compassion while allowing her body to be consumed by fire. Following her death, it was discovered that she had written many other poems and letters. When a Catholic friend who was also involved in the peace movement tried to publish her writings, he was attacked by other Catholics who saw her action as communist propaganda.[44] Those who participated in the peace effort, it seems, were able to understand and appreciate her action, while those outside of the movement could not.

Nhat Hanh has retold this story on other occasions, but what is striking about this particular telling is the context. Eight years earlier when he tried to explain the self-immolation of Buddhist monks in an open letter to Martin Luther King, he did so in primarily Buddhist terms by relating the act with the monk's ordination vows. Now, talking with someone who is both a Catholic priest and a companion in the struggle for peace in Vietnam, he gives the event a Christian as well as Buddhist interpretation. He suggests that there might be an analogy between the death of this young woman and the death of Jesus. Like Jesus, Chi Mai died for others.

Berrigan was deeply moved by the whole discussion, and commented at the end that he had been led to see something he had not seen before.

> I think it's because of our worship together and Holy Week and the very deep things in this community which I have gained some sense of. I see how these deaths would be much better understood in the Buddhist community than in the Christian community. And this says something very deep about how our communities understand the offering of Jesus.[45]

If Berrigan gained new insight from this exchange, so did Nhat Hanh. As the contrast between his two explanations of the Buddhist self-immolations shows, he had grown considerably in his understanding of the Christian faith and his capacity to converse empathetically with a representative of that faith.

The Nhat-Hanh-Berrigan Dialogue

The meeting with Berrigan in which this exchange occurred came at a crucial time in the life of Thich Nhat Hanh, a time of transition.

The year was 1974 and the war was coming to an end, but the future was uncertain. He knew that he would no longer be needed as an advocate for peace in Vietnam, yet it was not clear what role, if any, he would have in rebuilding his country after the war. He and Berrigan had a great deal in common. Both were priests within their respective religious traditions, both were poets, and both had been leaders in the peace movement for many years. They had opposed the official policies of their governments and been severely criticized by the leadership of their religious communities. They had also been pressured to leave their homelands—Berrigan not long after his comments at the memorial service for the young peace worker and Nhat Hanh when his reform efforts were rebuffed by the conservative Buddhist hierarchy. The Buddhist activist could have said of his Christian counterpart what Merton once said of Nhat Hanh: he is my brother. Although they had met before, they now had a rare opportunity for extended discussion on a wide range of issues—not just war and peace, but issues of genuine concern to any spiritually engaged person in the latter half of the twentieth century. When their dialogue was published, it was given the appropriate subtitle: "Conversations toward a Buddhist/Christian Awareness." It could well serve as a model for interreligious dialogue in a time of global interdependence.

In his book *Living Buddha, Living Christ*, written twenty years after this meeting, Nhat Hanh sets out what he considers the essential conditions for authentic dialogue between religions. To begin with, he says, the participants must faithfully represent their own traditions, and they must be willing to learn from one another. "For dialogue to be fruitful, we need to live deeply our own tradition and, at the same time, listen deeply to others."[46] Only in this way will we be able to appreciate the values inherent in one another's traditions. In order for the dialogue to be authentic, the participants must be aware of the positive and negative aspects of their own tradition. It will not do to present one's own religion in the best possible light while emphasizing the faults of another's. We must be honest and self-critical regarding both traditions. As an aside, he says that it is sometimes more difficult to have a dialogue with someone from one's own tradition than with someone from another tradition, because of the feeling we often have of being misunderstood or betrayed by those within our tradition. Respecting differences within our own religious community and seeing how those differences have enriched us can help us be more open to the richness and diversity of other traditions. Yet in the end we must be prepared to change; otherwise any attempt at dialogue will be a waste of time. Nhat Hanh concludes:

> If we think we monopolize the truth and we still organize a dialogue, it is not authentic. We have to believe that by engaging in dialogue with the other person, we have the possibility of making a change in ourselves, that we can become deeper. . . . We have to allow what is good, beautiful, and meaningful in the other's tradition to transform us.[47]

Nhat Hanh's dialogue with Daniel Berrigan exemplifies these principles. It is a reflection of the degree of openness the Buddhist monk had achieved at this time in his life that he could enter into such a dialogue. It is also indicative of the kind of ministry he would pursue following the war.

The opening exchange between these two men is representative of their dialogue as a whole. Berrigan begins the conversation with an observation about "remembrance." He says that this idea had always fascinated him. It figures prominently in the Bible, but also has contemporary relevance because of the importance it had for Martin Luther King and the civil rights movement. Remembrance, as Dr. King understood it, does not bind one to the past, but serves as a creative power to unlock the future. "In some mysterious way the bitter and unpromising past" was transformed by him into a "vision of an entirely new future," according to Berrigan.[48]

Nhat Hanh responds with a different sense of "re-membering." He sees it as a way of reconnecting with oneself, of not being so dispersed, of becoming whole again. He associates this sense of remembrance with the Buddhist experience of awakening to oneself. "It is not something very difficult to understand," he says. "Each of us has undergone that kind of experience in our own life, several times in our own life."[49] He then makes an intuitive leap and relates the Buddhist understanding of remembrance to the Christian Eucharist. He recalls how he was able to understand and appreciate this sacrament after hearing the story of Jesus breaking bread and pouring wine with his disciples. Jesus said to them: "This is my flesh, my blood. Drink it, take it, eat it and you will have eternal life." Instead of mindlessly eating bread and drinking wine, they were awakened by this action from their forgetfulness and illusion and brought to a recognition of who Jesus really was. "I think," he tells Berrigan, "when you perform the rite of Eucharist, you have a role that is very similar to the act of Jesus. Your role is to bring back life and reality to a community that is participating in the worship."⁵⁰

The discussion then turns to the subject of death, with Berrigan first reflecting on the gospel accounts of Jesus' death and then recalling a near-death experience of his own while he was in prison. Nhat Hanh notes that such experiences often bring "an awareness that what you have thought of as death is not death. And maybe you have the realization that if one doesn't know how to die, then one doesn't know how to live either."⁵¹ He proceeds to offer an interpretation of death that sees it as integrally related to life, concluding that there is a reality that transcends what we call both life and death. For Buddhists, it is "emptiness" and for Christians "eternal life." Berrigan follows by recalling something Merton once said to the novices at Gethsemani. "He said the only thing that relieved the life of a monk from absolute absurdity was that his life was a joyful conquest of death." Merton, he thought, embodied this joy. "He had a true sense of God and the world, and I think people came from him with a sense of the possibilities life held—enlightenment maybe."⁵²

Berrigan next reflects on America's "obsession with death" as evidenced by the emphasis on violence in our culture and our preoccupation with preparation for war. "Our real shrines are nuclear installations and the Pentagon," he contends. "This is where we worship, allowing ourselves to hear the obscene command that we kill and be killed." Nhat Hanh responds with some observations of his own about living under the conditions of war. "During the periods when the war was very intensive in Vietnam, most of us meditated on death every day, because death was a matter of every second, every minute." He is reminded of his Master who died during the war, who even when he was very old continued to share in the work of the community. He sadly observes that he was supposed to succeed his Master as head of the community, but now since he cannot return someone else has taken his place. Berrigan concludes this phase of the dialogue with the suggestion that since it is Holy Thursday they celebrate the Eucharist together, to which Nhat Hanh replies: "Sure. We'll make some bread."⁵³

It is intriguing to follow this conversation and to observe how easily it flows from reflections on sacred texts to recollections of personal experiences and back again; how freely the speakers merge the spiritual and the political, the sacred and the profane; and how comfortable they are with references and allusions drawn from each other's religious tradition. Nhat Hanh shows himself to be unusually conversant with both traditions; he is in that sense "bilingual." He does not equate Buddhist and Christian terms, but he is able to use them inclusively to interpret his own and others' experiences. His willingness to share the Eucharist, a Christian sacrament, with his Catholic friend at the conclusion of the dialogue is an indication of the level of trust that had developed between them, not only as a result of the dialogue, but also because of their shared involvement in the peace movement.

The most revealing moment in the dialogue for me came when the discussion turned to a comparison of Buddha and Jesus. It became apparent at this point how much each of them had been affected by the other. Berrigan brings what might be called a Buddhist perspective to bear on the interpretation of Jesus. He says that if only people would "breathe with the silence of Jesus," go into the desert with him, be with him in prison, and penetrate his silence before Herod, "when he refused to answer as another way of answering," they would better understand him. He is reminded once again of Merton—and of the young Buddhist woman who burned herself. "These are people who have met the eyes of Jesus or Buddha through some understanding of silence," he says.[54] Nhat Hanh, for his part, offers an interpretation of Buddha that is distinctly Christian in the way it attempts to place him in a historical context. He compares the reaction of people in Buddha's time to his teachings with the reaction of Jesus' contemporaries to his message. Buddha was born into a society that was less overtly violent than that of Jesus, yet his criticisms of the social practices of his day were no less radical. If he had been born into a society more like that of Jesus, "he would have been crucified also."[55] Jesus and Buddha, Nhat Hanh concludes, were both social activists. They showed the same courage in confronting and challenging the values of their respective societies, even though the outcome was different. What I find so interesting about this particular exchange is that the Christian offers a contemplative interpretation of Jesus and the Buddhist an activist interpretation of Buddha—not what one would expect in either case, and certainly not the traditional interpretation of either religious figure.

Both participants in this dialogue were able to represent their own tradition faithfully and creatively, while listening attentively and sympathetically to the other. As a result, each was profoundly affected by the other in ways that could not have been anticipated. They were able to look deeply into each other's tradition, but they were also able to see their own traditions reflected through the eyes of the other. This dialogical approach to understanding gave each one fresh insight into his own tradition without taking him outside it. Berrigan could appreciate the sacrificial deaths of the Buddhist monks and the American peace worker, in a way he had not been able to previously, by viewing them from a Buddhist/Christian perspective, while Nhat Hanh could see something in the life of Buddha that was not evident to others in his tradition because he saw it in relation to the life of Jesus. In neither case could it be said that adopting the perspective of the other detracted from or compromised the person's own faith; instead it opened up a further level of meaning and provided a basis for greater understanding.

Both men were realistic enough to know that this sort of communication does not always occur when persons of different religions come together. Berrigan had recently returned from a visit to Israel and recalled how difficult it was to get a genuine dialogue going with representatives of the various factions of Judaism. He actually found it easier to converse with secular Jews than with religiously committed Jews. "The religious people we met were very closed in their suppositions about the state, in obedience to the state, and in [their attitude toward] violence," he said. When Nhat Hanh asked if their common suffering had possibly drawn people of different religions closer together, Berrigan replied that it had not. Suffering had made them extremely rigid and reactionary; they "resist any possibility of living together and of welcoming Christians and Moslems and unbelieving people to an equal ground." But did they feel no tension between their religious ideals and their loyalty to the state? Again Berrigan's answer was no. As far as he could tell the traditional religious language of Judaism had been pretty much co-opted by the state. "In that case," Nhat Hanh said, "religion plays only the role of an ideology to preserve the identity of a race, of a nation, of a group of people." In his view, "genuine religious life must express reverence toward life, nonviolence, communion between man and man, man and the absolute."[56] Where religion functions only as an ideology, there is no real possibility of dialogue.

Nhat Hanh had his own encounter with this kind of resistance to dialogue at an international conference on religion in Sri Lanka not long before his meeting with Berrigan. At this conference, which he

described as one of the most difficult religious meetings he had ever
attended, he engaged a rabbi from Tel Aviv in an extended conversation about the political situation in Israel. The rabbi asked what Nhat
Hanh would do if he were in the rabbi's place. Nhat Hanh said it
was a hard question to answer because the most one can do is imagine,
and imagination is not the real thing. The rabbi then asked what Nhat
Hanh would do if it came down to a choice between peace in Vietnam
and the survival of Buddhism. When he replied that he would choose
peace, the rabbi was shocked. Yet for Nhat Hanh "it was quite plain
that if you have to choose between Buddhism and peace, then you
must choose peace. Because if you choose Buddhism you sacrifice
peace and Buddhism does not accept that." Buddhism, in his view,
does not consist of temples and organizations. "Buddhism is in your
heart. Even if you don't have any temple or any monks, you can still
be a Buddhist in your heart and life." But what about your loyalty to
Vietnam as a nation? he was asked. Nhat Hanh thought that question
"touched the very core of the problem in the Middle East." When he
said that he would choose the survival of the Vietnamese people over
the survival of the nation, the rabbi concluded they could not agree.
And if they could not agree on that point, he felt they could not agree
on other things.[57] There the dialogue ended. They had reached an
impasse, as much political as spiritual.

But this was not the only difficult situation Nhat Hanh confronted
at the conference. He was also involved in an incident that showed
the obstacles to dialogue are not always political; they may be rooted
in the religious practices of a community. At one point, a Catholic
priest who was responsible for leading a session on varieties of religious experience came to him for help. He thought it would be hard
to have a discussion of religious experience, so Nhat Hanh proposed
that they put together an "interfaith program of meditation" and invite
a Hindu swami to join them. In the first part of the program, Nhat
Hanh led a guided meditation on a pebble. In the second part, the
priest presented everyone with a flower and recounted a legend about
St. Francis of Assisi coming upon an almond tree in winter and
questioning it about God, when "suddenly the tree blossomed." They
were asked to think of their flower as that tree and try to get a message
from it. After that the swami led the group to a nearby hospital for
crippled children where they presented the children with a bouquet
of flowers together with their messages. The reaction to this program
was intense. A number of participants withdrew halfway through the

program, and others objected to having a prayer not of their own tradition imposed on them. They were particularly disturbed that they could not object "because of the silence and meditation." After that incident, morning prayers, which had been led each day by a representative of a different faith, were canceled. "It's too bad," Nhat Hanh said, "but that's what happened."[58]

He and Berrigan knew that the kind of dialogue they were having was special. They would probably not have been able to share in the Eucharist had it not been for the sufferings they shared over a period of many years. "The sufferings brought us together," Nhat Hanh observed, "our worship didn't come out of light discussions or anything like that."[59] Underlying their conversation was a wealth of shared experience, which enabled them to discuss some very sensitive matters. For instance, at one point in the conversation Berrigan asked Nhat Hanh what it meant for him to be an "exile." He had been away from his country for seven years, and it looked as though it might be some time before he was able to return. How was he dealing with this situation? Nhat Hanh said he was not prepared to live in a different culture and society, separated from people with whom he had worked so intimately and for so long. It was hard enough that he could not share their difficulties, but he also had to live with the knowledge that many of them were in prison and some had been killed. He wondered why he was not permitted to go home and continue his work there.[60] Berrigan then asked if there was a Buddhist tradition that dealt with being an exile. In Christianity, he said, there is the story of exile from the Garden of Eden, the loss of original innocence and love. Nhat Hanh replied that there was something like that in Buddhism: a tradition that holds that enlightenment is a kind of returning home, a recovery of oneself and one's integrity.[61]

Later in the conversation, he recounts a recurring dream about returning home. In the dream, he is standing on a hill, a hill of green grass where he used to play as a child. The place is northern Vietnam. "I have returned to that hill, that land, several times in dreams," he says. "Every time I leave, I leave things on that hill." When he returns, he finds the hill has grown. "The hill is not a static image, it's growing like myself; and every time I come to the hill I see that it's the place where I should be." It happens sometimes in the dream that something stands in the way, and he is not able to reach the hill. "Very sadly I have returned, and each time like that I woke up with a feeling of sadness." Even in dreams, he observes, "you are not allowed to come back." Commenting on the dream, he says that "the hill represents something like my homeland." Yet he knows that if he were to go back and actually stand on that hill, it would not be the hill he had been dreaming of. "One feels less a stranger when one returns to oneself, even in dreams," he concludes.[62]

Going Home

Nhat Hanh did not return to Vietnam when he thought he would—at the conclusion of his speaking tour in 1966 or at the end of the war in 1975. His exile, if we may call it that, continues to this day. It is possible that he could get permission to visit his homeland, but not to teach or conduct the kind of ministry he once envisioned for himself there. This situation continues to be a source of great personal anguish for him. "I have offered teachings and practices in 35 countries," he was recently quoted, "and yet in Vietnam, my books are still banned."[63] He trains a growing number of Vietnamese monks and nuns at Plum Village and would very much like to return with them to Vietnam, but he knows he cannot. It has been suggested that he might be permitted back if he would accept sponsorship by the government-sanctioned Buddhist organization in Vietnam. But this "official" Buddhist organization, in his opinion, has no credibility with most Vietnamese Buddhists. He wants to be recognized as a teacher in his own right and be free to teach as he thinks best, so he has chosen not to pursue that avenue. In the meantime, his influence outside Vietnam continues to grow. Denied a ministry in his own country, he has developed a *global* ministry not limited by politics or religion.

When Nhat Hanh first began coming to the United States to teach and lead retreats, it was at the invitation of some American Buddhists. His intention at that time was to help strengthen the newly developing Buddhist community in America, but his teaching attracted the attention of non-Buddhists as well. Since then his trips to the States have become an annual occurrence, and his audience has expanded to include persons of many different religious faiths. Increasingly he finds himself addressing people with little or no background in Buddhism, but with a deep spiritual hunger. His travels have also taken him to other parts of the world, to cultures as diverse as India, China, Africa, and the Middle East. Over the past twenty years, he has probably had conversations with representatives of all the world's major religions. Yet it is with Christianity that he has had his most extended dialogue.

In 1995, Nhat Hanh made a major contribution to Buddhist–Christian dialogue with the publication of *Living Buddha, Living Christ*. He followed it four years later with *Going Home: Jesus and Buddha as Brothers*, a collection of "Christmas talks" delivered over a period of several years to the residents of Plum Village during their winter retreats. In both works it is apparent that his dialogue with Christianity—carried on in a very interpersonal way with Berrigan—had become internalized. He was now able to reflect on the meaning of Christian teachings in the manner of one who had "made them his own," and with good reason. He had by then incorporated Christian symbols into his own religious practice and made friends with some of the leading Christians of his day. He had also "listened deeply" and allowed himself to be affected by what he heard. If anyone outside the Christian tradition could claim to understand Christianity from within, he could.

In his "internal dialogue" with Christianity, Nhat Hanh explores some of the different ways Buddhists and Christians have of speaking about ultimate reality. He discusses concepts such as God, Nirvana, the Pure Land, and the Kingdom of God, yet he keeps coming back to the subject of practice. As we might expect, he considers the practice of mindfulness a key component of both religions. Christians may not speak of it as such, but they speak of living fully in the presence of God, and he thinks that amounts to the same thing. "Mindfulness is to be aware of everything you do every day," he writes. "Mindfulness is a kind of light that shines upon all your thoughts, all your feelings, all your actions and all your words."[64] A more *theological* term for mindfulness might be the Holy Spirit. He once asked a Catholic priest for his understanding of the Holy Spirit and was told that it is "the energy sent by God."[65] He liked that answer, as it provided a practical way of relating to God. Mindfulness, he concluded, is the energy of the Buddha just as the Holy Spirit is the energy of God. Both have the capacity "to make us present, fully alive, deeply understanding, and loving."[66] Through the practice of mindfulness or the gift of the Holy Spirit—whatever one may choose to call it—we are able, he thinks, "to touch the ultimate."[67]

In his opinion, Buddhist-Christian dialogue has not gotten very far because it has not been sufficiently grounded in practice. We are hung up on philosophical differences that are not "real." If we would look deeply enough we would discover that we have many things in common.[68] This is not to say there are no real differences. There are differences even within the same tradition. He has noted that when Christians come to Plum Village to practice with him, they frequently find that they have more in common with Buddhists than they have with many of their Christian brethren back home. Likewise, he finds that he often feels a greater affinity for some Christians than for certain members of his own tradition. He is convinced, however, that the encounter currently taking place among religious traditions can help to renew *every* religious tradition.[69] Through dialogue with representatives of another religion, we are brought to recognize elements in our own that we may have forgotten, overlooked, or ignored. He thinks, for instance, that Christians could benefit from Buddhist insights in regard to interbeing and non-duality. To bring these insights to Christianity would "radically transform the way people look on the Christian tradition," but it could also enable "valuable jewels in the Christian tradition to be rediscovered."[70]

In recent years, Thich Nhat Hanh has introduced countless people to the practice of mindfulness. Most of them are not Buddhist, and he has not encouraged them to become Buddhists. He would prefer that they return to their religious roots. We all need roots, he says, in order to stand tall and grow. "When young people come to Plum Village," he writes, "I always encourage them to practice in a way that will help them go back to their own tradition and get rerooted. If they succeed at becoming reintegrated, they will be an important instrument in transforming and renewing their tradition."[71] He even takes this approach with the Vietnamese who come to Plum Village, because they may be just as alienated from their cultural and religious traditions as any young American. They have suffered so much, he feels, that they often do not want to have anything to do with their families, their government, their society, or their culture. They want to become "someone other than themselves," but they cannot. They are "hungry souls," hungry for something to believe in and something to belong to. We try to embrace them in our practice of mindfulness, he says, "like the damp soil embracing the cutting of a plant, giving it a chance to put forth a few tiny roots." Gradually they recover "their confidence, their faith, and their capacity to accept love."[72]

Rootedness, Nhat Hanh is convinced, is essential for true dialogue as well as for personal growth. We need to return to ourselves, if we are to be genuinely open to others. He and Merton were able to have the kind of meeting they had in which each was deeply affected by the other and in which a genuine spiritual bond developed between them, because each was deeply rooted in his own tradition. They were able to hear one another and respond to one another from a very deep place in their respective traditions, a place to which their spiritual practice, carried on over a period of many years, had taken them. This place, as we have seen, is a place beyond words, yet words are sometimes necessary in order to get to it. Words, he would say, are "skillful means" for arriving at an experience that often cannot be put into words.

Merton had his deepest experience of Buddhism at Polonnaruwa, an experience truly beyond words. Only then could he say that his Asian pilgrimage had "come clear and purified itself." Nhat Hanh recounts a similar experience in respect to Christianity. He begins by recalling how, as a boy growing up in Vietnam, he frequently heard the sound of Buddhist temple bells and occasionally the sound of Catholic church bells. Later, as a young monk, he was taught to "invite the bell to sound" and to listen attentively to the sound while breathing deeply. In this way he learned to appreciate the sound of a temple bell. But he did not hear the church bell in the same way. Years later, while leading retreats in Western Europe, he would sometimes encourage the retreatants to practice listening to church bells in the way he listened to temple bells. Yet he himself was not deeply touched by the sound of a church bell. Then one day, in 1992, something unexpected happened:

> Suddenly I heard the church bells. This time it went very deeply into me. As you know, I had been listening to church bells before, many times everywhere, in France, in Switzerland, and in many other countries. But this was the first time a church bell touched me very deeply. I felt that it was the first time I was able to touch the soul of ancient Europe. I had been in Europe for a long time. I had seen a lot. I had learned a lot about the civilization, the culture, and had met with many Europeans. Only this time, walking in the city of Prague, was I able to touch the soul of Europe in a most profound way because of the sound of a church bell.[73]

Because of the depth of their spiritual practice within their own tradition and their genuine openness to other traditions, Thomas Merton and Thich Nhat Hanh were able to touch the soul of another culture, even another religion, in often profound and sometimes unexpected ways.

Merton did not live to see his journey to Asia bear fruit in the lives of others, so we do not know what he might have been able to accomplish had he lived longer. Yet there is a sense in which his vision for interfaith dialogue has found expression in the work of Nhat Hanh. The Buddhist whom Merton called "my brother" has done in the post–Vietnam War period what we might imagine Merton to have done if he had lived another twenty or thirty years. Nhat Hanh has brought the practice of meditation to large numbers of people of diverse religious backgrounds as a way of helping them deepen their spiritual lives, but also as a way of empowering them to act responsibly in the world. He has promoted the formation of communities of practice, similar in some ways to the traditional monastic communities of Buddhism and Christianity, yet open to persons of all faiths. And he has continued the interfaith dialogue that Merton began, with the same emphasis on inner renewal and spiritual transformation that Merton called for. Both men have been—and still are—exemplars of a new era in religious dialogue.

5

Engaged Spirituality in an Age of Globalization

S
OMETIME IN THE mid-1970s, I realized that I was developing a deep fascination with Buddhism, particularly Zen Buddhism. Teaching Buddhism was no longer something I did as an assignment; it had become for me a matter of intense personal interest. Though I continued to regard myself as a Christian, I remember saying to someone that if there was such a thing as reincarnation, I would like to come back as a Buddhist. It was my view at the time that one religion is enough for a lifetime. It is not that I thought there was only one true religion. I simply did not think it possible to enter into another religion with sufficient depth to experience its truth. That view began to change as I took up the practice of meditation, first under the direction of a Roman Catholic priest and later a Zen Buddhist roshi. Without ceasing to be a Christian, I found myself looking at the world more and more through Buddhist eyes. I was for the first time experiencing Buddhism as a living religion. This personal experience has helped me to understand some of the new ways in which religions are coming together in this age of globalization. Thomas Merton and Thich Nhat Hanh have been pioneers in this development, but others have followed the path they laid out.

Contemplative Renewal

Thomas Merton did not go to Gethsemani expecting to discover Buddhism. He had already been exposed to Eastern religions, initially through the writings of Aldous Huxley and later through a personal encounter with a Hindu monk by the name of Bramachari. The monk did not try to convert Merton to Hinduism, but rather, sensing his contemplative interest, referred him to the mystical strand in his own religion. "There are many beautiful mystical books written by Christians," he said. "You should read St. Augustine's *Confessions* and *The Imitation of Christ*."[1] The irony of this situation was not lost on Merton. He had turned to the religions of the East to learn about mysticism, and here was a man from the East pointing him to his own religious tradition, albeit one he had largely neglected. By the time he reached Gethsemani, Merton had put aside his interest in Eastern religions and was focused single-mindedly on realizing the essence of the Christian contemplative tradition. Neither the active life pursued by his friends at Columbia nor the ascetic life represented by his Hindu acquaintance appealed to him any longer.

Only after he had gone deeply into his own tradition was Merton able to fully appreciate the Eastern mystical tradition, which he rediscovered through the writings of D. T. Suzuki. His contemplative practice had by then brought him onto the dark path, beyond words and images, and this development undoubtedly made him more receptive to the teachings of Zen. He could recognize in these teachings a shared vision of reality. In his initial letter to Suzuki, Merton acknowledges that in reading his books on Zen, especially his translations of verses by the great Zen masters, he felt a "profound and intimate agreement." Yet he would not at that time have known much about the actual practice of meditation in the Zen tradition. Suzuki's writings tend to be rather poetic and philosophical and not much given to practical instruction. In that respect, they are not unlike Merton's own writings, which present the fruits of contemplative practice rather than the practice itself. So when Merton says in the same letter that he "has his own way to walk, and for some reason or other Zen is right in the middle of it," he is not speaking of the formal practice of Zen, but rather the spirit of Zen, a contemplative outlook that he intuitively recognized as congruent with his own.

It is not clear from his published writings what form Merton's own contemplative practice took. We know that he followed the daily offices of his religious order, which consisted mainly of psalms and prayers recited at prescribed times during the day; that he devoted some time each day to Bible reading; and that he celebrated the Mass every day. But what about the practice of meditation? After taking up permanent residence in the hermitage especially built for him on the grounds of Gethsemani Abbey, he was able to devote more time to what he called meditation—three to four hours a day according to a letter written to a Muslim correspondent by the name of Abdul Aziz in January 1966. He did not, however, like to talk about his personal practice, so we know very little about the procedure he followed.

One of the few times Merton wrote specifically about his contemplative practice was in this same letter to Aziz. Asked about his method of meditation, he wrote:

> Strictly speaking I have a very simple way of prayer. It is centered entirely on attention to the presence of God and to His will and His love. That is to say that it is centered on *faith* by which alone we can know the presence of God. One might say this gives my meditation the character described by the Prophet as "being before God as if you saw Him." Yet it does not mean imagining anything or conceiving a precise image of God, for to my mind this would be a kind of idolatry. On the contrary, it is a matter of adoring Him as invisible and infinitely beyond our comprehension, and realizing Him as all. My prayer tends very much toward what you call *fana*. There is in my heart this great thirst to recognize totally the nothingness of all that is not God. My prayer is then a kind of praise rising up out of the center of Nothing and Silence. If I am still present "myself" this I recognize as an obstacle about which I can do nothing unless He Himself removes the obstacle. If He wills He can then make the Nothingness into a total clarity. If He does not will, then the Nothingness seems to itself to be an object and remains an obstacle. Such is my ordinary way of prayer, or meditation. It is not "thinking about" anything, but a direct seeking of the Face of the Invisible, which cannot be found unless we become lost in Him who is Invisible.[2]

This is an extraordinary reply that places Merton squarely within the mystical tradition. Yet he says at the conclusion of this account, "I do not ordinarily write about such things." One can only speculate why he was so reluctant to speak about his practice. Was he concerned that he might be misunderstood, that his practice might be perceived as out of bounds for a Christian monk? Or was it simply too personal, too intimate a matter to be talked about? In his earlier writings, he had declined to provide a technique for meditation. Perhaps he thought that would cheapen it. In any case, he did not offer much practical advice to his readers, many of whom had awakened to the contemplative life under the influence of his writings.

That task was taken up in the 1970s, several years after Merton's
death, by the Trappist monks of St. Joseph's Abbey in Spencer,
Massachusetts. With the encouragement of their abbot, Thomas Keating, they devised a form of contemplative practice, based on the
fourteenth-century spiritual classic *The Cloud of Unknowing*. They
called it centering prayer—a prayer of the heart, a prayer of faith
and simplicity, a prayer of simple regard. In his book *Open Mind,
Open Heart*, Keating summarizes the practice as follows:

> First, choose a sacred word as the symbol of your intention to consent to
> God's presence and action within. Then, sitting comfortably and with eyes
> closed, settle briefly and silently introduce the sacred word as the symbol
> of your consent to God's presence and action within. When you become
> aware of thoughts, return ever-so-gently to the sacred word. At the end
> of the prayer period, remain in silence with eyes closed for a couple
> of minutes.

The object is to quiet the mind and direct attention inward. Thinking
continues. In fact, thinking goes on all the time, whether we are aware
of it or not. But by "returning to the sacred word," we are able
to break the relentless sequence of thoughts that might otherwise
preoccupy us and direct our attention to the deeper silence within.
The sacred word, according to Keating, "is a simple thought that you
are thinking at ever deeper levels of perception." Eventually you
should be able to pass beyond it to "pure awareness." When this
happens, the "interiorization" process is complete. You are then, he
says, "beyond the sacred word into union with that to which it points—
the Ultimate Mystery, the Presence of God, beyond any perception
that we can form of Him."[3]

There is a close fit between the practice of centering prayer, as
Keating describes it, and Merton's method of meditation. Merton's
"simple way of prayer," as he called it, was "centered entirely on
attention to the presence of God." He does not seem to have needed
a sacred word or mantra to focus his attention or bring his awareness
back to God, though he may sometimes have used the Jesus Prayer.[4]
He was able, it seems, simply to be before God—without thoughts,
words, or images. He sometimes spoke of this practice as "resting in
God." But then Merton was a very experienced meditator. He had by
this time been following the dark path for more than twenty years.
Keating, on the other hand, is writing for persons with little or no

experience of contemplative practice. For most of them, centering prayer was their first exposure to a nonconceptual form of meditation. They needed some kind of support in order to sustain the level of concentration required by this form of practice. Besides most of them did not live in a monastery and needed a form of meditation that was compatible with an active life, and centering prayer offered that possibility.

Keating does say that it should not be a person's sole means of spiritual practice. He advises those following this path also to practice *lectio divina*, the spiritual reading of scripture. In this way, they will have a conceptual context for the nonconceptual act of attending to "God present within." That accords with Merton's experience, which included the daily reading of scripture along with the recitation of psalms and prayers in conjunction with the daily offices that are a regular part of the life of a monk. So even though the dark path was at the heart of Merton's contemplative practice, it would be a mistake to ignore the larger context of Christian devotion within which it was set. The language of the Christian religion was deeply embedded in his consciousness, even as he extended his awareness beyond the reach of language in search of the "Face of the Invisible." Merton, it would be fair to say, carried the process of going into silence in search of God further than most people could; yet his practice, according to Keating, was not different in principle from the practice of centering prayer supplemented by reflection on scripture.

The spread of centering prayer and similar forms of contemplative practice among Christians has not been confined to the Catholic Church. Keating's retreats and workshops have attracted Protestants as well. The one I attended included a Methodist minister who entered fully into the practice of centering prayer, yet argued vigorously with Father Keating about the goal of "union with God." He was uncomfortable with the implication that one's personal identity might be completely submerged in God. In his tradition, he said, it would be more acceptable to speak of "communion with God." What was striking about this exchange was not that there was a difference of interpretation between the Protestant student and his Catholic teacher, but that it did not seem to interfere with their practicing together. This incident is not atypical of what is happening today: Christians are increasingly crossing denominational lines to participate in the spiritual practices of other Christians. What is even more remarkable is that they are going outside of the Christian tradition altogether to expand their repertoire of spiritual practices. It is no longer unusual to find Christians practicing *zazen*, the Buddhist form of sitting meditation, in the company of Buddhists, and even under the direction of a Buddhist teacher.

That would not have been possible when Thomas Merton first took up the study of Zen in the early 1950s, for there were no teachers of Zen practicing in the United States at that time. Anyone who wanted instruction in the practice of Zen, as distinct from the philosophy of Zen, was required to go outside the country. It was during this period, for instance, that Gary Snyder, the Beat poet featured in Jack Kerouac's novel *Dharma Bums*, went to Japan to study with a traditional Zen teacher. The situation began to change in the 1960s as Buddhist teachers of various nationalities and traditions took up residence in this country. One of the first teachers of Zen to establish residence in the United States was, coincidentally, another Suzuki. Shunryu Suzuki came to the United States from Japan in 1959 to be the priest of a small Zen Buddhist temple in San Francisco. Within a year he had a cohort of young Americans sitting regularly with him in what was to become the San Francisco Zen Center. He did not philosophize about Zen; he practiced it and taught others how to practice it. In this way he carried on the ancient Buddhist tradition of transmitting the teachings directly from teacher to student.

There were, and still are, significant differences of interpretation and practice among Zen practitioners. D. T. Suzuki, for instance, belonged to the Rinzai tradition of Zen Buddhism that makes extensive use of koans in the practice of meditation, whereas Shunryu Suzuki came from the Soto tradition, which emphasizes posture and breathing, or what they call *shikantaza* (just sitting). Shunryu Suzuki taught his students to sit on a cushion with their legs crossed in the time-honored lotus position for extended periods of time and gave them techniques for meditation that concentrated primarily on the breath. He taught them to focus their attention on breathing so completely that nothing else mattered. "When we practice zazen," he wrote, "all that exists is the movement of the breathing, but we are aware of this movement." A person's awareness during meditation should be centered not in the "small self," but rather in the "large self," what Buddhists call the Buddha nature. "Our usual understanding of life," he said, "is dualistic: you and I, this and that, good and bad. But actually these discriminations are themselves the awareness of the universal existence. 'You' means to be aware of the universe in the form of you, 'I' means to be aware of the universe in the form of I."[5] In typical Buddhist fashion, Suzuki does not speak explicitly of God, but he does imply union with a greater reality, what Keating calls the "Ultimate Mystery."

Shunryu Suzuki was not alone in bringing the practice of meditation from Asia to America. Representatives of many different Eastern religious traditions came to the United States during 1960s and 1970s, some to take up residence, others to give lectures and conduct retreats. They brought with them a rich diversity of meditative practices developed and refined over hundreds of years in countries as diverse as India, Korea, Thailand, Burma, and Tibet. The combined effect of this influx of religious practices from abroad was considerable and continues to the present day. The practice of meditation in America, a country known more for its activist lifestyle than for contemplative practice of any kind, has grown at an astonishing rate. There are now centers of practice throughout the country, and not all of them are identified with Zen. In the city of Colorado Springs, where I live, there are three Buddhist groups practicing distinct forms of meditation: a Zen group that combines Rinzai and Soto elements, a Theravadan group practicing the Vipassana form of meditation, and a Tibetan group with its own unique form of practice. Moreover, since the early 1980s a second generation of Buddhist teachers—Americans who have trained with Japanese teachers but do not share all of their cultural assumptions—has begun to emerge. It would appear that the practice of meditation is actually taking root in American soil.

Thomas Merton would have been fascinated by this development. The circumstances of his life at Gethsemani prior to his Asian journey and his untimely death prevented his participating in it. But that was not true of David Steindl-Rast, a Benedictine monk whose life in many ways parallels Merton's. Born in 1926, the same year as Nhat Hanh, he is a native of Austria. He was drafted into the Nazi army, but did not see combat. After serving for a year, he deserted and hid out until the war ended. Following the war, he worked for a time in art restoration before earning a doctorate in psychology at the University of Vienna. In 1953, he came to the United States and shortly afterwards joined a small community of monks in upstate New York. The monks of Mt. Saviour Monastery, as the community is called, are committed to living according to the original Rule of St. Benedict, but they are also open to fresh currents of thought. It was there that Brother David was introduced to the writings of D. T. Suzuki. Like Merton, he

recognized an immediate affinity with this Zen Buddhist whose experience was so similar to his own. Yet unlike Merton, he was not confined
to the monastery. So when he heard that a Zen teacher by the name
of Tai-Shimano had recently come to New York from Japan, he was
free to seek him out and, with the approval of his religious community,
to practice with him at his zendo in New York City.

    In an interview with journalist and social activist Catherine Ingram,
Steindl-Rast tells how it came about that he received this approval.
He had initially approached his abbot with a request to study Zen,
but before acting on this request the abbot suggested that Tai-Shimano
come to the monastery for a couple of days. During that time, the
Zen teacher was subjected to rigorous questioning by members of
the Benedictine community. Brother David was sure they would not
approve of his answers. Yet following the visit, they took him aside
and said that though the Zen monk's answers made no sense to them,
they had observed his actions and concluded from the way he walked,
sat, and ate that he was a "true monk," and that was good enough
for them.[6]

    It was highly unusual at that time for a Catholic monk to study
Zen, much less practice with a Buddhist monk. Yet Steindl-Rast
continued this practice for three years, and subsequently studied
with other Zen teachers, including Shunryu Suzuki. Through these
associations he has become one of the major contributors to Buddhist-
Christian dialogue. At a point early in his practice of Zen, Brother
David's abbot suggested that the two of them pay a visit to Thomas
Merton. Recalling that visit some years later, Steindl-Rast observed
that Merton, with all of his reading, was "way ahead of me in understanding the relationship between Buddhism and Christianity." Yet
Merton lacked the personal experience of his younger friend, so
the "practical aspects" were particularly interesting to him.[7] They
continued to interest him, as we saw in his meetings with the Tibetan
lamas during his Asian journey. Merton was impressed with their
practice and speculated that he might return some day to study with
one of them. His untimely death prevented that, but we can imagine
that his life might have followed a course similar to that of Brother
David if he had lived longer. He certainly would have wanted to
participate in the contemplative renewal he helped to spawn and to
contribute in whatever way he could to the Buddhist-Christian dialogue he also helped to initiate.

The Secularization of Contemplation

Thomas Merton and Thich Nhat Hanh were, as the Christian contemplative observed in his moving tribute to his Buddhist "brother," both monks. They received their primary religious training in monasteries—not exactly the preparation you would expect of someone who was to become a major influence in the modern world, but an ideal setting in which to be introduced to contemplative practice. The monastic traditions of Buddhism and Christianity have a long history of preparing men and women for the contemplative life. For all their differences, they have many things in common. One is that they provide an environment conducive to the practice of meditation. Monks and nuns of both traditions are largely separated from worldly responsibilities and distractions and are provided with an order and structure that supports their contemplative practice. There is also a tradition of instruction by which this practice is passed on from one generation to the next. The monastery of Our Lady of Gethsemani did not always support Merton's contemplative practice in the way he thought it should, any more than the Institute at Hue provided Nhat Hanh with the kind of education he sought. Yet for both men, the monastic community was a place of refuge where they could follow their contemplative yearnings.

For all of his criticisms of monastic life, Merton never abandoned the community where he first went in search of inner peace. He remained a Trappist monk and a loyal member of the Gethsemani community to the end of his life. It was from this base that he addressed the world and shared with others his contemplative vision. He would have been the first to acknowledge that he occupied a privileged position in relation to the world, that he was protected in many ways from the afflictions of his day; yet he was not indifferent to the suffering of others. As we have seen, he spoke out against war and social injustice and the conditions of alienation in modern life. Though he was not the social activist that Nhat Hanh was, he was an influential social critic. Yet first and foremost, he was a monk committed to a life of contemplation. With the support of his community, he was able to spend a great deal of time in solitude and to practice a form of contemplation unknown to most of his contemporaries. Through his writings he was able to evoke a contemplative longing in people whose lives were not as sheltered as his, but it remained for others to devise ways of taking the practice of contemplation outside the monastery and making it an integral part of secular life.

Thich Nhat Hanh has made this his life work. For although he received his initial training in a traditional Buddhist monastery, from an early age he had the dream of taking the practice of meditation beyond the confines of the monastery and into the lives of ordinary people. He is given credit for coming up with the term "engaged Buddhism." Yet he rejects the idea that this means anything other than "living Buddhism." A religion that is truly alive will *engage* people. It will affect them deeply and transform their lives. Since meditation is integral to the Buddhist religion, as he understands it, meditation must have a place in any vital expression of the religion. Engaged Buddhism must include meditation in a form that is meaningful and practical for people who are living responsible lives in the world; otherwise it is not true to its heritage.

Nhat Hanh's greatest contribution to the contemplative renewal of our time may well be his genius for adapting traditional meditative practices, originally intended for monks, to everyday life with its many adversities. His first such undertaking to reach a worldwide audience began as a letter to his students who had remained in Vietnam to carry on his work in the midst of war. This "manual on meditation for the use of young activists" offers guidance in the practice of meditation as an integral part of an active life of service. Under the title *Miracle of Mindfulness*, it has been translated into many languages and even now serves as a practical guide to meditation and a source of inspiration for bringing the contemplative dimension into ordinary life. In the quarter-century since the book first appeared, Nhat Hanh has conducted hundreds of retreats and workshops, extending his message of engaged spirituality to all parts of the world. It is a universal message arising out of the particularity of monastic life, yet transcending it.

Thay, as he is known to his students, recalls his early training as a monk, and in particular the training he received in mindfulness through the discipline of reciting gathas. There were gathas for virtually every action one might perform in the course of a day. When washing his hands, for instance, he would think, "Washing my hands, I hope that every person will have pure hands to receive reality." The purpose of the gathas, he says, "was to help the beginning practitioner take hold of his own consciousness." Each time you did something like put on your robe, wash the dishes, fold your mat, or brush your teeth, you would use one of these thoughts to take hold of your consciousness and awaken your mind to what you were doing at the moment.[8] Yet how realistic is this practice for someone who does not live in a monastery? "If you spend all day practicing mindfulness," he asks, "how will there ever be enough time to do all of the work that needs to be done to change and to build an alternative society?" His reply is very simple: "Keep your attention focused on the work, be alert and ready to handle ably and intelligently any situation that may arise—this is mindfulness."[9]

Thus, there is no contradiction between practicing mindfulness and engaging in social action. You do not cease practicing mindfulness to engage in social action; you extend your contemplative practice to include it. Still, there must be a practice to extend. Faced with a difficult situation, one does not suddenly and without any prior preparation act mindfully. Thay recognized that his students might not have the well-established habit of mindfulness that he acquired in the monastery to bring to their social action. So he offered them some instruction in breathing. "In a Buddhist monastery," he writes, "everyone learns to use breath as a tool to stop mental dispersion and build up concentration power."[10] They learn to follow their breath by thinking to themselves as they breathe: "I am breathing in, I am breathing out." They practice this method of mindfully breathing during sitting and walking meditation and during other activities as well. Although he regards the practice as beneficial in itself, Nhat Hanh also sees it as a way of preparing for situations of crisis. "In those moments when you are upset or dispersed or find it difficult to practice mindfulness," he tells his students, "return to your breath: Taking hold of your breath is itself mindfulness."[11]

Still one wonders how young people who are deeply engaged in social service under the extreme conditions of war could find the time to prepare themselves for these inevitable moments of crisis. His recommendation is that they set aside one day a week and devote it exclusively to the practice of mindfulness. "Every worker in a peace or service community, no matter how urgent its work, has the right to such a day, for without it we will lose ourselves quickly in a life of worry and action, and our responses will become increasingly useless."[12] He proceeds to describe how one might spend this day of mindfulness. He suggests rising slowly and doing one's morning activities "in a calm and relaxing way, each movement done in mindfulness." No task, he says, should be done "in order to get it over with." For those who are new to the practice, he recommends maintaining "a spirit of silence" throughout the day. He envisions spending the morning cleaning house and the afternoon working in the garden. Then you should prepare a pot of tea.

> Allow yourself a good length of time to do this. Don't drink your tea like someone who gulps down a cup of coffee during a work break. Drink your tea slowly and reverently, as if it is the axis on which the whole earth revolves—slowly, evenly, without rushing toward the future. Live in the actual moment. Only this actual moment is life.[13]

In the evening, he suggests reading scripture, writing to friends, or doing anything you enjoy but do not have time for during the week. He thinks it is a good idea to eat lightly in the evening in order to get the most out of your sitting meditation and then to do some walking meditation before retiring for the night. Somehow, he says, we must find a way to allow each worker such a day of mindfulness. "Its effect on the other days of the week is immeasurable."[14]

Nhat Hanh spoke from experience. Ten years earlier, he and the small community of workers who made up the Order of Interbeing had followed just such a practice—and it had gotten them through some difficult times. But now he could not be with his students in person and had to rely on written communication to explain the techniques of meditation, rather than the more traditional method of direct communication from teacher to student. He had no other choice. It was nonetheless effective and became the model for subsequent presentations of his ideas about meditation. He has elaborated these ideas over the years, yet the basic message remains the same. *"Meditation is not an evasion; it is a serene encounter with reality."*[15] (Italics added.) It enables one to look deeply into situations, to see the interdependence of all things, and to let go of the notion of a separate self that inevitably leads to suffering for oneself and others. It is both healing and liberating. By restoring a sense of one's true self, it frees one for service of others. "Only by practicing mindfulness," he contends, "will we not lose ourselves but acquire a bright joy and peace. Only by practicing mindfulness, will we be able to look at everyone else with the open mind and eyes of love."[16]

These words were written not to monks, but to peace workers laboring under conditions of extreme adversity. In subsequent years, Nhat Hanh has brought his message to Vietnam War veterans, environmentalists, and psychotherapists. But in his view it is not limited to persons engaged in social work or dealing with the ravages of war.

As he observes near the close of his treatise: "We talk about social service, service to the people, service to humanity, service for others, who are far away, helping to bring peace to the world—but we often forget that it is the very people around us that we must live for first of all."[17] In the retreats and workshops he has conducted throughout the world, Nhat Hanh has addressed the universal condition of suffering in all of its manifestations and reached out to people in all walks of life. In this way, he has helped to secularize the practice of contemplation.

The term "secularization" is sometimes used to mean a flattening out of reality, a denial or at least a setting aside of the transcendent, a purely "worldly" point of view. But that is not the original meaning, nor is it the one I wish to give it in the present context. The term was originally used to differentiate monastic clergy from clergy not affiliated with a monastery, clergy who worked "in the world." This distinction between monastic clergy and secular clergy is similar to one that a Korean monk, Samu Sunim, has made between a monastic bodhisattva and a worldly bodhisattva. Worldly bodhisattvas, he says, "are ordinary persons with 'great hearts,' who involve themselves enthusiastically in worldly affairs."[18] He sees a trend toward fewer monastic bodhisattvas and more worldly bodhisattavas in the period ahead. The Christian theologian Dietrich Bonhoeffer noted a similar trend in his famous "letters from prison." Writing from a German prison camp during the closing days of World War II, shortly before his execution for participating in the resistance movement, he speaks of a "religionless Christianity" and a Christian faith "come of age." He says that he has "come to appreciate the 'worldliness' of Christianity as never before." The Christian, he writes, "is not a *homo religiosus*, but a man, pure and simple, just as Jesus was man"[19]

We may recall that Thich Nhat Hanh was reading Bonhoeffer's account of his final days when he had one of his most profound experiences of awakening. The experience came in the wake of a major identity crisis. It was, he noted, the last link in a chain of experiences that led him to conclude that he could endure even greater suffering than he had previously thought possible. Yet, profound as the experience was, this worldly bodhisattva did not consider it a religious experience. "What I felt," he wrote in his journal, "was totally and utterly human." In this sense the practice of mindfulness is not a strictly religious practice. It is certainly a spiritual practice, but a spiritual practice suitable for secular life, which is to say, life in the world.

Thich Nhat Hanh did not abandon the monastic life, or even the religious life, when he took his contemplative practice out of the monastery and into the world. He remained a practicing Buddhist and in recent years has devoted an increasing amount of his time to the monastic community he helped found at Plum Village. This monastery, as he sees it, is not just a refuge from the world. It is a place of practice, where monks and nuns receive training so they can, in turn, train others. It is also a laboratory, where meditative practices are developed and refined and where procedures are worked out that can enable people to live together in greater peace and harmony. These practices and procedures are not confined to the monastery but are meant to be taken out into the world and shared with others.

I was privileged to see the fruit of the community's work, not only on my visit to Plum Village but a year later at a workshop I attended in Boulder, Colorado. The workshop was led by Sister Annabel Laity, a senior student of Thich Nhat Hanh and currently abbess of Forest Monastery in Vermont. She instructed participants in the practice of mindfulness as a way of dealing with anger and conflict in ordinary life. Some of those attending the workshop were Buddhists, but most were not. Religious affiliation was, in any case, irrelevant. What she taught was a way of using meditation to transform anger—something everyone has had to deal with at sometime or other. She also showed how conflicts are resolved at Plum Village using a practice known as Beginning Anew. While grounded in Buddhist principles, this practice, as she presented it, is not specifically Buddhist. We could readily see how it applied to our own lives and not just to life in a Buddhist monastery. Because I had been to Plum Village, I could also see from Sister Annabel's presentation how well Thay had succeeded in transmitting his teaching to his student. The dharma he embodies was present in her as well.

So along with contemplative renewal has come a secularization of contemplation. The practice of contemplation is flourishing as never before, but it is not tied to a particular religious tradition, nor is it the prerogative of a particular religious community. It continues to be rooted in religious tradition, but it belongs as much to the laity as to the clergy. Increasingly it is finding its way into the lives of ordinary people everywhere. Thomas Keating was surprised to discover twenty years ago that lay men and women were as receptive to the practice of centering prayer as clergy are, if not more so. Largely on

account of that perceived interest, he founded Contemplative Outreach, a primarily lay organization with lay teachers and students.
Not only does this organization of Christian contemplatives include
laity, it also recognizes an affinity with contemplatives of other religious traditions. In their mission statement, the members of Contemplative Outreach explicitly identify with the "Christian contemplative
heritage," yet also affirm their "solidarity with the contemplative
dimension of other religions and sacred traditions, with the needs
and rights of the whole human family, and with all creation." The
contemplative movement has, in the words of Dietrich Bonhoeffer,
"come of age."

The Legacy of Gandhi

One of the seminal figures of the twentieth century—possibly the
most influential political leader of this era even though he did not
hold political office—was Mahatma Gandhi. What is even more remarkable is that he was one of the century's most influential spiritual
leaders. He pioneered in the use of nonviolent action to effect fundamental social change. He began by challenging the practice of discrimination in South Africa and ended up taking on the British rulers of
India, calling for an end to colonialism and a restoration of national
independence. He also challenged his own people to live up to the
fundamental ethical principles of their religion, which were often
obscured by social convention. Without resorting to violence but
appealing instead to conscience, he led a successful campaign of
massive resistance to the prevailing power structure. It was a bold
course of action for anyone to undertake and utterly without precedent
in the Hindu religious tradition, which is not known for social activism
of any sort. Gandhi's movement of nonviolent social action was successful in large measure because it was spiritually grounded, although
at the time it seemed to have no clear basis in Hindu religion. He
created a basis for it by re-visioning the tradition.

As a young man, Gandhi was not a particularly devout Hindu; he
was a seeker after truth who openly explored other religious traditions,
including Christianity. He acknowledges in his autobiography that it
was not until he went to London to study law that he seriously read
the sacred classics of his own tradition, in particular the Bhagavad-
Gita and the Upanishads. But then he also read the Old and New

Testaments and the Koran. When he came to South Africa to practice law in 1893, he still had not settled upon a primary religious commitment. He was given several books by Christian apologists, yet none impressed him so much as a work by Tolstoy entitled *The Kingdom of God Is Within You*. Years later he acknowledged that this book had made a lasting impression on him; yet it did not make a Christian of him. He read other books by Tolstoy, which helped him "to realize more and more the infinite possibilities of love," but it was from the Bhagavad-Gita that he took his primary spiritual orientation.[20] From this deeply spiritual work, which espouses the "way of action," he found a way to practice love while actively opposing injustice.

Gandhi's method of nonviolent resistance developed while he was in South Africa as a response to situations that he perceived as an affront to his dignity and that of other Indians living there. At first he only spoke against discrimination, but when the government imposed an oppressive registration law upon the Indians, he organized a mass resistance. Years later in India, he adopted similar nonviolent tactics to oppose British colonialism. And he also fasted. He did so as a way of appealing to the conscience of the British and communicating with his fellow Indians, who recognized fasting as an accepted spiritual practice within their religious tradition. It was a form of practice used by holy men for spiritual purification. In the eyes of ordinary Hindus it demonstrated a willingness to suffer, and even die, for a higher cause. Fasting and prayer marked Gandhi as a spiritual leader and not just another politician out to advance his career at the expense of others. It enabled him to appeal to the deeper values of his religious tradition and at the same time reach out to persons of other traditions. He fasted in protest of British restrictions on the civil liberties of Indians but also on behalf of the untouchables, the outcasts of traditional Indian society who were discriminated against by their own people. On one famous occasion, he was prepared to "fast unto death" in order to bring an end to a bloody conflict between Hindus and Muslims. By fasting he hoped to bring the warring parties to their senses and inspire them to look beyond themselves to their common humanity.

Mahatma Gandhi was not a mystic, but he was an activist with a contemplative vision. Thomas Merton, who acknowledges having first learned about nonviolence from him, recognized this quality in him and wrote about it in a personal tribute to one he called "a gentle revolutionary."

Gandhi's whole concept of man's relation to his own inner being and to the world of objects around him was informed by the contemplative heritage of Hinduism, together with the principles of Karma Yoga [the way of action], which blended, in his thought, with the ethic of the Synoptic Gospels and the Sermon on the Mount. In such a view, politics had to be understood in the context of service and worship. . . . Political action was not a means to acquire security and strength for one's self and one's party, but a means of witnessing to the truth and the reality of the cosmic structure by making one's own proper contribution to the order willed by God. One could thus preserve one's integrity and peace, being detached from results (which are in the hands of God) and being free from the inner violence that comes from division and untruth. . . . These perspectives lent Gandhi's politics their extraordinary spiritual force and religious realism.[21]

As for his contemplative practice, Merton notes that Gandhi saw, as no other world leader of his time did, "the necessity to be free from the pressures, the exorbitant and tyrannical demands of a society that is violent because it is essentially greedy, lustful and cruel." Gandhi preserved his inner peace by fasting, observing days of silence, and living frequently in retreat. He knew, writes Merton, "the value of solitude, as well as of the totally generous expenditure of his time and energy in listening to others and communicating with them."[22] He was a social activist with deep roots in the ethical principles and contemplative practices of his religion.

Gandhi's life was a model of engaged spirituality before there was such a term. He brought spiritual practices ordinarily associated with self-purification to bear on the reform of society, drew on the highest ethical principles of his religion to challenge the prevailing social structure, and tapped into the wisdom of diverse religious traditions in an effort to heal the deep divisions within his country. He was not always successful, yet his example inspired others. One of those to take up the cause of nonviolent resistance in the years following Gandhi's death was Martin Luther King. When the famous Montgomery, Alabama, bus boycott first attracted international attention, marking the beginning of the civil rights movement in America, commentators were quick to make comparisons between this act of civil disobedience and similar actions initiated by Gandhi in the Indian struggle for national independence. King himself did not initially make that connection. Only gradually did he come to acknowledge a close relationship between his work and Gandhi's, and then only at the urging of supporters from the Fellowship of Reconciliation.

When it came to explaining his cause to others, King preferred to draw on sources from his own culture and religious tradition. His well-known "Letter from a Birmingham Jail" is typical in this regard. He cites the prophet Amos and the apostle Paul, Augustine, Thomas Aquinas, Reinhold Niebuhr, and Paul Tillich, but also Thomas Jefferson, Abraham Lincoln, and the United States Constitution. He appeals to a "higher law" above the civil law and a "sacred tradition of freedom" in support of his acts of civil disobedience. He defends the practice of nonviolent direct action as a response to injustice based on love rather than hate, and affirms his belief that brotherhood will ultimately prevail over prejudice, ignorance, and fear. He sees both brotherhood and love as expressions of the Christian faith that he shared with his opponents. If there is an underlying theme to his writings, it is his appeal for *reconciliation*. In a penetrating essay written shortly after King's assassination, the Protestant theologian Herbert Richardson argues that reconciliation was his answer to the destructive forces of ideological conflict generated by relativism. The civil rights leader's deep conviction that the power of reconciliation transcends ideological conflict enabled him to direct his struggle against "the forces or structure of evil itself rather than against the person or group who is doing the evil."[23]

To arrive at this unifying vision and also move people to action, King drew on a source not ordinarily considered a part of mainstream Christianity, the Negro spiritual. The genius of the spirituals, as he recognized, is that they contain a political meaning embedded within a spiritual message. Because this music is deeply spiritual—a primary expression of the aspirations of an oppressed people—yet implicitly political in the challenge it poses to the institution of slavery, it has the power to inspire social action. While the Negro spirituals are profoundly Christian in their use of biblical concepts and imagery, they have also proven to be universal in their ability to touch the hearts of people everywhere. The spirituals did for the civil rights movement what Gandhi's fasts did for his own reform movement: they brought people together and gave them the courage to resist oppression, while also affecting the consciences of people outside of the movement.

Both Gandhi and King spoke the language of their respective religious traditions, yet in a way that enabled them to communicate with persons outside that tradition. By going deep within their own tradition, they found a way to make it relevant to the social conditions of their day, while at the same time eliciting a sympathetic response from persons of other backgrounds. They may have differed on matters of religious belief, but generally agreed on the principles of religious ethics. Above all they shared a commitment to the practice of nonviolence. Although their respective religions have a long history of violence, these men were personally convinced that at the deepest spiritual level the religions stood for peace and reconciliation. Early in his career King did not associate his work with Gandhi's, yet following a trip to India he founded the Gandhi Society of Human Rights to help raise money for the civil rights movement. When the editors of the *Christian Century*, a liberal publication, criticized him for adopting an "un-Christian" name for his organization, he replied that surely God also worked through Gandhi.[24] In spite of their cultural and religious differences, the great civil rights leader could recognize a kindred spirit in the "gentle revolutionary."

As for Thich Nhat Hanh, he too followed the way of Gandhi, though he did not deliberately choose Gandhi as his model. His engaged Buddhism is yet another expression of the socially engaged spirituality represented by Mahatma Gandhi and Martin Luther King. He has been accused of going outside his religious tradition in his advocacy of social change, but he does not see it that way. Like Gandhi and King, he has made creative use of elements from his own tradition to respond to the social challenges of his day. He has retrieved elements of historical Buddhism that largely had been forgotten or ignored and made them part of a living Buddhism. One of the leading authorities on Vietnamese Buddhism, Nhat Hanh sees the origins of engaged Buddhism in the earlier history of Vietnamese Buddhism, including the Bamboo Forest School of the fourteenth century. In his *History of Buddhism in Vietnam*, a scholarly work currently available only in Vietnamese, he gives an account of how this unusual "school of meditation" came to be.

Its founder was Tran Nhan Tong, one of the most successful kings in the history of Vietnam. Ruling at the end of the thirteenth century, he repelled an invasion by the Mongols under Kublai Khan and made peace with the neighboring country of Champa. There was a tradition at that time for Vietnamese kings to abdicate the throne when they had a son who was of an age to succeed them. In this case, the king chose to become a hermit upon abdication, withdrawing to a mountain retreat to pursue the study and practice of Buddhism. This was a bit unusual, but not unprecedented. More remarkable was his decision, following ordination, to travel about the country teaching a distinctive form of Buddhism. His religious name was Bamboo Forest, and his teachings were not directed solely toward the enlightenment of the individual, but rather were closely linked to matters of government and social morality. The Bamboo Forest School, as his lineage came to be known, remained influential for half a century following his death and then declined. For Nhat Hanh, it survives as "one of the foundation stones for engaged Buddhism."[25]

Thich Nhat Hanh was not a leader in the Vietnamese struggle for national independence in the way that Gandhi was in the Indian struggle against Great Britain. The war with France began while he was still a novice, and it ended about the time he began teaching and writing. He knew many monks and nuns who supported the resistance, some of whom were killed, and has said that his own life was threatened during this time. Later, he knew he was taking a personal risk in opposing the government of South Vietnam. He was probably never fully safe, even while living abroad. So it is fair to say that his commitment to social justice has been as severely tested as that of Gandhi and King, even though it has not resulted in his death.

Nhat Hanh's method of nonviolent resistance is different from Gandhi's or King's. His activism has primarily taken the form of writing and speaking on behalf of peace. During his first stay in the United States, when the war in Vietnam was starting to intensify and America was just beginning to get involved, he conducted a five-day fast at the United Nations building in New York City and led a mass demonstration in Washington, D.C. But these actions were not particularly characteristic of him. He has preferred to appeal to reason rather than emotion and has endeavored by word and example to show people that there are better ways of resolving conflict than by killing one another. He was, as we have noted, critical of the antiwar movement with its mass demonstrations and angry rhetoric, because it did not seem to manifest an "inner peace." Nhat Hanh eventually came to the conclusion that the leaders of the movement used nonviolence mainly as a technique. They were willing to use any means necessary to end American involvement in the war, though this was not true of Martin Luther King. Nhat Hanh could see that King possessed great inner strength. For him nonviolence was not merely a technique: it was a manifestation in the political sphere of a spiritual way of being in the world.

During his second trip to the United States, in the spring of 1966 when American involvement in the war was accelerating, Nhat Hanh had an opportunity to meet Dr. King. Soon after, King called a press conference and announced his opposition to the war. It was a controversial decision that provoked criticism from other civil rights leaders who felt that it would compromise their movement to be associated with the antiwar cause. But in King's mind the two causes were inseparable. There could be no reconciliation of the races at home as long as America was waging ideological warfare abroad. A strong personal bond developed between King and Nhat Hanh, not unlike that between Merton and Nhat Hanh. Their relationship helped to transform the Buddhist's view of Christianity as well as strengthen his appreciation for the practice of nonviolence. At the time of their last meeting, not long before King's assassination, Nhat Hanh recalls saying to him: "You know, Martin, in Vietnam they consider you a bodhisattva."[26] He could apply this Buddhist title of honor to a Christian leader because he recognized in him the same spirit of peace and love so important to his own religious tradition.

To Nhat Hanh, peace and love must originate from within. We cannot bring peace to the world unless we first discover peace within ourselves. That is why he considers meditation so important for social action. To meditate, he says, is "to see deeply into things, to see how we can change, how we can transform our situation."[27] Meditation functions for Nhat Hanh in much the same way that fasting did for Gandhi. It helps bring one to greater self-awareness and greater empathy for others. Still, it is no guarantee of success. Looking back on the nonviolent struggle for peace in Vietnam, Nhat Hanh has concluded that it was not entirely successful, "not because it was wrong, but because it did not have all the conditions needed" for success.[28] The same could be said for his efforts on behalf of the boat people. That operation, too, was carried out in a spirit of mindfulness. We lived, he says, "like holy people, in the mode of prayer, of meditation, all the time, because we knew that human lives depended on our mindfulness." Yet the project did not succeed.[29] Since meditation teaches a person to act without regard to consequences, one should not be surprised that social action inspired by a contemplative vision is not always efficacious. The important thing is that it be carried out with integrity. On this, all three activists would agree.

The Globalization of Engaged Spirituality

Although his campaign to free India from British colonial rule received international attention, Gandhi's objectives were national in scope.

He sought to raise the spirit of his own people, restore their sense of national dignity and honor, and bring justice to the oppressed within their borders. He did not address the problem of colonialism in general or call upon people of other nations to join the struggle for social justice. In the years following his assassination his influence extended well beyond India, but that was not his intention. He addressed problems indigenous to his own culture in terms his own people could understand. If, in the words of George C. Marshall, the American secretary of state at the time of Gandhi's death, he was a "spokesman for the conscience of mankind," that was incidental to his purpose. Likewise, Martin Luther King challenged his fellow Americans to live up to the highest ideals of their nation and their religion by putting an end to racial discrimination in the United States; he did not mount a crusade against all forms of discrimination everywhere. When he joined the movement to end the war in Vietnam, it was because he considered it contrary to American ideals. Although both men clearly commanded the respect of people throughout the world, neither could be said to have had a global agenda.

That was not true of Thomas Merton, who from the outset brought a global perspective to the issues that most concerned him. His earliest social writings were on the subject of war, more specifically nuclear war, which he saw affecting all of humanity. His own life was deeply affected by the two World Wars. Born in France a few months after the start of World War I, he entered the monastery at Gethsemani a few days after the bombing of Pearl Harbor. The First World War forced his family to move to the United States, beginning a practice of moving around that took him to several different countries before he was an adult and no doubt helped to form him as a world citizen (it was only after many years in the monastery that he applied for American citizenship). The seclusion of monastic life prevented him from knowing very much about what went on during World War II (even though he lost a brother in the war and includes a moving tribute to him in his autobiography). He learned about the atrocities of the war (as did many Americans who were *not* living in a monastery) after it was over. He responded with horror and revulsion to reports of the Holocaust and the American decision to use the atomic bomb against Japan. But it was the prospect of global nuclear war that elicited his most passionate and sustained writing on the subject of war.

In his seminal essay "Nuclear War and Christian Responsibility," Merton begins with the thesis, which he acknowledges had become

something of a cliché, that "the world and society of man face destruction."[30] Destruction is *possible*, he contends, because nuclear, bacte-
rial, and chemical means exist "to wipe out the entire human race."
It is *probable* because the world's leaders are committed to policies
that are built on the threat to use these agents of extermination.
War under such conditions cannot be a purely national concern. But
neither, he believes, should the decisions that might lead to war be
left to an anonymous power elite. Merton is troubled by the general
moral passivity characteristic of his time. He imagines a situation in
which nuclear war might appear inevitable and the world's leaders
found to be morally incapable of preventing it. At such a time it
would be "legitimate and even obligatory for all sane and conscientious
men everywhere" to resist. But could they? "It would be folly," he
writes, "to suppose that men hitherto passive, inert, morally indifferent
and irresponsible might suddenly recover their sense of obligation
and their awareness of their own power when the world was on the very
brink of war."[31] He concludes by calling upon responsible Christians to
make themselves heard, to protest clearly and forcibly, before it is
too late, against trends that could lead to "global suicide."

Although Merton addresses this essay to Christians and draws to
some extent on Christian sources to support his argument, his appeal
is primarily to moral reason and to a spiritual sensibility not confined
to Christians. In a letter to his Muslim correspondent Abdul Aziz, he
writes as follows:

> It is my belief that all those in the world who have kept some vestige of
> sanity and spirituality should unite in firm resistance to the movements
> of power politicians and the monster nations, resist the whole movement
> of war and aggression, resist the diplomatic overtures of power and develop
> a strong and coherent "third world" that can stand on its own feet and
> affirm the spiritual and human values which are cynically denied by the
> great powers.[32]

Merton framed many of his arguments in terms of the Christian theory
of the just war, but only to show that it was no longer applicable in
an age of total war. In an essay entitled "Christian Action in World
Crisis" published in *Blackfriars*, a British publication, in June 1962,
he calls upon Christians to "manifest the truth of the Gospel in social
action," but to do so on the basis of a "mature moral conscience."
Such a conscience, he contends, "derives its strength and its light

not from external directives alone but above all from *an inner spiritual connaturality with the deepest values of nature and grace.*"[33] So it cannot be the exclusive prerogative of Christians.

Merton the Christian contemplative was deeply affected by the problem of war, which he saw as having spiritual roots. But he also recognized that war had become a global phenomenon. It could no longer be approached in strictly national terms. If the United States were to be drawn into a nuclear war with Russia, it would affect the entire world. He imagines a scenario in which a mass movement spontaneously arises in all parts of the world—in Russia and America, China and France, Africa and Germany—to save the world from destruction.[34] Though he acknowledged that such a development is highly unlikely, he clearly saw that the only way to deal with war in an age of globalization is by mounting a global response. He understood that this would entail appealing to people of different religions for their support, which in turn would mean communicating with them at a deep spiritual level. He was confident that this could be done, in large part because of his own experience with interreligious dialogue. He had discovered in his encounters with representatives of other religions, albeit largely through their writings, an "inner spiritual connaturality" that encompassed the deepest human values.

Thich Nhat Hanh came to a similar conclusion by a different route. He too was deeply affected by war. But for him, it was war that first brought him into contact with Christians who shared his values. The experience taught him that persons of different religions could work together for peace. It also served to enlarge his social vision. Nhat Hanh's work, as we have seen, was initially focused on bringing about a social transformation within his own country, but the war forced him to redirect his efforts. He came to the United States in 1966 with the purpose of promoting greater understanding of the war. He wanted Americans to see it from the viewpoint of the Vietnamese people. When it became apparent that he could not safely return to his homeland, he made his headquarters in Paris and spent the remainder of the war meeting with political leaders and concerned citizens throughout Europe in an effort to bring about an end to the conflict and secure relief for its victims. The Vietnam War made him an international figure and required him to think globally.

In the years since, Nhat Hanh has found other issues besides peace that could unite people across cultural and religious lines. In 1971, even before the war was over, he joined with several individuals of

different nationalities to mount one of the first international conferences on the environment.[35] Since then he has led workshops for
environmentalists as well as peace workers and others engaged in
social action. Though no longer the social activist he once was, he
continues to travel around the world giving talks, presenting workshops, and conducting retreats. The focus of his present work is the
practice of meditation, but with the understanding that in order for
it to be authentic it must relate to society. "The purpose of meditation,"
he has said, "is not to get out of society, to escape from society, but
to prepare for a reentry into society."[36] We may think we are leaving
society behind when we take up the practice of meditation, but that
is an illusion. We have no "separate self" to retreat to through the
practice of meditation. We "inter-are" with everything that is. Rather
than diminish our sense of social responsibility, meditation should
enlarge it. Not long ago Nhat Hanh was invited to attend an international conference on AIDS in Washington, D.C. So even though he
may be less actively involved in social causes than he once was, he
remains a global thinker sensitive to social issues.

Others, meanwhile, have taken up many of his causes, actively
pursuing engaged spirituality on a global basis. An outstanding example is A. T. Ariyaratne, founder of a movement similar in some ways
to the School of Youth for Social Service. A Buddhist layman in the
Theravada tradition, Ariyaratne started out as a science teacher. In
1958, he began organizing student work camps, which he called
shramadanas, meaning "the gift of time and labor." He established
these work camps in some of the most remote, impoverished villages
of Sri Lanka so that students could experience firsthand the living
conditions of people in the rural areas and thereby develop greater
appreciation for them. He also hoped to inspire the students to use
their education to help these people build a better life. In the work
camps, he developed ways to transmit Buddhist values as well as
improve the general quality of life for people. The students cleaned
latrines and built roads, but they also convened community gatherings
where Buddha's social teachings were discussed. The villagers were
encouraged to practice *metta*, a form of loving-kindness meditation,
on a daily basis.

In the late sixties, Ariyaratne traveled to India to study with one
of the leading disciples of Gandhi. As a result of this study, he
was able to combine the Gandhian philosophy of nonviolence with
Buddhist social ethics. In 1972, he expanded the work camps into a

full-blown social movement called Sarvodaya Shramadana. By the end of the decade this movement had grown into a major force in national life, involving thousands of people and more than a third of the island's villages. The primary emphasis of this movement is on decentralization and self-reliance. Like Gandhi and Nhat Hanh, Ariyaratne wants villagers to assume primary responsibility for their economic development. But there is also a strong spiritual emphasis to the movement. Sarvodaya considers the cultivation of spiritual and cultural values as important as programs to improve education, health care, transportation, and sanitation.

Along with a deep devotion to his own people and their indigenous culture, Ariyaratne has a global outlook. When asked in an interview with Catherine Ingram how he saw the world's problems as interrelated, he replied:

> We are living in an interdependent world. Communications and various technologies have brought us together. . . . Also we see that the world's resources are being used interdependently. . . . The other ways that our problems are connected is that the superpowers are building nuclear armaments. If anything happens, an accident, it's not only they who are going to suffer, but everybody in the world. . . . Whatever we are doing in whatever part of the world, we have to keep in mind this global perspective. In the Sarvodaya Movement, while we may be working in the most remote village in Asia or Africa, we always try to keep a global vision.[37]

Ariyaratne is not alone. He is one of a growing number of engaged Buddhists with a global vision, Buddhists who represent the new form of socially engaged spirituality.

Another such individual is Joanna Macy. She is an American, raised in the Christian tradition, who first discovered Buddhism as an adult while living with her husband in India. After a stint with the Peace Corps in Africa and a job with the National Urban League in Washington, D.C., she undertook graduate study in Buddhism at Syracuse University. What made her study unique was that she combined it with general systems theory, an interdisciplinary approach to the explanation of social phenomena. This theory gave her special insight into the Buddhist concept of interdependence, which provides the intellectual and spiritual basis for her social activism. In the years since she completed her degree, she has been actively engaged with a wide range of social issues centering around nuclear power and the environment, always approached from a global perspective.

If systems theory served as a theoretical basis for her work, Macy acquired her practical know-how from Ariyaratne and the Sarvodaya Movement. She first encountered it in 1976 while on a four-month pilgrimage tour of sacred sites in India and Sri Lanka. She returned to Sri Lanka in 1979 on a Ford Foundation grant to serve as a Sarvodaya volunteer, studying the way in which "religious beliefs and aspirations are reflected in the goals of the movement."[38] She has carried what she learned into the area of social action on behalf of peace and the environment. One of her most creative contributions to the evolving practice of engaged spirituality, coming directly out of her work with Sarvodaya, is the "Despair and Empowerment" workshop she developed in the 1980s to help people cope with the dire prospects for human survival in the face of the nuclear arms race and the destructive effects of modern life on the planet. The workshop employs meditative practices designed to deal honestly with despair in order to foster a greater sense of human community and a stronger commitment to the future.

There are also Christians who are carrying on this kind of work. Earlier we spoke of David Steindl-Rast in connection with contemplative renewal and interreligious dialogue, but he has also been engaged in social action on a worldwide scale for the past three decades. He has marched for peace, spoken out about hunger in Third World countries, and addressed problems of the environment in much the same way that Joanna Macy has. On one occasion, he and his Zen teacher together took part in a teach-in at the University of Michigan to protest the war in Vietnam.[39] He clearly sees a connection between contemplative practice and social action. Spirituality, he has said, is a "special kind of aliveness" that includes social commitment. It is "faulty spirituality" when a person "gets stuck in meditation" and cannot see "how it relates to social responsibility."[40] As for the globalization of engaged spirituality, he recognizes that we can "no longer do something in any part of the world that does not influence people in other parts of the world," but adds realistically that "we are not really a world community yet." In order to become a world community, he thinks we will need "global heroes." These are people who dare to put into practice "deep human values."[41] One thinks immediately of Thomas Merton and Thich Nhat Hanh.

Toward a Unifying Spirituality

Merton and Nhat Hanh, as we have noted, met only once, and then
for a very short time; yet in that brief meeting a true friendship was
established. They both acknowledged in subsequent writings that they
had made a genuine spiritual connection in spite of their social,
cultural, and religious differences. They appreciated the depth and
sincerity of each other's faith and realized that neither one fit the
other's stereotype of his religion. According to Merton, Nhat Hanh
showed that "Zen is not an esoteric and world-denying cult of inner
illumination," but has a "rare and unique sense of responsibility in
the modern world." Nhat Hanh was impressed with Merton's openness,
especially his nondogmatic, non-dualistic outlook. "One of the most
difficult things concerning the understanding between East and West,"
he observed, "is that the West tends to think in a dualistic way."

Yet for all his openness and willingness to learn from others, Merton
encountered at least one point of difference between Zen Buddhism
and Christianity, which he could not resolve to his satisfaction. He
had a serious problem with the "impersonal" language that Zen Buddhists use to speak of the Transcendent—whether or not they call
this reality "God." Thus, at the conclusion of his dialogue with Suzuki,
he notes that "the strongly personalistic tone of Christian mysticism,
even when it is 'apophatic,' generally seems to prohibit a full equation
with Zen experience."[42] Suzuki could, as we have seen, speak of "the
Godhead," as distinct from God the Creator, but he could not conceive
of God as a personal being. Godhead, for him, meant "ultimate emptiness"—not the emptiness of nothingness, to be sure, but emptiness
nonetheless—and one does not enter into a personal relationship with
Emptiness. Christians, on the other hand, typically seek union with
God through a personal relationship with Christ. They conceive of
God as Love and, according to Merton, find in God's "free gift of
love" the ultimate basis for union with God. Lest this idea of gift be
interpreted in a divisive dualistic sense, he is careful to point out
that "God is His own Gift" and "the Gift of the Spirit is the gift of
freedom and emptiness." The Christian contemplative agrees with
Suzuki in rejecting "an emptiness that is merely empty, and merely
the counterpart of some imagined fullness standing over against it in
metaphysical isolation," yet holds out for a personal dimension to the
"emptiness of fullness," insisting that it is none other than the "fullness
of love."[43]

Though Merton ended his exchange with Suzuki on a positive note, acknowledging a "unity of outlook and purpose" in spite of differences in religious beliefs, he was not done with this problem. At a retreat he led for a group of contemplative sisters at Gethsemani in May 1968, just a few months before his departure for Asia, he was asked: "Does it make any difference if you're a Catholic or not if there's so much good spirituality in all these other traditions?" In his reply, he makes it clear that he still considered the lack of a personal relationship to God a deficiency in Buddhism, yet he held out hope that with greater understanding the deficiency could be overcome. "Something that has to be explored in the relations between Catholicism and Buddhism," he said, "is the fact that there's room for a personal understanding of what they call the 'void.' " The true ultimate for Buddhists, he explained, is the void or emptiness. "But it's not a negative emptiness, it's a positive emptiness which is fullness." Reiterating what he had said earlier in his response to Suzuki, he assured the sisters that there is a place for a personal understanding of this fullness.[44]

Merton had been reading the work of a Zen Buddhist philosopher named Nishida, who he thought succeeded in bringing a personal dimension into his philosophy.[45] But he had also been giving consideration to the phenomenon of "Buddhist converts to Christianity."[46] What did they find in Christianity that was lacking in their own religion? he wondered. What they were looking for, he concluded, was this "personal element," the relationship to a personal God. "It was in Buddhism, but it was not explicit, and so the personal revelation of God was the final thing they needed." Buddhists who convert to Christianity, he observed, "often seem to have a deeper appreciation for what this personal relationship to God means" than most Christians. He thought this was because they do not convert to the Western idea of individualism when they become Christians and so do not get caught up in the "rudimentary idea of the soul being saved by Christ." They may find in Christianity an "elaboration of Buddhism," but not necessarily a deepening of their own Buddhist faith. Buddhism, he thinks, does not need deepening as much as "rethinking in personal terms." Buddhists would do well to retain "their pure kind of consciousness" and "within this deep emptiness" to seek "a personal relationship with God." When this occurs, he said, "they really have it made."[47]

For Nhat Hanh, the chief barrier to mutual understanding from the side of Christianity has been, and continues to be, its dogmatic claim to absolute truth. Responding to a statement by Pope John Paul II that "Christ is absolutely original and absolutely unique . . . the one mediator between God and humanity," the Buddhist observes that underlying this statement is the idea that "Christianity provides the only way of salvation and all other religious traditions are of no use." This attitude, he thinks, "excludes dialogue and fosters religious intolerance and discrimination."[48] The very first precept of his Order of Interbeing, we may recall, was the one regarding absolutism: "Do not be idolatrous about or bound to any doctrine, theory, or ideology, even Buddhist ones. Buddhist systems of thought are guiding means; they are not absolute truth." Nhat Hanh clearly prefers a pragmatic approach to truth, one based on experience rather than doctrine, and he is opposed to any attempt to put forward a religious absolute. He is especially critical of the Christian claim that Christ is the one and only way to salvation. In the gospels, Jesus speaks of himself as the door of salvation and everlasting life, but according to Nhat Hanh there are many doors. "Buddha is also described as a door, a teacher who shows us the way in this life," and there are other doors as well. If we are fortunate, he says, we will find one of these doors, but "it would not be very Buddhist to say that ours is the only door." Our task should be "to open even more doors for future generations."[49]

The way Christians can honor Jesus, he believes, is by living as Jesus did—with "love, understanding, courage, and acceptance."[50] This is not just a matter of ethics. The ethical principles of Buddhism and Christianity are similar in many respects and they are important, but they are not the whole of the matter. There is that in every religion that makes it a living religion. Christians call it the Holy Spirit, and Buddhists speak of it as mindfulness. It is the spiritual dimension of the religion that opens a person to the Transcendent. Nhat Hanh is aware that it is a matter of some controversy whether to speak of this transcendent reality in personal terms, but he does not consider resolution of this issue crucial for spiritual practice. It turns on a conceptual difference, and as far as he is concerned, "all concepts have to be transcended if we are to touch the ground of our being deeply."[51] The important thing is to look deep within our own tradition for an underlying spiritual reality. *"When we understand and practice deeply the life and teachings of Buddha or the life and teachings of*

*Jesus, we penetrate the door and enter the abode of the living Buddha
and the living Christ, and life eternal presents itself to us.*"[52]

One of Nhat Hanh's major insights regarding Buddhism and Christianity is that there are non-Christian elements in Christianity and
non-Buddhist elements in Buddhism. He thinks this is one of the
major reasons why persons of different traditions are able to communicate with one another. Because their traditions are not totally self-
contained but include elements from other religions, they can understand one another. There are, moreover, many forms of Buddhism, as
there are many forms of Christianity. We cannot say that either religion
has been unchanged throughout its history or unaffected by other
religions. Although he does not deny that there are real differences
between the two religions, Nhat Hanh is convinced that if we look
deep enough we will discover that we have many things in common.
We should not be afraid to acknowledge this commonality. One is
reminded of Merton's statement in his tribute to Nhat Hanh that
he had more in common with this Buddhist monk than with many
Americans. "It is vitally important," he insisted, "that such bonds
be admitted."

The Gethsemani Encounter

As we have noted, the period since the historic meeting of Thomas
Merton and Thich Nhat Hanh has been one of increased communication between and among religions. For Catholics, the Second Vatican
Council was a major factor. Not only did this unprecedented gathering
of theologians and church leaders provide the impetus for general
reform within the Catholic Church, it was also the occasion for a
major papal encyclical calling upon the church to enter into dialogue
with other religions. For Buddhists, the Dalai Lama has played a
major role in bringing about meetings with persons of other faiths.
For instance, he once initiated a meeting with Jews in order to learn
more about the experience of "living in exile." Over the past three
decades, people of many different religious traditions and backgrounds
have come together out of a genuine desire to know one another better,
but also out of a shared concern for global developments such as
nuclear proliferation and environmental pollution that threaten human
survival. With further advances in information technology on the
horizon, we can anticipate even more engagements of this sort.

One noteworthy event in this whole development was the week-long conference of Buddhist and Catholic monks convened at Gethsemani Abbey in July 1996. Representatives of three distinct traditions within Buddhism were invited to participate, along with a number of lay participants and observers. The Catholic delegation comprised Benedictine monks and nuns from several different orders as well as representatives of the Catholic hierarchy. A special effort was made to include women from both traditions. The general theme of the conference, called the Gethsemani Encounter, was the spiritual life, but discussions covered a broad range of topics, including an examination of diverse forms of spiritual practice, consideration of the place of spiritual direction within different traditions, the role of women in the religious orders, and the relationship of spiritual awakening to social transformation. By the end of the week the participants agreed, in the words of Father Pierre-Francois de Bethune, secretary general of the Monastic Interreligious Dialogue, that they had achieved "a new climate of openness and unity" as the result of "a process of interior evolution."[53]

When I first began teaching a course on Buddhism after many years of studying Christian theology, it was like entering a foreign country. I did not know the language and did not share a history with those whose tradition I was trying to expound. It was difficult even to make a connection. The participants in the Gethsemani Encounter faced a similar dilemma. They could only speak from within their own traditions, yet they were curious about each other's and questioned the features they had trouble understanding. Buddhists, for instance, asked about the suffering of Christ. One participant, a Zen Buddhist, observed that it made him sad to see a crucifix, with its image of Jesus on the cross, prominently displayed in the room where they met every day. This observation led to a discussion of the place of sacrifice and the role of forgiveness in the two religions. Christians, on the other hand, were interested in knowing more about the Buddhist concept of mind. They were intrigued by the way it was used to explain both the origin and end of suffering. A particularly interesting exchange occurred on the subject of anger. Though generally agreeing that anger is destructive of human relationships, Christians tended to regard righteous anger as an appropriate response to injustice, while most Buddhists did not. They were inclined to think it would exacerbate the situation. But there was not complete unanimity *within* either tradition on this issue, and there was some agreement across traditions.

In reading the published account of this meeting, I was struck by the freshness and authenticity of the responses. The participants did not merely give textbook answers to questions from their religious counterparts. They drew upon their own traditions in ways that were often creative and transformative. Diana Eck, professor of comparative religions at Harvard and the only Protestant participant in the encounter, observed that monks and theologians in the past had not had the benefit of this kind of open, face-to-face dialogue with representatives of other religions. In light of this new situation, she thought there was a need for "a new theological language that is forged out of this dialogue situation." Though acknowledging that there is probably room for a new interfaith vocabulary, one of the Catholic sisters expressed a feeling (no doubt shared by others) that "we only speak truly if we speak from our own spiritual idiom, our own spiritual place in the universe." This observation led a Buddhist to remark that in his view "what happens in an encounter such as this is that by hearing terms from another tradition we bring them into our own tradition. . . . So perhaps rather than creating another terminology, it is a matter of stretching one's own to take in the other's terminology."[54] In future dialogues, we will probably see all three things happening simultaneously. A new interreligious vocabulary, a higher-order way of speaking about religious matters that is not the prerogative of any particular religious community, will undoubtedly emerge *even as* the participants in religious dialogue continue to speak the language of their own traditions *and* look for innovative ways to incorporate the terminology of other traditions into their own discourse.

If there was one thing the participants in this conference agreed on, it was that sharing in each other's spiritual practices provided a way for them to come together. Each day began with sitting meditation followed by a Buddhist or Christian ritual. The morning sessions were devoted to presentations on a particular aspect of the spiritual life as seen from a Buddhist perspective, while the afternoon sessions were given over to presentations on the same topic from a Christian viewpoint. Interspersed between sessions were further opportunities to participate in each other's spiritual practices. Although these practices were by no means identical, they were sufficiently similar to constitute, in the words of a Korean monk, "a common ground," a meeting place for the two religions.[55] Moreover, everyone agreed that they contributed to a general climate of openness. The participants in the encounter, both Buddhist and Christian, could discern a unity beyond words, because they had through their respective practices experienced a reality beyond words.

It should come as no surprise, therefore, that one of the main topics of the conference was a comparative discussion of meditative practices within the different traditions. A Burmese monk from the Theravada tradition led off with a presentation on mindfulness and loving-kindness meditation, followed by an American Zen practitioner's discussion of the more austere practice of zazen. Talks by Christians opened with a general treatment of the place of contemplative practice in Catholic life, but then focused on lectio divina and centering prayer. Even more remarkable to my mind was the attention given to social action as an expression of contemplative practice, particularly by the Buddhists. The Dalai Lama said that for many years he had been "attracted to those Christian brothers and sisters who are involved in social services—particularly in the fields of education and health care." In the mid-sixties, he told his monks that they should take a lesson from these Christian bodhisattvas.[56]

The most moving statement on the subject of social action, however, came from Maha Ghosananda, supreme patriarch of Buddhism in Cambodia. Speaking as one who has been actively involved for many years in the struggle for social justice within his own country, he said that the most important thing Buddhists can do is "to foster the liberation of the human spirit in every nation of the human family." This will necessarily mean a new role for monks outside of the temple.

> We Buddhists must find the courage to leave our temples and enter the temples of contemporary human experience, temples that are filled with suffering. If we listen to the Buddha, Christ, or Gandhi, we can do nothing else. The refugee camps, the prisons, the ghettos, and the battlefield will then become our temples. We have so much work to do.[57]

A Christian social activist might have said it differently, but could not have said it any better.

Near the conclusion of the conference, Kevin Hunt, a Benedictine monk who had trained with a Zen master in the seventies and who had participated in the Monastic Interreligious Dialogue from the beginning, observed that something unusual was taking place. We Christians, he noted, "are very interested in discussing meditative practices as aids to returning to our spiritual source of prayer and meditation," while "Buddhists seem to express the need for social engagement in their tradition."[58] He called it "two conversations going on at the same time," but it could also be seen as a sign of *convergence*, the coming together of two distinct strands within the two religious traditions and the coming together of the religions themselves. Through shared spiritual practices and joint efforts to address social issues, these two ancient religions are discovering a commonality they did not know they had—and they are being transformed in the process.

Walking the Labyrinth

Merton once envisioned himself as embodying the convergence of East and West, thus serving as a model for others.[59] He was thinking at the time of uniting the eastern and western branches of Christianity, although as we have seen his vision gradually expanded to include Buddhism and other Asian religions. Unlike the Gethsemani Encounter and similar meetings in recent years, Merton's dialogue with Buddhism was largely an internal one. With the exception of his meeting with Nhat Hanh and a brief visit with D. T. Suzuki a few years earlier, it was not until the last year of his life that he had an opportunity for face-to-face meetings with Buddhists, and by then he had so internalized the spirit of Buddhism that he could engage his Buddhist counterparts at a very deep level. His experience may seem unique, so much so that he would not be an appropriate model for others. On the contrary, I think he is a model for a new form of interfaith dialogue, one that is as much internal as external, a form of dialogue occurring with increasing frequency as much outside the monastery as within.

It is understandable that Buddhist-Christian dialogue had its beginnings in the monastic setting. For all of their religious differences, and they are not inconsiderable, Buddhist and Christian monks share a sufficiently similar lifestyle, particularly in respect to the importance given to contemplative practice, that they can fairly readily make a spiritual connection with one another. They may very well be our scouting party as we explore this new terrain. Yet it would be a mistake to suppose that Buddhist-Christian dialogue is confined to monastics. It is taking place in a variety of settings with people of varying degrees of religious commitment.

There are many factors contributing to this development, but one factor certainly is the growth of departments of religious studies in colleges and universities throughout the United States, dating from the mid-1960s. It is one of the ironies of recent American history that the Supreme Court decision that put an end to prayer in public schools opened the door for the academic study of religion in public institutions of higher education. The court made it clear that, although the state could not sponsor religious practices of any kind, it could support the academic study of religion as long as it did not favor one particular religion. Following this decision, many public and private universities began offering courses in religion. At first they were taught by local clergy—priests, ministers, and rabbis—but increasingly they were staffed by academics with no necessary religious affiliation but with considerable expertise in a particular religious tradition. Students began taking courses not only in Judaism and Christianity, but in many other religions such as Islam, Hinduism, Buddhism, Confucianism, and Taoism. Thus it is now possible to have an informed discussion of religious traditions that until recently were largely unknown in this country. Interreligious dialogue at a very sophisticated level has begun to occur on college campuses and in community forums throughout the country.

Another factor contributing to the growth of Buddhist-Christian dialogue is the large influx of immigrants from Southeast Asia following the Vietnam War. Asians still make up a small portion of the U.S. population, but their numbers are growing and they are assuming a more prominent place in American society. Since a large proportion of Asian-Americans are at least nominally Buddhist, it is much more likely now that the average American will at some time come into contact with Buddhists. Contact does not necessarily translate into dialogue, but at least the opportunity is there in a way that it was not even twenty-five years ago.

As we have noted, there are also Buddhist meditation groups of various sorts (Japanese Zen, Korean Zen, Tibetan, Theravadin, and even some that are distinctly American) springing up nearly everywhere. These groups generally welcome persons of diverse persuasions into their practice. Because Buddhists do not as a rule proselytize, one can usually hold onto one's previous religious commitment—be it Jewish, Christian, or Muslim—while taking part in Buddhist meditative practice. Buddhists and Christians practicing together may or may not choose to engage in interreligious dialogue. In most cases they probably do not, yet it has been my experience that sometimes study groups are formed from these experiences or informal conversations spontaneously arise in which interfaith issues do get discussed. This sort of thing may not be commonplace, but it is happening—certainly more now than ever before.

Yet, important as these developments are, I do not see them constituting the new form of dialogue that Merton modeled and Nhat Hanh, in his own way, has come to exemplify. This form of dialogue goes beyond mere curiosity about the other. What do Buddhists believe about the afterlife and why do they think suffering is universal? Is the concept of nirvana similar in some ways to the idea of God? Did Christ die for Buddhists as well as Christians? These are interesting questions; but the way in which they are usually asked does not pose a serious challenge for the questioner. They do not call into question his core beliefs or affect in any significant way her spiritual practice. Interreligious dialogue carried on at this level is purely external. It becomes an internal dialogue—what Raimon Panikkar calls *intra*religious as distinct from *inter*religious dialogue—when it "catches hold of our entire person and removes our many masks."[60] When this happens, dialogue with the other becomes dialogue with oneself. It is ourselves we are questioning and not just the other; our own ultimate meaning we are seeking, not just knowledge about someone else's. This was clearly the case with Merton, as he acknowledges in the preface to *Mystics and Zen Masters*, a compilation of essays about Christian and Zen practitioners of the mystical way. The author of this work, he says, was not content to write about these traditions "without making them, as far as possible, *his own*."[61]

It was once assumed that taking up a new religion meant giving up one's old religion. But that is not how I have come to see it. When my wife and I moved to Colorado a few years ago, we chose as our primary spiritual community a Zen meditation group that meets twice weekly—one evening a week in the chapel of a liberal arts college and every Saturday morning for up to half a day in a house belonging to the local Unitarian-Universalist Church. We retain our Christian affiliation (she is an Episcopalian and I am a Methodist), yet we have become, for all intents and purposes, practicing Buddhists. Not only do we sit with the group whenever we can, we also join in their monthly sutra service, even taking our turns leading the service. We work with a recognized Zen teacher within a somewhat untraditional

Zen lineage, one that combines Rinzai and Soto practices. Several times a year, we attend a week-long retreat led by this teacher.

Two years ago we took the additional step of "taking refuge," the Buddhist equivalent of Christian confirmation. In preparation for the refuge ceremony, which in Japanese is called *jukai*, we spent several months in weekly discussions of the Ten Precepts with members of our group. These precepts are the guiding ethical principles of Zen Buddhism and are in many respects similar to the ethical teachings of Christianity. For instance, we vowed to follow *the way of not killing, the way of not stealing, the way of not speaking falsely, the way of not discussing the faults of others*, and *the way of not praising oneself while abusing others*. We also promised *not to spare the dharma assets* and *not to defame the three treasures*, which is another way of saying we agreed to respect the teachings of Buddha and to make them available to others. By entering into this commitment, neither of us felt that we were betraying our Christian heritage. We thought rather that we were strengthening and deepening it in some subtle and mysterious way. We saw no contradiction in being Buddhist *and* Christian.

When we attend a church service, as we sometimes do, we feel that we still belong. Taking communion does not seem inconsistent with taking refuge. The two practices may touch a different part of us, but the one seems as genuine as the other. There is, no doubt, an internal dialogue going on between these two parts of ourselves. I sense it sometimes in conversations with others or while listening to a Buddhist talk or a Christian sermon. I hear the Buddhist in me responding to the Christian, the Christian in me responding to the Buddhist. But until recently I would not have said that anything like a convergence of the two religions was taking place. I certainly would not have said with Merton that I was "uniting in myself" these two traditions. Then something unusual happened, which even now I do not fully understand. It occurred while I was "walking the labyrinth" at a local Congregational church.

Elizabeth and I had recently visited Chartres, the magnificent medieval cathedral located near Paris, not far from Versailles. We went mainly to see the famous stained-glass windows, which have survived centuries of war and civil strife; but we discovered while we were there that the cathedral is also the site of the oldest intact labyrinth in Europe. The labyrinth is marked off with stones set into the floor of the nave. You can see it as you walk down the central aisle, although when we were there it was largely obscured by chairs. Circular in shape, it is characterized by a path sixteen inches wide and 861.5 feet in length that winds its way gradually around the circumference of the circle, sometimes moving towards the center, sometimes away, continuously turning back on itself until finally it reaches the center. To walk the labyrinth is to follow this path into the center of the circle and out again. We did not walk the labyrinth at Chartres, though we were certainly intrigued by it. Only later did we learn of an effort within the past ten years to revive this practice and create replicas of the Chartres labyrinth (usually made of canvas) in churches throughout the United States, including the one in Colorado Springs near where we live.[62]

When we heard that the labyrinth at the First Congregational Church would be open to the public on Ash Wednesday, we decided to walk it together. I was curious, but I did not expect anything out of the ordinary. Walking meditation has always been important to me, even when I would not have known to call it that. (Merton was once asked about his practice and replied that his practice was walking in the woods. I could say the same thing, although my woods are on the mountainside near my home, where several generations of my family have walked.) I looked forward to walking the labyrinth as I would to any kind of walking meditation. I was working on a Zen koan at the time and decided to hold the koan in my awareness during my walk, which took about forty-five minutes. I did not realize a breakthrough in my koan work, but I did find the walk a satisfying experience.

That night I had a vivid and powerful dream. In it I was walking after dark through a park I used to take on my way to and from grade school more than fifty years ago. (The grade school is long gone, and for all I know the park is too.) I found it somewhat frightening, but there was a sense that I was going home, and I felt myself carried along effortlessly. I also sensed that I was enclosed within an almost invisible container—not quite invisible, because I could just make out the outline of the container. It was a luminous blue, not unlike the dominant color in the stained-glass windows of Chartres Cathedral. On waking I felt an intense excitement coupled with awe. I knew somehow that I was being carried by my two spiritual traditions, both very powerful and both moving in the same direction—toward home.

On reflection I have come to think that the labyrinth is a good metaphor for what is happening spiritually for many people today. We find ourselves walking a path that we do not fully understand.

Sometimes it seems to be moving toward the center and sometimes away from it. There are others on the path, but we are not always walking together, and we cannot be sure we are always going in the same direction. When we reach the center, as we inevitably do if we persist, we find that we cannot stay there. We are propelled outward, moved to retrace our steps back into the world we came from, knowing we have been transformed but in ways we cannot explain. It is reassuring to think that there are others on the path, even if we are not always walking together. We may hope that when we finally emerge from our respective labyrinths, we will recognize one another as brothers and sisters, members of the same human family, and will find creative ways of working together for the resolution of the world's problems.

Epilogue

Global Heroes

A T THE HEIGHT OF the Vietnam War, Thich Nhat Hanh was
nominated for the Nobel Peace Prize by Martin Luther King,
the acknowledged leader of the civil rights movement in
America and a Nobel Peace laureate in his own right. Though the
Buddhist peace activist did not receive this highly acclaimed international award, his nomination was an indication that he had begun to
emerge as an international figure, a "global hero" to use Steindl-
Rast's term. In a troubled time he exemplified peace in a way others
could appreciate, even if they came from a different culture, nationality, or religious tradition. The same could be said for Thomas Merton.
Though not the activist Nhat Hanh was at that time, this deeply
contemplative man was even then on the way to becoming a modern-
day hero. He had become for many the exemplar of a new kind of
spirituality, a spirituality that could transcend historical and religious
differences and touch the hearts of people the world over.

What would it mean to speak of these men as global heroes? Joseph
Campbell, in his classic work *The Hero with a Thousand Faces*,
discerns a common pattern in the hero myths of the world's great
religions. "The hero," he writes, "is the man or woman who has been
able to battle past his personal and local historical limitations to the
generally valid, normally human forms. Such a one's visions, ideas,
and inspirations come pristine from the primary springs of human
life and thought."[1] Merton and Nhat Hanh are not in any sense
mythological. They belong to the history of their time. Yet their lives,
to a remarkable extent, fit the pattern of Campbell's mythological
hero. They battled personal and local historical limitations to realize
a life perceived by many to be universally valid. Both men, for

instance, lost a brother in war, experienced rejection by the authorities of their religious order, and questioned their vocation at one time or another. The spiritual vision that emerged from these struggles is rooted in tradition, yet is profoundly original. It is a shared vision, arising out of what Campbell calls the "primary springs of human life and thought." Independently of one another, they seem to have tapped into a source of inspiration not confined to either of their religious traditions.

In noting the almost mythic status that Merton and Nhat Hanh have achieved in the eyes of many throughout the world, we should not fail to recognize their ordinary humanity. Neither one puts forward, in person or in writing, a particularly idealized view of himself. That is especially obvious in the case of Nhat Hanh with his considerable reluctance to speak about himself. He would much rather talk about his practice. When specifically asked, he will sometimes reply, "If you want to know about me, look at my community." Merton, on the other hand, writes freely about himself, but in a way that is not self-aggrandizing. He has a penchant for self-observation, but also for self-criticism. The picture he paints is of someone struggling to find himself and often stumbling in the dark.

In the period since his death, a number of facts have come to light that might seem to reflect unfavorably on Merton's image as the "perfect monk." In particular, there is the disclosure of a romantic relationship with a young nurse, which began shortly before his meeting with Nhat Hanh and ended a few months later. It came as a great surprise, a shock to many, when this incident was first revealed in Michael Mott's biography of Merton published in 1984.[2] Yet it is not as though he had tried to hide it. The whole affair is fully documented in his personal journals, along with his agonizing ruminations about it. He clearly intended the matter to be made public, though he requested that the journals themselves not be made available to the general public until twenty-five years after his death. Like nearly everything else in his life, Merton used this affair as an occasion for ruthless self-examination in pursuit of greater self-integration. Far from detracting from his broad appeal, this disclosure has, if anything, made him more appealing by casting him in a more human light. The same could be said for his tendency to excess in the use of alcohol and his somewhat immature attitude toward authority. Thomas Merton was no saint in the conventional meaning of that word; yet in spite of his failings, perhaps even because of them, he was able to touch a deep spiritual chord in others.

Nhat Hanh is much less self-disclosing than Merton, at least in his public utterances. There are a few places in his writings, however, where he provides a window into his inner struggles. In one place, he tells about a time when as a young monk he fell in love with a Buddhist nun. In a series of talks, first given at Plum Village and later published under the title *Cultivating the Mind of Love*, he describes his tender feelings for this young woman and the problem they posed for his commitment to the life of a monk. "As a monk," he observes, "you are not supposed to fall in love, but sometimes love is stronger than your determination."[3] In the end he restrained himself, acting as her protector from the strong desire they felt for one another. When they finally separated, it was with a feeling of deep sadness. Eventually he was able to transform this romantic love into a larger and more inclusive love through compassionate service on behalf of others. The initial attraction he felt for this woman, together with the inner conflict that accompanied it, was nonetheless real and helps to show his true humanity.

In a somewhat different vein, there is Jim Forest's account of an incident cited earlier, the one in which Nhat Hanh, speaking to an American audience about the need to put an end to the killing in his homeland, was confronted by a very angry man who exclaimed, "If you care so much about the people of Vietnam, what are you doing here?" The Buddhist monk could have replied in anger, but instead, after a long pause, replied calmly that he was there because it was where the roots of war were. Having spoken these words, he immediately left the auditorium. Forest followed him out and found him "struggling for air—like someone who had been deeply underwater and who had barely managed to swim to the surface before gasping for breath."[4] It turned out that the man's words had upset him greatly. In order not to respond in anger, he had practiced deep breathing, so deep that it took him some time to recover. For the young American, it was the first time he had seen a connection between the way one breathes and the way one responds to the world. For me, the incident is indicative of Nhat Hanh's humanity, his vulnerability, and his constant struggle to maintain equanimity in the face of uncertainty, hostility, and even defeat.

In speaking of Merton and Nhat Hanh as heroes, it is important not to lose sight of the fact that they failed in most of the causes to

which they committed themselves. Merton did not bring about an end
to the nuclear arms race, any more than Nhat Hanh effected a peaceful
end to the Vietnam War. The Buddhist peace activist has said many
times that he did not seek a communist takeover of his country, yet
that is what happened. After the war, he wanted nothing so much as
to return to his country of origin and help the people there build a
new life for themselves, but he was forced instead to live in exile. In
the years since the war, Nhat Hanh has put together an effective
ministry that touches the lives of a great many people in all parts of
the world, but it is not the ministry he sought. He still longs to return
to his homeland.

What does make these men heroes is that they were able to resolve
one of life's fundamental problems in a way that has benefitted others.
To frame the issue in Western religious terms, they found a creative
way to resolve the tension between contemplation and action. When
I first presented this thesis at an international conference in Tokyo
several years ago, I did not present it as a distinctly Western dilemma.
One of the members of the audience said that he did not see it as a
problem for Zen Buddhists. It is one of the basic tenets of Zen, he
observed, that there is no separation between contemplation (or as
they would say, meditation) and action. He quoted the words of a
famous Zen teacher. When asked what is Zen, the teacher replied:
"When hungry, I eat. When tired, I sleep." I explained that this is a
characteristically Christian way of formulating the issue that goes
back to the Middle Ages. It reflects a separation in Christian thinking
that occurred around that time between the contemplative life, reserved for monks, and the active life, experienced by everyone else.
It may not be a problem for Buddhists, I acknowledged, but it is a
problem for Christians, who have for the most part lost touch with
the contemplative dimension of their own religion.

When Thomas Merton left his teaching position at St. Bonaventure
to join the Trappists at Gethsemani, he was seeking the contemplative
life in the only way he knew: by withdrawing from the world and
entering a monastic order. But even then he was not satisfied. To his
way of thinking, the monks of this austere religious order were altogether too busy; there was not enough time for true contemplative
practice. He was, it seems, always looking for more solitude, whether
in the form of a hermitage within the confines of the monastery or
some other setting altogether. To the credit of his religious superiors,

he was given a considerable degree of freedom to explore the contemplative life and experiment with various forms of spiritual practice. He had no living models for the kind of practice he wanted to pursue, so he mined the monastic literature of previous generations—the Desert Fathers, the Spanish mystics, and the German mystics. As we have seen, his explorations even took him into other religious traditions, notably Zen Buddhism. His practice eventually took him beyond solitude and back into the world. Almost in spite of himself, he became an active participant in the great social controversies of his day.

In the words of Robert Frost, Merton took the road less traveled. He followed the dark path of contemplation, which even most monks would tend to eschew, and it opened up for him a depth of love he did not know existed, what he came to call "the hidden ground of love." In speaking of the mythical hero, Campbell says that his passage may be "overground," but that is only incidental; "fundamentally it is inward—into the depths where obscure resistances are overcome, and long lost, forgotten powers revivified."[5] That is certainly what happened with Merton. His struggle was basically with himself, his contemplative practice the means by which he overcame his own internal resistances and gained access to this hidden ground of love. Once he reached this place within himself, as evidenced by his epiphany at Fourth and Walnut, he was free to engage the world on an entirely new basis. His contemplative practice opened a whole new perspective on the world, one in which he was able to love others freely and act courageously on their behalf. He could no longer remain silent. He would become an advocate for peace, even if it meant circumventing the censors within his religious order. Merton was still following the road less traveled; but instead of taking him even deeper into silence, his contemplative practice drew him into the public arena. He did not cease to be a contemplative when he assumed this more active role; he simply became a more complete and fully integrated contemplative. In this way he resolved, for himself at least, the seeming contradiction between contemplation and action.

Nhat Hanh confronted a different problem. Coming from a contemplative tradition that combined meditation and action, his primary concern was to bring this practice to bear on the lives of ordinary people and the social conditions in which they lived. He envisioned monks and nuns administering schools, taking care of orphans, running health-care centers, and teaching peasants new agricultural methods—all the while practicing meditation. When he proposed these reforms, he met with resistance, not only from the religious hierarchy but from lay people who were not prepared to accept such a radical change. His primary support came from young people—monks, nuns, and lay persons alike. In time, many of his proposals were accepted, but then came the war. His energies were redirected toward ending the war and preparing to rebuild the country once it was over. Yet once again he faced intense opposition, this time from his own government. As American involvement in the war increased, it became evident that he would have to contend with forces more formidable than any he had faced previously.

According to Campbell, the hero's adventure begins with a "call." The call may take the form of a "religious awakening," as it did with Merton, or it may summon the hero to "a high historical undertaking," as with Nhat Hanh. In any case, the call signals the beginning of a transformation. "The familiar life horizon has been outgrown; the old concepts, ideals and emotional patterns no longer fit."[6] We see the beginning of this transformation in Nhat Hanh with his first visit to the United States when he underwent a profound personal crisis mirroring the one in his own country. "I became a battlefield," we may recall his saying. "I couldn't know until the storm was over if I would survive, not in the sense of my physical life, but in the deeper sense of my core self." What he experienced was the falling away of social expectations and a realization of the freedom to be himself, even when faced with fierce opposition from others. Nhat Hanh emerged a changed person, prepared to assume a larger role in the struggle to end the war in his own country. He also became a major player on the international stage, no longer just a reformer within a particular strand of Buddhism. Even his engaged Buddhism took on new meaning as he outgrew his "familiar life horizon."

In his early writings and his work with young people, Nhat Hanh stressed the need for Buddhism to engage current social conditions if it was to retain its vitality as a living religion. Meditative practice was not emphasized at this time, though it was certainly not ignored. In the midst of the struggle to bring an end to the war in Vietnam, while also ministering to its victims, his emphasis began to shift. He took the anger and violence of the peace movement as an indication of what happens when activism, even on behalf of a good cause, is not grounded in meditative practice. "If we look deeply," he wrote, "we will observe that the roots of war are in the unmindful ways we have been living."[7] In order not to perpetuate the violence and injustice in the world, he believed, we must find a way to transform our anger into love. Meditation may not be the only way to accomplish this transformation, but it is a proven way. It is also a way of dealing with fear. So he exhorted his students, many of whom had remained in Vietnam to continue the work he began, to practice mindfulness as a way of maintaining peace within themselves, even in the face of death. Sometimes, he said, the most we can *do* on behalf of peace is simply to *be* peace.

Nhat Hanh's activism carried him deeper into the practice of meditation, even as Merton's contemplative practice drew him out into the world of action. Thus, there is a convergence in their two lives that is really quite remarkable. Starting from different positions, they managed to end up in a very similar place. What is more remarkable, they did so by going against the grain of their respective religious traditions. Merton might well have become a social activist straight-away had he not felt so strongly the pull toward contemplation. But if he had gone directly into a life of service, as he considered doing and as many Christians have done, it would have been without the deep spiritual grounding that his contemplative practice provided. It is questionable just how effective he would then have been. In any case, he would not have resolved for himself or others the seeming contradiction between contemplative life and the active life.

As for Nhat Hanh, he might have followed the traditional path of the Buddhist monk by remaining in the monastery or taking a position as a temple priest. He says in one place that he was expected to succeed his teacher as abbot of the monastery where he trained. But instead he followed the path of the worldly bodhisattva. In this way he modeled the engaged Buddhism he espoused. What made him such an effective leader in charting a new direction for his religion was his capacity for incorporating meditative practice into everything he did. Like Merton in his later years, Nhat Hanh has come to epitomize engaged spirituality, a form of spirituality that combines contemplative practice and social action.

As we have said many times, these two men were pioneers in working out this unique synthesis. But to say they were pioneers is also to say they did not do what they did just for themselves. They would certainly not be the global heroes we take them to be if they had not done it for others as well. The "second solemn task" of the hero—after battling through to a resolution of his own personal conflict—is, according to Campbell, "to return to us, transfigured,

and teach the lesson he has learned of life renewed."[8] Both Merton
and Nhat Hanh were and are consummate teachers, committed to
sharing what they have learned. What Merton sought by way of the
contemplative path was nothing less than union with God. Yet it was
clear from the outset that he did not intend to travel this road by
himself. He planned to bring others with him, though without leaving
the monastery. His writing was the vehicle for introducing others to the
contemplative experience. What he learned through his contemplative
practice, he shared with them through his many books, articles, essays,
and letters. As for Nhat Hanh, as near as I can tell, he has always
been a teacher. Before he left the monastery, he was writing books
and giving lectures. With a freedom to move around that Merton did
not have, he was able to take his message to many more places. But
he did not simply talk about engaged Buddhism: he lived it. He
inspired others as much by his example as by his words. Both Merton
and Nhat Hanh modeled what they learned, and in that way "returned
to us transfigured" to teach of "life renewed."

At the conclusion of his book, Campbell offers the opinion that the
hero today must transcend the factionalism and nationalism historically associated with institutional religion because "the community
today is the planet."[9] The contemporary hero, in other words, must
be a global hero. Once again Merton and Nhat Hanh fit that definition.
Not only have they been able to rise above the factionalism and
nationalism historically associated with their own religions; they have
been able to communicate in depth with representatives of other
religions. Their extraordinary capacity for interreligious and intrareligious dialogue sets them apart from most of their contemporaries and
marks them as belonging to the age of globalization.

Merton, for instance, maintained a far-flung correspondence that
included Muslims and Jews as well as Buddhists, while Nhat Hanh
has made a career of traveling around the world and meeting with
persons of all faiths. Both men have clearly been deeply affected by
those they have engaged in dialogue. David Steindl-Rast once asked
Merton whether he thought he could have presented Christian teaching
in the way he did without his exposure to Buddhism. Merton thought
about the question for a while and then replied, "You know, I think
I couldn't understand Christian teaching the way I do if it weren't in
the light of Buddhism."[10] Nhat Hanh surely would not regard Jesus
as one of his "spiritual ancestors" if his understanding of Buddhism

had not been profoundly affected by his encounters with men like Merton and Berrigan.

So it is not only engaged spirituality that these two men model, but interfaith dialogue as well. Moreover, theirs is no ordinary dialogue; it is dialogue carried on at the deepest human level. Merton and Nhat Hanh are global heroes first and foremost because their common humanity transcends their religious identity. They are global heroes at a time when the world desperately needs men and women who can model a way of life that is authentically human and also deeply spiritual. Neither of them, I am sure, set out to be heroic, yet in faithfully following where the spirit led they have fulfilled that role for all of us.

Notes

Chapter 1.   A Historic Meeting

1. *Merton by Those Who Knew Him Best*, ed. Paul Wilkes (San Franciso: Harper & Row, 1984), 151–2.
2. *Learning to Love, The Journals of Thomas Merton*, vol. 6, ed. Christine M. Bochen (San Francisco: HarperSanFrancisco, 1997), 76.
3. John Heidbrink in a personal letter to the author dated February 5, 2001.
4. Thomas Merton, *The Seven Storey Mountain* (Garden City, N.Y.: Image Books, 1970), 403.
5. Ibid., 472.
6. Ibid., 471–2.
7. Ibid., 482.
8. Ibid., 509.
9. Thomas Merton, *The Sign of Jonas* (New York: Harcourt Brace, 1953), 3.
10. Thomas Merton, *Conjectures of a Guilty Bystander* (New York: Image Books, 1965), 5.
11. Ibid., 7.
12. The original of this tape belongs to the Merton Legacy Trust. It is currently in the archives of the Thomas Merton Studies Center, Bellarmine College, Louisville, Ky.
13. *Passion for Peace: The Social Essays*, William H. Shannon, ed. (New York: Crossroad, 1997), 260–1.
14. Ibid., 261.
15. Ibid., 261–2.
16. Wilkes, *Merton by Those Who Knew Him Best*, 153.
17. This is the central theme of *Being Peace*, a collection of talks he gave to peace workers and meditation students during a U.S. speaking tour in the fall of 1985, subsequently published by Parallax Press.
18. Donald W. Mitchell and James A. Wiseman, eds., *The Gethsemani Encounter: A Dialogue on the Spiritual Life by Buddhist and Christian Monastics* (New York: Continuum, 1997), 260.
19. Samuel P. Huntington, "The Clash of Civilizations?" *Foreign Affairs* (Summer 1993): 22–49.

20. Thomas L. Friedman, *The Lexus and the Olive Tree* (New York: Farrar, Straus & Giroux, 1999), 7–8.

21. Ibid., 27.

22. H. Richard Niebuhr, *The Responsible Self* (New York: Harper & Row, 1963), 88.

Chapter 2.   Thomas Merton: Christian Contemplative

1. *Sign of Jonas*, 328.

2. See William H. Shannon, *Silent Lamp: The Thomas Merton Story* (New York: Crossroad, 1992), 291–2, where he quotes from an unpublished journal entry dated December 18, 1965.

3. *Sign of Jonas*, 110.

4. Ibid., 175.

5. Ibid., 181.

6. Ibid., 183.

7. Ibid., 193.

8. Thomas Merton, *What Is Contemplation?* (Springfield, Il: Templegate, 1978), 27.

9. Ibid., 29.

10. Ibid., 33–34.

11. Ibid., 36.

12. Ibid., 38.

13. Ibid., 40.

14. Ibid., 51.

15. Ibid., 52–53.

16. Ibid., 63.

17. Ibid., 70–71.

18. Ibid., 77.

19. See William H. Shannon, *Thomas Merton's Dark Path* (New York: Farrar, Straus & Giroux, 1981).

20. *Sign of Jonas*, 230.

21. Ibid., 106.

22. Thomas Merton, *Seeds of Contemplation* (New York: New Directions, 1949), 126.

23. Ibid., 17.

24. Ibid., 185.

25. Ibid., 60.

26. Ibid., 57–59.

27. Ibid., 40.

28. Ibid., 67.

29. Ibid., 133.

30. Ibid., 134.

31. Ibid., 138–9.

32. Ibid., 146.

33. Ibid., 147–8, italics added.

34. Ibid., 149.

35. Ibid., 87.
36. *Sign of Jonas*, 203.
37. Ibid., 233.
38. Ibid., 234.
39. Ibid., 134.
40. Ibid., 334.
41. Ibid., 337.
42. Ibid., 197.
43. *The Hidden Ground of Love: Letters of Thomas Merton*, selected and edited by William H. Shannon (New York: Harcourt Brace Jovanovich, 1985), 561.
44. Thomas Merton, *New Seeds of Contemplation* (New York: New Directions, 1972), ix.
45. Ibid., 1.
46. Ibid., 1, 3.
47. Ibid., 84.
48. Ibid., 141.
49. *Seeds of Contemplation*, 27–29.
50. Ibid., 34.
51. Ibid., 47.
52. Ibid., 194–6.
53. *New Seeds of Contemplation*, 7–8.
54. Ibid., 9.
55. Thomas Merton, *Zen and the Birds of Appetite* (New York: New Directions, 1968), 71–72.
56. Ibid., 76.
57. Ibid., 77.
58. *New Seeds of Contemplation*, 114–5.
59. Ibid., 119–20.
60. *Passion for Peace*, 11–13.
61. William Shannon, in his introduction to this article, traces its history through numerous rewrites and republications in order to show its central importance for Merton's peace writings (*Passion for Peace*, 37–38).
62. Ibid., 39–40.
63. Ibid., 47.
64. Ibid., 170.
65. Ibid., 318.
66. Ibid., 288.
67. Ibid., 293–4.
68. Ibid., 255.
69. *Seeds of Contemplation*, 115; *New Seeds*, 192 (italics added).
70. *New Seeds of Contemplation*, x.
71. *Sign of Jonas*, 91–92.
72. *A Search for Solitude, The Journals of Thomas Merton*, vol. 3, ed. Lawrence S. Cunningham (San Francisco: HarperSanFrancisco, 1997), 181–2. Compare *Conjectures of a Guilty Bystander*, 156–7.
73. *Conjectures of a Guilty Bystander*, 158.
74. Ibid., 158.

75. *Seeds of Contemplation*, 42.
76. *Search for Solitude*, 366.
77. *Passion for Peace*, 204.
78. Ibid., 175.
79. Ibid., 250.
80. Ibid., 324.
81. Shannon, *Silent Lamp*, 181.
82. *Hidden Ground of Love*, 73.

Chapter 3.   Thich Nhat Hanh: Engaged Buddhist

1. Thich Nhat Hanh, *Cultivating the Mind of Love* (Berkeley, Calif.: Parallax Press, 1996), 8–9.
2. Thich Nhat Hanh, *Zen Keys* (New York: Doubleday, 1974), 24–25.
3. Ibid., 86.
4. Ibid., 25–26.
5. *Cultivating Mind of Love*, 32.
6. Thich Nhat Hanh, *Vietnam: Lotus in a Sea of Fire* (New York: Hill and Wang, 1967), 42.
7. Thich Nhat Hanh, *Aujourd'hui le Bouddhisme*, trans. (from Vietnamese) Le Van Hao (Cholon, South Vietnam: La Boi, 1965).
8. *Cultivating Mind of Love*, 57–58.
9. *Lotus in Sea of Fire*, 57.
10. Chan Khong, *Learning True Love* (Berkeley, Calif.: Parallax Press, 1993), 29.
11. Thich Nhat Hanh, trans. Mobi Warren, *Fragrant Palm Leaves: Journals 1962–66* (Berkeley, Calif.: Parallax Press, 1998), 7.
12. Ibid., 19.
13. *Learning True Love*, 30.
14. *Fragrant Palm Leaves*, 65–66.
15. Ibid., 69.
16. Ibid., 82–83.
17. Ibid., 84–85.
18. Ibid., 86.
19. Ibid., 87–88.
20. Ibid., 93.
21. Ibid., 109.
22. Ibid., 106–7.
23. Ibid., 101.
24. Ibid., 176.
25. Ibid., 80.
26. *Learning True Love*, 49.
27. Ibid., 60.
28. *Fragrant Palm Leaves*, 137.
29. *Learning True Love*, 70.
30. Daniel Berrigan and Thich Nhat Hanh, *The Raft Is Not the Shore: Conversations toward a Buddhist-Christian Awareness* (Boston: Beacon Press, 1975), 93–94.

31. *Learning True Love*, 90.
32. Thich Nhat Hanh, *Interbeing: Fourteen Guidelines for Engaged Buddhism* (Berkeley, Calif.: Parallax Press, 1993), 17–20.
33. *Learning True Love*, 85.
34. Ibid., 67.
35. Ibid., 87–88.
36. Thich Nhat Hanh, *Love in Action: Writings on Nonviolent Social Change* (Berkeley, Calif.: Parallax Press, 1993), 57.
37. Ibid., 58.
38. Ibid., 60.
39. *Lotus in Sea of Fire*, vii.
40. Ibid., 47.
41. Ibid., 92.
42. Ibid., 93.
43. Sallie B. King, "Thich Nhat Hanh and the Unified Buddhist Church of Vietnam: Nondualism in Action," in *Engaged Buddhism: Buddhist Liberation Movements in Asia*, ed. Christopher S. Queen and Sallie B. King (Albany, N.Y.: State University of New York Press, 1996), 335.
44. Ibid., 326.
45. *Love in Action*, 39.
46. Ibid., 40.
47. Ibid., 44–45.
48. Thich Nhat Hanh, trans. Mobi Warren, *The Miracle of Mindfulness: A Manual on Meditation*, rev. ed. (Boston: Beacon Press, 1987), 11.
49. Ibid., 14.
50. Ibid., 58.
51. Ibid., 76 (italics added).
52. *Learning True Love*, 170.
53. This 16-page booklet published by The Hoa Binh Press in October 1972 is no longer in print. I was able to obtain a copy from Jim Forest.
54. *Learning True Love*, 141.
55. Ibid., 147–8.
56. Ibid., 187–9.
57. Ibid., 190–5.
58. Ibid., 176.
59. This quotation is from the introduction to the edition of the book first published in 1976. It was then titled *The Miracle of Being Awake*. The 1987 edition, *The Miracle of Mindfulness*, does not contain this introduction by the translator.
60. *Raft Is Not Shore*, 122.
61. Ibid., 119.
62. Ibid., 125. See also *Fragrant Palm Leaves*, 6.
63. *Learning True Love*, 29.
64. *Raft Is Not Shore*, 125.
65. Ibid., 124.
66. *Learning True Love*, 178.
67. *Raft Is Not Shore*, 126.
68. Ibid., 118.

69. Thich Nhat Hanh, *Being Peace* (Berkeley, Calif.: Parallax Press, 1987), 25.
70. *Learning True Love*, 220–1.
71. Ibid., 222–3.
72. Ibid., 225.
73. *Being Peace*, viii.
74. Ibid., 53.
75. Thich Nhat Hanh, *Teachings on Love* (Berkeley, Calif.: Parallax Press, 1997), 5.
76. *Zen Keys*, 44.
77. Ibid., 88.
78. *Cultivating Mind of Love*, 32.
79. Thich Nhat Hanh, *Living Buddha, Living Christ* (New York: Riverhead Books, 1995), 83.
80. *Interbeing*, 6.
81. *Zen Keys*, 93.
82. *Interbeing*, 17–20.
83. *Call Me by My True Names: The Collected Poems of Thich Nhat Hanh* (Berkeley: Parallax, 1999), 72–73.

Chapter 4.   Entering into Dialogue

1. Thomas Merton, *Mystics and Zen Masters* (New York: Noonday Press, 1967), 203.
2. *Zen and Birds of Appetite*, 114.
3. Ibid., 115.
4. *Hidden Ground of Love*, 566.
5. *Zen and Birds of Appetite*, 117–8.
6. Ibid., 131–2.
7. Ibid., 133–4.
8. Ibid., 137–8.
9. Ibid., 139.
10. Thomas Merton, *The Way of Chuang Tzu* (New York: New Directions, 1965), 9.
11. Ibid., 11.
12. *Zen and Birds of Appetite*, 38–39.
13. Ibid., 57.
14. Thomas Merton, *The Asian Journal* (New York: New Directions, 1968), 4.
15. Ibid., 313.
16. Ibid., 47, n. 21.
17. Ibid., 305–7.
18. Ibid., 308.
19. Ibid., 82.
20. Ibid., 143.
21. From an interview with Harold Talbott in *Tricycle: The Buddhist Review*, Summer 1992, 14–24.
22. The meetings were held on three separate days (November 4, 6, and 8). Merton's observations are recorded in the *Asian Journal*, 100–2, 112–3, and 124–5.
23. Ibid., 125.
24. Wilkes, *Merton by Those Who Knew Him Best*, 145–6.
25. Ibid., 147.

26. *Asian Journal*, 316.
27. Ibid., 148.
28. Ibid., 152.
29. Ibid., 233–6.
30. Ibid., 343.
31. *Living Buddha, Living Christ*, 5.
32. *Lotus in Sea of Fire*, 30.
33. Ibid., 93.
34. Ibid., 109.
35. Ibid., 93–94.
36. Ibid., 106–7.
37. Ibid., 107.
38. *Hidden Ground of Love*, 285–6.
39. "Blessed Are the Meek: The Christian Roots of Non-Violence" was written in the two months immediately following the LaPorte incident and first appeared in German. It later appeared in English as an article in *Fellowship* and as a booklet published by the Catholic Peace Fellowship (See *Passion for Peace*, 248–259.)
40. *Raft Is Not Shore*, 60.
41. Ibid., 60–61.
42. Ibid., 61.
43. Ibid., 63.
44. Ibid., 64.
45. Ibid., 65.
46. *Living Buddha, Living Christ*, 7.
47. Ibid., 9.
48. *Raft Is Not Shore*, 1.
49. Ibid., 2.
50. Ibid., 3.
51. Ibid., 5.
52. Ibid., 7.
53. Ibid., 9–10.
54. Ibid., 108.
55. Ibid., 111.
56. Ibid., 13–18.
57. Ibid., 18–20.
58. Ibid., 25–27.
59. Ibid., 27.
60. Ibid., 38.
61. Ibid., 39.
62. Ibid., 47.
63. *The New York Times*, October 16, 1999.
64. Thich Nhat Hanh, *Going Home: Jesus and Buddha as Brothers* (New York: Riverhead Books, 1999), 17.
65. *Living Buddha, Living Christ*, 13.
66. *Going Home*, 5.
67. Ibid., 9.
68. Ibid., 17.

69. Ibid., 143.
70. Ibid., 98.
71. *Living Buddha, Living Christ*, 89.
72. *Going Home*, 182–3.
73. Ibid., 176.

Chapter 5.   Engaged Spirituality in an Age of Globalization

1. *Seven Storey Mountain*, 242.
2. *Hidden Ground of Love*, 63–64.
3. Thomas Keating, *Open Mind, Open Heart: The Contemplative Dimension of the Gospel* (Rockport, Mass.: Element Books, 1992), 110–1.
4. See David Steindl-Rast, "Man of Prayer," in *Thomas Merton/Monk: A Monastic Tribute*, ed. Patrick Hart (Kalamazoo, Mich.: Cistercian Publications, 1983), 87.
5. Shunryu Suzuki, *Zen Mind, Beginner's Mind* (New York: Weatherhill, 1970), 29.
6. Catherine Ingram, *In the Footsteps of Gandhi* (Berkeley, Calif.: Parallax Press, 1990), 253–4.
7. Ibid., 254.
8. *Miracle of Mindfulness*, 7.
9. Ibid., 14.
10. Ibid., 16.
11. Ibid., 22.
12. Ibid., 27–28.
13. Ibid., 30.
14. Ibid., 31.
15. Ibid., 60 (italics added).
16. Ibid., 65.
17. Ibid., 75.
18. *Gethsemani Encounter*, 144.
19. Dietrich Bonhoeffer, *Letters and Papers from Prison* (London: SCM Press, 1953), 168.
20. Mohandas K. Gandhi, *An Autobiography: The Story of My Experiments with Truth* (Boston: Beacon Press, 1957), 160.
21. *Passion for Peace*, 205–6.
22. Ibid., 208.
23. Herbert W. Richardson, "Martin Luther King—Unsung Theologian," *Commonweal*, May 3, 1968. Reprinted in *New Theology No. 6*, ed. Martin E. Marty and Dean G. Peerman (London: MacMillan, 1969), 181.
24. David J. Garrow, *Bearing the Cross: Martin Luther King, Jr. and the Southern Christian Leadership Conference* (New York: William Morrow, 1986), 200.
25. This account of the Bamboo Forest School is taken from Sister Annabel Laity's unpublished translation of Nhat Hanh's history. I heard him say that engaged Buddhism derives in part from this school in a lecture he gave during the Winter Retreat at Plum Village in February 1999.

26. Ingram, *Footsteps of Ghandi*, 87.
27. *Being Peace*, 74.
28. Ingram, *Footsteps of Ghandi*, 89.
29. Ibid., 90.
30. *Passion for Peace*, 38.
31. Ibid., 47.
32. *Hidden Ground of Love*, 50–51.
33. *Passion for Peace*, 84, 90 (italics added).
34. Ibid., 46–47.
35. *Learning True Love*, 139–40.
36. *Being Peace*, 45.
37. Ingram, *Footsteps of Ghandi*, 129.
38. Ibid., 147.
39. Ibid., 253.
40. Ibid., 265–6.
41. Ibid., 257.
42. *Zen and Birds of Appetite*, 135.
43. Ibid., 137–8.
44. Thomas Merton, *The Springs of Contemplation* (Notre Dame, Ind.: Ave Maria Press, 1997), 167.
45. See his review essay entitled "Nishida: A Zen Philosopher" in *Zen and the Birds of Appetite*, 67–70.
46. He cites the example of a Trappistine nun in Belgium who was a Vietnamese Buddhist and whose uncle was a Buddhist monk. *Springs of Contemplation*, 167.
47. Ibid., 168.
48. *Living Buddha, Living Christ*, 193.
49. Ibid., 38–39.
50. Ibid., 35.
51. *Going Home*, 12.
52. *Living Buddha, Living Christ*, 56.
53. *Gethsemani Encounter*, xii.
54. Ibid., 202.
55. Ibid., 243–4.
56. Ibid., 243–4.
57. Ibid., 139.
58. Ibid., 243.
59. "If I can unite *in myself* the thought and the devotion of Eastern and Western Christendom, the Greek and the Latin Fathers, the Russians with the Spanish mystics, I can prepare in myself the reunion of divided Christians. From that secret and unspoken unity in myself can eventually come a visible and manifest unity of all Christians. If we want to bring together what is divided, we can not do so by imposing one division upon the other or absorbing one division into the other. But if we do this, the union is not Christian. It is political, and doomed to further conflict. We must contain all divided worlds in ourselves and transcend them in Christ." *Conjectures of a Guilty Bystander*, 21.
60. Raimon Panikkar, *The Intrareligious Dialogue*, rev. ed. (New York: Paulist Press, 1999), xvi.

61. *Mystics and Zen Masters*, ix.
62. See Lauren Artress, *Walking the Sacred Path: Rediscovering the Labyrinth as a Spiritual Tool* (New York: Riverhead Books, 1995) for an account of this development and a fuller explanation of the labyrinth.

Epilogue: Global Heroes

1. Joseph Campbell, *The Hero with a Thousand Faces*, 2nd ed. (Princeton, N.J.: Princeton University Press, 1968), 19–20.
2. Michael Mott, *The Seven Mountains of Thomas Merton* (Boston: Houghton Mifflin, 1984), 435–58. See *Learning to Love* for Merton's journals dealing with this period of his life.
3. *Cultivating the Mind of Love*, 21.
4. James Forest, "Nhat Hanh: Seeing with the Eyes of Compassion" in *Miracle of Mindfulness*, 104.
5. Campbell, 29.
6. Ibid., 51.
7. *Love in Action*, 66.
8. Campbell, 20.
9. Ibid., 389.
10. Robert Aitken and David Steindl-Rast, *The Ground We Share: Everyday Practice, Buddhist and Christian* (Boston: Shambhala, 1994), 47.

Index